The Transverse Information System

The Transverse Information System

New Solutions for IS and Business Performance

François Rivard
Georges Abou Harb
Philippe Méret

First published in France in 2008 by Hermes Science/Lavoisier entitled: *Le système d'information transverse : nouvelles solutions du SI & performance métier* © LAVOISIER, 2008
First published in Great Britain and the United States in 2009 by ISTE Ltd and John Wiley & Sons, Inc.

ISTE Ltd
27-37 St George's Road
London SW19 4EU
UK

www.iste.co.uk

John Wiley & Sons, Inc.
111 River Street
Hoboken, NJ 07030
USA

www.wiley.com

© ISTE Ltd, 2009

Library of Congress Cataloging-in-Publication Data

Rivard, Francois, 1971-
 [Système d'information transverse. English]
 The transverse information system : new solutions for IS and business performance / François Rivard, Georges Abou Harb, Philippe Méret.
   p. cm.
 "First published in France in 2008 by Hermes Science/Lavoisier entitled: Le système d'information transverse : nouvelles solutions du SI & performance métier."
 Includes bibliographical references and index.
 ISBN 978-1-84821-108-7
 1. Management information systems. 2. Information technology--Management. I. Abou-Harb, Georges. II. Méret, Philippe. III. Title.
 HD30.213.R58 2009
 658.4'038011--dc22

                                                                                          2009001027

British Library Cataloguing-in-Publication Data
A CIP record for this book is available from the British Library
ISBN: 978-1-84821-108-7

Printed and bound in Great Britain by CPI Antony Rowe, Chippenham and Eastbourne.

FSC
Mixed Sources
Product group from well-managed
forests and other controlled sources
Cert no. SGS-COC-2953
www.fsc.org
© 1996 Forest Stewardship Council

Table of Contents

Preface

The transverse information system is gradually taking shape in the business information systems environment. Whatever you call it, and even if some people continue to reduce it to the level of middleware, it is time to take notice of the predominant, central role played by this domain, as well as its impact, firstly on information system architectures and secondly on the implementation of new business applications. Inbetween applications there are parts of the information system which businesses must undertake to build and optimize without delay, that is unless they intend to miss out on opportunities and lag behind their competitors, just at a time when IS managers have to justify how they actively contribute to creating value.

This information system is based on major architecture and technology systems combined under the name of new information system solutions (NISS), some of which will probably be familiar to many readers:

– master data management (MDM), for data which is the basis of the information system;

– service-oriented architecture (SOA), a dominant architecture paradigm, perfect for transformation, modernization and enterprise architecture; and

– business process management (BPM), the driving force for value creation and business innovation intermediaries.

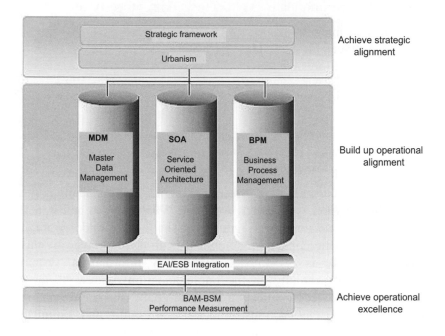

Figure 1. *The new information system solutions*

Each at their own level, these domains respond to the issues that IT managers are exposed to: contributing to the company's growth, increasing the alignment capabilities between the business and the available IT resources, and safeguarding investments whilst managing innovation. Together, these technologies form a new information system, the transverse information system, which is the subject of this book.

These technologies do not compete with each other. They are complementary resources that help to make up this integrated whole. To achieve this, other resources may be called upon:

– modeling systems and systems for managing information assets;

– solutions for measuring operational performance, which ensure that the transverse information system is working properly; and

– dedicated integration layers (EAI/ESB), to facilitate transversal exchanges between the application systems.

In other words, whatever the quality of the technologies involved, they cannot function on their own. It is necessary to think about the method and organization systems which will genuinely ensure the success of the technologies concerned, in addition to showing how all of these factors will interconnect to provide an integrated, organized system in the long term.

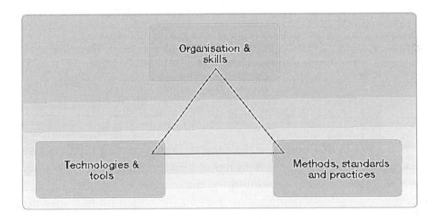

Figure 2. *Organization-method-technology triptych*

How to use this book

This book is divided into three parts which are aimed at all business professionals such as IT personnel, decision-makers and managers who are anxious to gain a better understanding about how to optimize the services provided by the information system.

1st part – Issues	**About the business: the new issues facing IT managers** Chapter 1 - Innovation for Business Value and Cost-killing Chapter 2 - The Transverse Information System
2nd part – Solutions	**New Information System Solutions** Chapter 3 - Master Data Chapter 4 - Service-Oriented Architectures Chapter 5 - Business Process Management Chapter 6 - Exchange Platforms Chapter 7 - Complex, Innovative Business Architectures
3rd part – Methods and organization	**Managing new information system solutions** Chapter 8 - The Impact of NISS on Software Implementation Chapter 9 - From Implementation to Measurement Chapter 10 - Contribution and Impact of NISS on Organization Chapter 11 - How to Get the Best Out of NISS

Throughout this book we shall use the acronym IT to indicate what happens on the information systems management side. The initials CIO will also be used, depending on the context, to indicate either the information systems manager or the unit for which he is responsible, the information systems department.

The transverse information system and the new information system solutions are an innovative, exciting subject and an opportunity to create value by means of safeguarded investments. Be the first to break the rules and venture into this new territory.

Acknowledgements

Considering the diversity of subjects tackled, a book such as this can only be representative. The authors would like to thank the EI²S team at Logica Management Consulting for its expertise and constant involvement, as well as the entire MIG business unit (information system consulting) for its quality. It is a real pleasure to be involved with them on a daily basis.

We would also particularly like to thank:

– Sébastien Durand, partner in charge of IT Governance at Unilog Management, who provided valuable assistance for Chapter 2;

– Franck Régnier-Pécastaing, MDM manager, whose generous contribution is widely used in Chapter 3;

– Eric Vendeville, a mine of information on service directories and reference systems, whose work is used in Chapter 4; and

– Olivier Lallement and Iarantsoa Rafitosoa, who provided a valuable contribution to Chapter 4, which deals with SOA management.

We would like to express our admiration for the managers of projects described in this book for having the intuition to promote innovative architectures and technologies and for convincing their clients to have faith in them:

– Hugues Lorez and Nicolas Pétain, the architects of the energy project described in Chapter 7; and

– Olivier Hochon, Sadaq Boutrif, Mohamed-Ali Razgallah and Clément Dhamelincourt, designers, architects and developers of the bank project described in Chapter 7.

We will inevitably leave out lots of people, but before doing so we would also like to thank the following for their daily contribution: Stéphane Breton, François-Xavier Brun, Youen Chené, Pierre Chiandusso, Eric Cohen, Marc Cortial, Sébastien Delayre, Thierry Desforges, Christophe Dewaele, Vincent Dorlhiac, Céline Falque, Gwladys Frémand, Thierry Hehunstre, Stéphane Jaubert, Chantal Legrand, Sanaà and Séverin Legras, Jean-Michel Lemaire, Thomas Lepere, Grégory Le Henry, Fabrice Losson, Agnès Lucot, Emmanuel Manceau, Olivier Roubertie, Patrick Saint-Jean, Benoît Tournel, Stéphane Toutlouyan, Raphaël Troude, Nicolas Ullmo, Pierre Verger, Andreea Vuta and Ali Zlaoui.

We would also like to thank our boldest, most visionary clients, whose innovative projects are described in this book. Since we are not allowed to name them all, we hope that they will recognize themselves.

Guillain Issartel's contribution on skill centers was invaluable. Pierre-Dominique Martin and Benoît Leboucher brought the authors up to speed on good sourcing practices and the eSCM framework. In this capacity they must be duly gratified.

Thanks to Jean-Louis Bénard, Cyril Dhénin, Christophe Berly, Leda Pavlouchenko and the whole Brainsonic team for their contribution and proofreading.

Very special thanks to Patrick Guimbal, Philippe Bouron, René Napoli, Jean-François Bodin, Vincent Colombani, Jean-Pascal Boutier and to Jean-Jacques Maillard – *so long*, JJ.

François Rivard would like to thank Cécile and Joséphine for their support and patience during the long evenings spent writing this book.

Chapter 1

Innovation for Business Value and Cost-killing

It is February 2000. A top-selling European daily paper is starting to enter all the day's sports results into its database. The aim is to make the process of retrieving results from its website more reliable, as well as to make it easier to produce the statistics that its readers are so fond of. Until now, individual journalists recorded the results themselves, on media and in formats of their own choosing: notebooks, Excel sheets, sometimes their own memory, etc.

Fast forward to the year 2004. A large French mutual insurance company is taking a fresh look at the tools it uses to monitor the exchange of company data at its processing center. Staff must always know what is happening with transactions between departmental funds, trust funds and parent organizations, so that they can identify those that are late without needing to chase them up urgently through the system. These five brave people have had enough of manually ticking off miles of lists giving the names of prompt payers, deducing the stragglers for themselves.

In August 2007, a break in the chain processing remittances and transactions between customers of a large German bank and the clearing houses held up €1 billion in the payment facilities chain, all in a single day. The penalties incurred were in keeping with the amount held up. As a result, this bank is now thinking about rolling out a system to monitor this process in real-time, a system they do not have at the moment, surprising as this may seem.

What is particularly significant is that examples like these occur again and again in every country in the world, in all business sectors, year after year. They perfectly illustrate the main areas for improvement of information systems, as well as the enormous scope for further enhancing their performance. When we teach our discipline in management or engineering schools, we amaze the students with cases like these. "What?" they exclaim incredulously. "How can we possibly still be running into this type of problem, even in 2009?" However, is it so difficult to believe? There are still a great number of value and performance improvements that can be achieved by intelligent, competent computerization of the information system. A company can end up losing vast amounts of energy and money as a result of its information system not being sufficiently robust to meet the requirements of the business.

In spite of an unparalleled degree of technological development, in spite of progress that is accessible, available and within reach, some companies make extensive use of computers, whereas others make less use of them. This discrepancy exists between all business sectors and even between companies within the same sector. Since only a very small part of the IT budget is devoted to developing and applying new technologies, it is first of all necessary to identify the right kind of technology, one which will be able to create value quickly, which will be reliable and which will provide a structure without being restrictive. In addition, between choosing the technology and making successful use of it every day comes the project, which itself must be successfully implemented. There are so many hurdles to get over and so many risks of failure!

But does that mean we have to resign ourselves to fate when faced with technological advances? Can you imagine working every day without word processors or spreadsheets? No, you would probably change your job because these days, the effort of carrying out office work manually seems unbearable to contemplate. So let's not accept that situations such as those described above should always be so. And let us implement ways of finding efficient solutions to them.

The actions of IT managers are guided by these thoughts. Major projects are no longer only rationalization projects, aimed at reducing the costs of what has for too long been regarded as a support function and a cost center. They must also create value, performance and a competitive edge. The will to rationalize may persist, but with new objectives in mind. Just as with other functions, such as marketing departments, IS departments are now responsible for driving the profitable growth of the business. Even in times of crisis, rationalization and cost-killing must come with performance improvement and added business value.

In itself, our students' reaction is justified. In spite of the enormous potential of IT for improving business performance, which can be exploited with proper innovation, successful projects and an *ad hoc* budget, we still allow these timeworn situations to persist. Instead, we must now try our utmost to reduce them. In its own way, this book proposes solutions and remedial action for all of these situations.

1.1. Supporting profit and growth

There have been less favorable times for IT. In particular, the aftermath of September 11th 2001 and the ensuing economic turmoil was a dark period in the history of IT, as it was in many other fields. As a result of budget restrictions imposed during these years, CIOs were forced to adopt defensive tactics and seek out drastic *cost-cutting* measures. Given that a belt-tightening policy does not form the ideal basis for implementing an action plan – far from it – running an IT department was no easy task in these years of famine.

Nevertheless, when it did come the recovery was well worth waiting for, since it enabled IT to finally assert itself. In spite of the crisis, businesses have undertaken to improve rather than just maintain their performance, spurred on by increasingly insistent shareholders and major geo-economic maneuvers. In the eyes of decision-makers, IT has to be a growth lever for the business. IT must once more sustain and improve performance in the business units, an objective which is now forced upon all the company's support functions to a general extent.

1.1.1. *A junction with the business*

1.1.1.1. *A thwarted ambition*

This is not the first time that IT has been tasked with the role of contributing to improved performance. In its early years, because it was something new, people thought that IT could do no wrong and placed all their hopes in it. Its development marked the start of a cycle of progress. During what was a period of apparently limitless growth, people could put up with a few transgressions, understandably tentative attempts to harness a discipline that was still new, the occasional over-eagerness to do well and to turn a situation to one's own advantage. This teenage crisis couldn't last long.

However, an increase in the number of failures brought this young pretender back down to earth. Delayed from entering the age of reason, IT became a mere support function once more. In the company organizational chart, the IT department lost its organizational component. Brushed aside but not easily forgotten, in an economic climate that had turned into a slump, IT retreated into the technician's domain, cutting itself off from the business to manage its own affairs, causing major discrepancies between strategic and operational expectations. This is how the enormous credibility which IT enjoyed was squandered, to the extent that its contribution was perceived as being wholly negative as far as the business was concerned. It was expensive, inappropriate and out of touch with the actual requirements of the business. This remains a common perception of IT in too many businesses, a perception which it is now taking great effort to shake off.

1.1.1.2. *The issues involved with an efficient information system*

Which businesses have built their reputation on the fact that their information system does not work? Not many, certainly. On the contrary, being efficient through an optimized design and use of the information system can be a way to differentiate. Dell and the direct model (which is, however, soon to lose its exclusivity), Amazon or eBay, are players who couldn't survive without an efficient information system. One of our models is Ikea. All of the store's business is based on an available, efficient information system where the business processes faithfully reproduce the customer's path. Thus, as the customer passes through the checkout, withdrawal slips are printed automatically. These are used by warehouse staff to bring the products as quickly as possible. An optimized process based on a just-in-time logic. A business process tool optimized by a value-creating IT tool.

Having an efficient information system is no longer a luxury. Nobody would disagree with the following statements: a "good" information system is a way for the company to set itself apart, whereas a "bad" information system may hold up the business's development. This leads to the conclusion that: the information system is a growth lever. Let us examine a simple convincing example of this in 2008 in France. Due to strong internal growth after acquiring several competitors in its sector, a real estate company experiences rapid development, increasing the number of staff from 40 to 600 in 5 years. However, the information system has not developed at the same rate. It must, however, definitely be modified to sustain current and future growth. Otherwise, managing the property transactions portfolio and clients portfolios based on Excel sheets and simple Intranet applications will soon seem outdated, if not detrimental. This company is looking for a powerful information system built on intangible foundations (the business assets of the company). What characteristics does it need? To integrate the new without having a major impact on the old (other than those that are clearly accepted and defined); to be able to design and roll out solutions to new business requirements quickly, in any case, more quickly than before; to control predicted expansion and rationalize costs; and finally, to provide justification to the business units regarding investments made, by justifying the contribution of IT in creating value.

Focussing the information system on the business unit has become a quest and a vocation for information system departments. According to an annual survey carried out by Gartner in 2007 on more than 1,000 IT departments in Europe and throughout the world, controlling IT costs remains high up in the list of priorities but has dropped from first to second position. Top priority is now reserved for improving business processes. Information system managers are now turning about-face and focussing more on the business units. Why? Because defining new ways of creating value for the business, thanks to new technologies and the information system, will allow them to set themselves apart and contribute to global performance and profitable growth by implementing innovative, successful systems. And when it is done in a proper manner, costs will be cut. Cost-killing is an inherent benefit of a proper IT strategy and the use of sustainable development technologies and practices.

1.1.1.3. *Numerous applications*

In 2003, in a previous publication[1], we listed some areas where information systems had an important role to play:

– reducing the time taken to bring new products or new product references to market;

– reducing costs and the amount of time taken to perform business processes;

---

1. G. Abou Harb, F. Rivard, *L'EAI au service de l'entreprise évolutive*, éditions Maxima, 2003.

– providing excellent customer relations thanks to a unique vision, a consistent image and consistent behavior throughout the different sales channels;

– improving the logistics chain by reconciling logistics with demand;

– assisting business integration in the event of mergers/acquisitions.

There is no denying that these issues are still as topical as ever. Although a lot has already been done and each of these areas has been developed in a number of businesses, progress is still ongoing. New business models are emerging and others are becoming established. New technologies are being used to support these models effectively and to reinforce, or even improve, the projects already started, in a continuous improvement cycle to which businesses must submit.

1.1.1.3.1. The importance of exchanging data in new business models

In this book we noted that each of the areas mentioned involved increasing and automating the exchange of information in the business. We also pointed out the importance of controlling these exchanges. Recent cases can be quoted that show that these subjects are still very important today. For example, in the energy sector, deregulation and opening the sector up to competition forced companies in this sector to open up their information systems and increase the number of data exchanges between players. In the insurance sector, the decoupling of back-offices channels from the distribution partners lead to data exchanges.

In some cases, controlling exchanges is an essential condition for success. Decide for yourself using an example of this business in the retail industry. To establish itself as an agent, the business offers its customers a wide range of products which it does not, however, intend to stock itself, so as not to incur massive storage costs and so that it can continue with the *drop shipment* distribution model, which it is currently implementing. It opens up its information system to its partners and, over all its sales channels, offers a wider range of products and a more up-to-date catalog, thanks to more frequent, regular exchange of data.

Information on availability is available in real-time, prices can be recalculated at any time depending on partner promotions or the customer's rating. By implementing new business processes, by setting up a real-time interoperability model between partners, by centralizing data in a data repository, and by sharing pricing services, the information system, technology and innovation provide solutions for this business and support its strategy.

This business has been able to align its business strategy and its information system strategy based on methods that will be described in detail later on in this book and which are based on the use of new technologies: business process management, service-oriented architecture and master data management. Data exchanges contribute to the success of the set-up but are not the only methods used. It is this acknowledgement that leads to the transverse information system.

1.1.1.3.2. The role of technology in improving performance

It is widely claimed that technology is playing a more and more important role in this development in terms of the place it now holds in businesses and in people's daily lives.

Let us take the case of RFID (*Radio Frequency Identification*) tags. In the future these chips will be fitted to so many things (public transport cards, passports, student cards, medicines, library books etc.) that the number of possible applications is, quite simply, difficult to imagine. In all these cases, this innovation will only become established in relation to the information system of the business, the institution, the body with which the relevant process is connected, then, in a networked economy, by integrating these different information systems into each other. In all cases, the information system is enhanced by this.

You have to examine the applications and open up the field of possibilities as wide as possible. RFID is a technology that has been around since 1948, when it was used to identify war planes from a distance. It was almost resurrected by the Wal-Mart distribution group in 2002. In 2007 it was a field that was constantly being developed and for which applications were increasing rapidly. Some of them were completely new. Others in boxes may never see the light of day, although the main reason for this may not necessarily be the technology. The characteristic favoring the development of one activity over another is its appropriateness for a situation, a market or a budget.

Mastering innovation, identifying where it may lead the business and how it is different is a role that falls just as often to innovation managers as to consulting companies. And having a good idea is very often, only the start, as one innovation leads to another.

1.2. Assessing innovation

1.2.1. *"Russian Ark", a universal example*

Russian Ark was released in 2003. A feature length film by the director Alexander Sokourov, its distinguishing feature was that it was filmed in a single 90-minute take. In the bonus material found on the DVD[2], right at the beginning of the *behind-the-scenes* documentary, the German producer, Jens Meurer, remembers being attracted immediately by the artist's ideas. From the length of the shoot to the absence of editing, everything seemed to indicate that risks would be taken and costs reduced. Filming in a single place (the Hermitage Museum in St. Petersburg, booked for a Tuesday when the doors were closed to the public), a skeleton film crew taken on short-term, etc., it was a technical challenge and an artistic prowess with almost all modern conveniences, for a guaranteed image effect (no pun intended).

---

2. Knut Elstermann, *In one breath, le making-of de l'Arche Russe*, Egoli Tossell Film AG & Hermitage Bridge Studio, 2003.

The reality of the undertaking was to prove more complex, taxing and ultimately more costly than you might have predicted for this wonderful idea which appeared to be very simple – although that is another subject which we shall deal with in more detail in Chapter 4. This is usually the case with IT. Everything looks easy and everything is always much more complex. Why? Because it is innovation!

For the time being, we may wonder how on earth none of Sokourov's numerous predecessors ever managed to come up with this idea, considering that cinema has been going strong for more than 110 years. Frustrated creativity? Inordinately high budget demands? A lack of suitable scriptwriters? Of course, nothing like that. In fact, it was technological constraints that stopped a project like this from being turned into reality: films weren't long enough to cover 90 minutes, batteries would not last long enough, and other similar problems.

As digital technology developed (and battery life grew longer), the deadlock was broken and Sokourov went off to find his producer and put forward his idea (or rather outline his gamble). In fact, choosing the right innovation is only the start of an adventure, a hole that opens up new questions with no answers. While some of these questions certainly related to a film context, others were clearly linked to the field of the new area. To see this project through to completion, it would take more than just the singular talent of the director, his crew and the thousands of extras and actors who were set to take up their positions in the museum and play their parts without any room for error. Most importantly, it would take innovation, innovation and more innovation.

1.2.2. *What does innovation involve?*

The term innovation normally sounds like something grand or pompous. It frightens people. Perhaps, for many people, this is because there is an almost revolutionary flavor to the term innovation. To innovate is to change, to disrupt, implicitly or explicitly. It means to discover something totally new, totally different, an unstoppable solution to a number of ills. Ultimately though, are we not confusing the term innovation with invention?

Innovation is not as inhibiting as invention and you don't always have to see revolution in what is often only a convergence of factors leading to progress. You just have to turn to our neighbours to convince yourself of this. The British, known for their pragmatism, readily make innovation accessible (in the absence of more modest terms, since marketing always confers upon it a somewhat magical image).

Innovation is continuous improvement. It is a vision of progress that incorporates the past to improve the future. It is the fruit of seeds which may have been planted a long time ago. Each of us will notice that we make innovations every day, in our own way, for example to save time or to make a repetitive task easier to perform. When applied to an individual, this is often called *changing one's habits.*

This is, in itself, an interesting expression. It indicates the desire to go against what we consider to be acquired behavior or, at least, behavior that it is difficult to cast doubt on. When applied to an industry or company, it may be called innovation.

This is what innovation is in the information sector. It is about making progress that helps us break away from tiresome, even mind-numbing practices. It is about implementing solutions that were previously inconceivable other than in science fiction novels but which progress, little by little, has eventually made possible. It is making every day's work more comfortable by pushing yesterday's limits a bit further away.

Thus, there are two levels of innovation:

– internalized innovation, used every day within the business, using ideas thought up by staff and management, which generally lead to continuous, more or less successful progress, depending on the change culture developed by the company;

– externalized innovation, supplied by business partners by means of new technologies and new solutions which normally leads to progress that breaks with the past. In the IT industry, the software vendor, the consultancy company and the service company play an important part in this model.

1.2.3. *A central mission for IT*

Companies are becoming increasingly reliant on computers. More and more areas of our working environment and our daily lives involve the use of new technologies. As a result, some far-reaching trends are emerging. Objects are becoming a means of communication and we are gradually becoming linked to each other, exchanging information in more and more varied situations. There is no lack of opportunity. New business models are constantly emerging that businesses may opt for, from start-ups to the most established corporation. How can we detect tomorrow's growth levers? How do we create the means to implement them? Who is responsible for this?

Increasing computerization, the multiplicity of technologies, constant innovation in terms of solutions such as technological architectures clearly indicate that responsibility lies with IT departments. Even if the business unit has its own input to give, you notice that staff members do not mention some requirements because they think that IT will not be able to support the new requirements:

– from a technological point of view: "a technological solution would be necessary but it probably doesn't exist";

– from an organizational point of view "we don't have the structure to manage this type of requirement effectively".

This point of view is no longer justifiable. The IT department now has a greater awareness of the business, even though there is not always the means to do anything about it. Since they are at the center of innovation, the IT teams must be able to detect the benefits to be derived from a technological innovation. The fact that large corporations appoint innovation managers within their IT departments bears witness to this. As far as the functional departments are concerned, the job of the business architect is gradually emerging to complete the system for detecting these types of opportunities.

Here is the response given by a panel of IS directors as part of a survey carried out by Logica Management Consulting and 01 IT department in mid-2006. If the question of adaptability is vital (we will return to this later in the chapter), the ability to create a more fluid relationship between the business unit and the IT department has become one of the innovation missions in the IT domain.

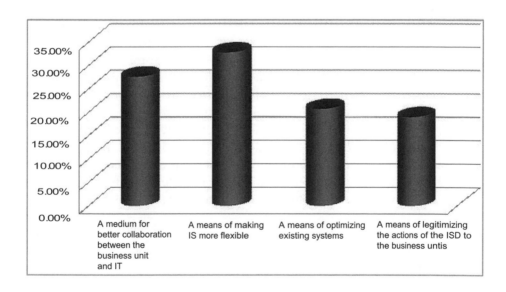

Figure 1.1. *The role of technological innovation for IT departments*

In terms of its connection with innovation, IT is supposed to know, or at least to have identified, solutions that can be best used to meet requirements, methods and practices. It is also supposed to be able to implement them and to be able to promote this solution so that it delivers the required value. Although promoting innovation is a role that has always been assigned to IT departments, they were sometimes suspected of promoting innovation for innovation's sake, of acting dogmatically, in order to make an impression, to experiment, to stockpile technological weapons, the reasoning being "let's get it. It's bound to come in handy sooner or later" or "my software supplier has slipped this new solution into the package that will be very useful to me one day". Too many years have gone by like this and even if this model still persists, it is also getting a little tired. These days nobody is in any doubt as to this model's inadequacy because the role of IT is undergoing a fundamental change.

Since it has become a contributor to the creation of value, IT must henceforth make rational, safeguarded, lasting investments in which technology is used incisively to provide a service for the business unit and to improve the performance of the business. This role will be played all the more objectively since IT, in collaboration with the business units, can show how innovation fits into their context and brings about progress: making users work easier and reducing the risk of errors in tedious tasks, increasing productivity when performing an activity, providing more monitoring solutions and transparency in the activity to make decision-making more reliable. As is traditionally the case, it will then be left to IT to implement the solution.

In its decisive role in the IT innovation cycle, from assessing the relevant innovation and implementing it, the IS department contributes to the performance of the business. What base should it build on and in which directions should it turn to deliver this value?

1.3. Agility and alignment

The development of a business passes through different cycles which are reflected in the information system. These cycles increase in speed, run in parallel and development requirements are permanent, creating constant pressure. The information system is a living being, constantly developing and always changing. Constructing and controlling an information system today means incorporating the unknown, foreseeing the unexpected, anticipating the unforeseeable. This applies just as much during the construction phase as it does during the day-to-day operation of the system. An information system must be compared with those Japanese buildings which, when hit by an earthquake, bend, twist and change shape but do not collapse.

It is under these conditions that the information system may respond to the major task it has been assigned: becoming a profitable growth lever. It is not as if it doesn't already meet these requirements: it would be a pity if companies didn't use it in this way. Nevertheless, it is important to show what methods to use and which objectives to pursue to maintain or strengthen this course.

The question of adaptability is essential. Figure 1.1 reminds us of the main role that IT departments play in innovation – providing more adaptability and alignment capacity for the information system. How do you set up an information system which can cope with short term modifications and, if possible, structural modifications?

Figure 1.2 answers these questions by supplying an organic vision based on several principles:

– improving the performance of the business by standardizing the integration of the innovation in question;

– improving the flexibility of the information system, so as to achieve operational alignment as quickly as possible and at low cost as soon as a request is formulated by the business units;

– controlling the complexity of the information system more effectively by rationalizing the use of business unit assets and reducing the associated costs; and

– measuring the information system operating indicators and proving the validity of the investments made.

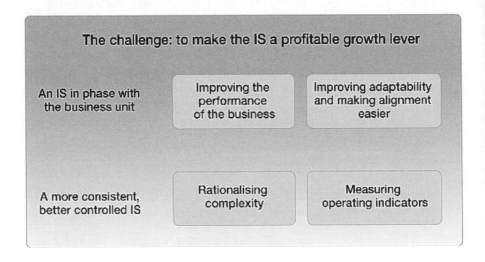

Figure 1.2. *Four objectives for a value-creating information system*

1.3.1. *Improving performance by innovation*

Optimized use of existing resources is not enough to optimize performance. The regular integration of innovations to speed up or strengthen the management of the business unit is decisive. It is necessary to be able to detect and evaluate this innovation. This is what is generally grouped together under the term vision. Jonathan Swift wrote along similar lines, "Vision is the art of seeing invisible things." And making them appear, we might add. There is actually an art to vision: knowing how to carry a project, sometimes just one against everybody, making it happen by achieving one or more successes, transforming it from a short-term investment to a long-term one by bringing the initiatives together, these are all characteristics of an undeniable expertise on several levels.

Vision is an essential prerogative of the Information System Director (and in this respect, times have changed since 2002-2003). As far as the detection and assessment of opportunities are concerned, it falls to IT to promote the innovation among the business units by compiling business cases which illustrate the total added value of a particular technology. This is vital because business units are reluctant to express what they really want, persuaded as they are that technology will not be able to meet their requirements. And yet who better than IT to demonstrate technological development, or suggest ways to meet current, future and even past needs that have been left by the wayside? Innovation is a subject which requires dialogue to be established between the business unit and IT, so that IT can show how good its proposal is. However, the establishment of such a dialogue is dependent on one condition: trust. In order to reassure the business units, IT must look for references that demonstrate the successful adoption of the technology in other contexts. It also has to show its ability to integrate the innovation effectively by means of past successful experiments.

At a given moment, this vision will become reality in the form of an investment budget, one which is duly defined and generally divided into several parts, to be allocated before and after the proof of the concept. This proof is normally established when, in the initial stages, the company has taken the time to look into the opportunity seriously and has carefully assessed it in context. This is the way to turn the vision into a business reality. This implementation stage includes a dimension that is all too often neglected: the integration of the innovation, into the information system. How do you integrate the innovation and supply the required value without destabilising the existing system? Onto what bases can the innovation be grafted?

One method is to treat the existing information assets with respect. This is the best way to adapt the new technology to the company's actual situation. Integrating also means exchanging: information exchanges – in whatever form – with existing applications must be created quickly, on a standardized basis, guaranteed by respect for information assets. This requires prior mastery in certain respects: knowledge of company data, assertive functions and orchestrated processes. If this is not the case, what then? An iterative process is needed which gives body to the assets by linking the new solution to them. When we claim to have an organic vision of the information system, this is mainly referring to those entities which, although they have a certain stability, must constantly integrate development requirements. However, the work involved in optimizing this asset base is not very great. If there is any work, it is often restricted to modeling, particularly for mapping purposes, and does not have any direct knock-on effect in the field.

Sometimes business partners (software publishers, consultancy companies, service companies) promote the innovation themselves. Although it is desirable to benefit from their initiatives, the question of integration remains. Prior mapping work will provide the partner with the means to co-ordinate his action with the existing system and to respect it. In addition, implementing a new technology requires a certain expertise that goes beyond the technology framework and is expressed in terms of methods. The methods must be mastered both by the partner and by the company who will have to take it over.

Iterating and assembling existing elements with a view to reusing them, are two basic means of integrating innovation. They mark out the terrain and ensure the intermediate production of results, as well as a regular measurement of performance in a validation process which is itself iterative.

1.3.2. *Improving adaptability and making alignment easier*

In the ever-changing environment of the 21st century economy, an ability to adapt is no longer a luxury but a necessity. For this reason the terms flexibility and upgradeability have been on everybody's lips for several years, which is reason enough to consider them legitimate.

These two terms must first of all be understood as a reply to the question: how easily can my information system constantly align itself and realign itself in response to new requirements and new demands? It is certainly about ensuring flexibility towards the business unit but, from a technological point of view: what resistance is there to changing my architecture and my applications? In a previous book we have already described an example taken from the financial sector,[3] where the combining of new financial products required weeks, even months and a complete project cycle, due to the great number of existing technologies and the integration of information system applications. The choice of architecture and technology restricted as much as influenced the business unit, an absurd situation which totally contradicts any notion of flexibility and alignment.

In a competitive environment, the bank in question looked for ways to roll out its new products much more quickly. To achieve this it acquired flexible technologies, methods and organization, saving a considerable amount of time in the management of its processes. Do not credit us with words we haven't written: a major project always remains a major project and it will take years before it is fully implemented. However, in some cases, releasing new products quickly, knowing the stock levels of a new shop in real-time or integrating a new partner into an exchange network quickly may provide a critical competitive edge and create value. We shall see that the conditions for this flexibility lie in the organization of the company's information assets and in the way that these assets are used.

Behind these aspects lies the relationship that the company has with change, both from a cultural point of view, and with regard to its information system. It matters not whether the information system describes the world exactly. However, it must represent *the vision that the company has of the world, its market and its ecosystem* (this is called the systemic principle) and adapt precisely to the required changes. If the vision is constantly changing, it is necessary to adapt constantly. If the vision is stable, the stranglehold of change can be

---

3. G. Abou Harb, F. Rivard, *L'EAI au service de l'entreprise évolutive*, éditions Maxima, 2003.

released. The company must retain control over the rate at which it changes. Furthermore, the information system must demonstrate a flexibility and upgradeability matching this rhythm. It cannot achieve this if it is always being broken up and overhauled. To incorporate flexibility as a component part of the information system, it is therefore necessary to find a stable state.

The very notion of an information system is about looking for a stable state. A company is made up of people. It is very unlikely that all of them will have the same point of view and equally unlikely that they will all have the same vision of the whole picture or its individual details. The more people there are, the more the roles and responsibilities increase, and the more difficult it is to establish a common point of view that everybody can share. The information system formulates a united vision of the environment and the business. Total agreement will not perhaps be obtained but the essential factor will have been achieved: a stable state for a certain length of time.

This stable condition is achieved by specific work on basic elements of the information system (not everything can change all the time): the information assets. Data, functions, processes: these describe what the business does and are not technological in themselves. However, from a technological point of view, these assets are often scattered, redundant, duplicated. Centralizing them and sharing them is one way to bring together, on the one hand, the function maps of the information system, and on the other hand, the application and technology maps. Bringing these maps together until they merge makes it easier for the business unit to accept IT, from the expression of a particular requirement to its implementation. The information system destabilization period is reduced. There is better alignment between the business unit and the information system.

You can see how business architecture or planning work becomes of crucial importance in this search, as well as in developing the ability to switch between stable states. This work does not just have to improve existing situations. It must also be used to maintain these gains for a long time.

1.3.3. *Rationalizing complexity*

For a long time we all believed and hoped, somewhat naively, that we could limit the expansion of the information system, see the number of applications decrease and see technologies rationalize themselves. This resulted in a boom in demand for integrated management software packages (or ERP standing for *enterprise resource planning*). The search for a single technology continued doggedly to the point that some people still think it can be achieved, to the point of sacrificing their capacity for alignment and flexibility just for the sake of technological homogenity.

We thought this for a long time and in the end we realized that it would be nothing of the sort. The business does not have all the cards in its hand to achieve this. The introduction rate of new technologies has hardly slowed down. More and more applications are emerging and, as a result of mergers and acquisitions and opening up to partners, information systems continue to expand.

The business unit itself is becoming more and more complex. To differentiate themselves, businesses are achieving unprecedented levels of sophistication. Since the information system reflects the business unit that uses it, it is difficult to imagine how this can be simplified. On the contrary, new technologies are being sought to cope with this, technologies which are more efficient but also more complex in themselves. Complex by nature, first of all, but also because the company will need to master new and unfamiliar procedures. It is normally to limit the risks when getting to grips with this complexity that a company calls on service companies or specialist consultancy companies.

Reducing complexity has therefore become a vain wish that we can barely cling onto any longer. Efforts are consequently focussed on mastering this complexity, in the sense that the complexity has been chosen and not imposed, being an explicit rather than creeping complexity.

Let us take the case of service-oriented architectures. Their aim is to reuse and share business services for the whole information system, with the intention of ironing out an imposed complexity. This imposed complexity is namely the redundancy of functionally identical components, which makes it difficult to roll out changes, carry out maintenance and, overall, undermines the flexibility of the information system. Creating a service-oriented architecture is not really easier: new technology, new design methods and more secure, more robust technical architectures. It is a chosen complexity, particularly since, in addition to making a fresh start, the technology will meet the business needs, that were previously difficult to address, with the same degree of finesse. However, the increase in services will require a degree of organization if they are to avoid gradually becoming more and more difficult to control. It is explicit complexity, if you have understood that you have to organize it and that you are implementing the means to control it. Even if the services are allowed to increase without an appropriate reference framework, problems may not necessarily appear during the first few months of implementation. However, as the number of services increases you will notice that the system will be less aligned and flexible. You will notice, for example, that some services are redundant. The integration of new base services will become slower. It then becomes creeping complexity, complexity that establishes over time and gradually slows down the system's performance.

Basically, complexity is rather like cholesterol. You could say that there is good complexity, complexity that you can foresee, master and control, and bad complexity that arises from a lack of control and inefficient practices. Bad complexity gradually makes the flexibility and alignment capabilities of the information system seize up to the point of undermining the very existence of certain applications. For example, when you use an inter-application exchange platform and, gradually, the average time to complete a flow increases, you can be sure that some practices have gradually paralyzed the performance of the platform. By that stage, back-pedaling is normally an extremely complicated exercise.

Replacing one technology with another, and therefore shifting points of complexity, is not only an admission of failure faced with creeping complexity that is too established. The need to evolve, to advance from a business point of view, may involve implementing new solutions. It is then important to grasp the opportunity to enable the new areas of complexity to be mastered in the long term. It is also important to determine accurately what these points of complexity are and how they might be controled.

Good complexity does not manage itself. Recent urbanization efforts have thus changed the objectives somewhat. Such efforts are no longer just about rationalization. They are also aimed at suggesting methods for controlling the information system and providing the means to control this complexity. To achieve this, they suggest development rules and, we would be tempted to add, sustainable development.

Meeting new requirements and creating new solutions in an existing environment becomes more difficult each time. How do you fit a new link into a chain without weakening it? How do you prove that it is easier to add a new link than to remake an existing one and resist the temptation to break everything? This is the new mission for planners and is sometimes akin to surgery, but it is the only way to guarantee the sustainable development of the information system.

1.3.4. *Measuring operating indicators*

Justifying the relevance of an action, as well as effectively measuring the contribution that the information system makes to performance, remain the ideal ways to prove the validity of the vision and to demonstrate what the information system actually contributes to value creation. There is a wide range of indicators to demonstrate all the benefit that can be drawn from an investment. The best known indicator is return on investment (ROI), which assesses the difference between the investment made and the results obtained, as well as the time required for the operation to pay for itself. ROI depends on the total cost of ownership of the solution, which includes recurring annual costs and is not just restricted to the construction phase of the first project.

One of the points perceived as difficult, is measuring the performance that would have been obtained if no investment had been made. If you consider obvious examples such as the evolution of transport over more than a century, it is not difficult to admit that certain processes have achieved extraordinary performance gains. Technology has made an undeniable contribution to such progress. This example is obvious with hindsight, but, in the initial stages, before the choices are made, it often is not easy to convince people of the success of an innovation. For this reason, it is vital to begin by first preparing the measurement indicators that will subsequently be observed, and to carefully study the associated *business cases*, or even to compile the business plan for the gradual roll out of the solution. To do this, the business units also have to be involved and give current performance data.

Once all these factors have been identified and recorded, it will be necessary to measure over time the values actually recorded on the ground and compare them with the forecasts. The aim is to increase the value of the information system by increasing the value of the assets. This increase in value is necessary to prove the system's contribution to performance but also, more prosaically, to define the financing and invoicing methods for using the assets.

1.4. Sustainable development and information assets

"20 years of sustainable development" was the headline of a French daily paper in the summer of 2007. 20 years is the right age for sustainable development to emerge from its cocoon, spread its wings and benefit from contact with other disciplines. The information industry, which by comparison is more venerable in age, is buzzing with ideas about sustainable development, some of which are gradually, patiently becoming established within the industry. A book devoted to this topic was even published in the autumn of 2007[4], which provides a welcome expansion to this subject of managing information systems.

Until then, sustainable development was all too often restricted to the subject of saving resources, the main aim being to limit the greenhouse effect: "Turn off your printers, switch your screens to standby and you will reduce your carbon footprint." In Britain they call this Green IT. Its scope is almost too superficial, in our view. We believe that there is a much better way of applying sustainable development principles: by using them to improve business performance. To make more with less. To reuse, recycle and reorganize existing business assets.

Major projects aimed at rationalizing network and telecom infrastructures, ERP applications and even messaging systems, have guided the actions of IT decision makers in recent years. Such projects are intended to achieve economies of scale: from the number of servers and the business software applications, to the sourcing of service providers, everything must be reorganized and rationalized. The drive to rationalize and reduce costs, which these days most frequently takes the form of virtualization initiatives, is implemented at IT system level.

Ensuring more fluid organization between the business unit and production makes little sense at IT system level, but rather more sense at information system level. The data and processes have few points in common with the hardware or even with the *software*. Is it therefore possible to rationalize information assets in the same way, to reduce the costs associated with these assets and thus achieve a real improvement in the information system? Generally, the idea is to control the expansion of information systems by relying on existing strengths. The idea, therefore, is to perpetuate past investments, not based on the level of technology but rather in terms of the information

---

4. P. Bonnet, J.-M. de Tavernier, D. Vauquier, *Le système d'information durable*, Hermes, 2007.

assets that they contribute. The innovation will only then be integrated into the landscape by bringing under control the assets that it intends to cover or replace. Then the development of the information system will become sustainable because it will take place with these assets covered.

It goes without saying that major rationalization projects are not going to disappear. Mergers and acquisitions, to mention just one of the many reasons for streamlining a business, will continue to occur, at a less sustained rate, of course, but a significant one nevertheless. Since there is still much to do in this respect, such projects are still going to be a permanent part of IT departments. Similarly, programes for standardizing internal IT department processes, and their associated certifications, still have a bright future.

Against this background, tasks associated with increasing the value of the information system and its assets are becoming more and more important. You must be aware that an information system will lose its qualities if nothing is implemented to control its contribution to value creation, if the assets are squandered by being duplicated many times over throughout the four corners of the business. If they are redundant and inconsistent, these assets will then require colossal efforts from the company to achieve what are sometimes very simple activities. To illustrate this, let us touch on the case of customer data, a major asset if ever there was one. Where is it located? How many applications spread all over the information system use it regularly? Who is responsible for it? How is a new application or a new system going to use or duplicate this information and how will its consistency be maintained?

These are among the many questions that henceforth require standardized answers. For example, how will the company develop a real customer management system? With a CRM ("customer relationship management") tool? Partly, but that is not enough. Will the CRM innovation write off or replace all or part of the current customer data managers? How do you ensure the consistency and exhaustiveness of the information with those that are going to be kept?

Who in the business unit is going to be the responsible for which part of the information? It is necessary to prevent the updating of customer information from creating dramatic overheating, or even a far-reaching greenhouse effect. This could be caused by, for example, several customer databases co-existing in multiple business departments, the absence of a standardized synchronization mechanism, information not being updated globally or some decisions being made by mistake. Furthermore, updates like this could be made hundreds of times in the same day, which means that the cost of the mistake could quickly turn out to be huge.

So is sustainable development a fad or a fundamental movement? Probably both, but it certainly is a deep-seated trend because if businesses do not integrate it quickly, information systems will continue to develop tactically, project after project, in spite of all the guiding principles or possible transformation programs. By contrast, an overall, transversal view would bring increased value.

Sustainable development of the information system can only take place if there is a constant balance between the strength of the business unit and the strength of the IT component, at the center of which are the information assets: data, functions and processes. These assets are transversal and used at numerous points in the information system, however, so little effort is devoted to the organization and co-ordination of this transversality of assets.

These assets can be organized using a wide range of solutions, both technological and organizational, innovative and based on existing systems, which enable companies to meet opportunities, threats and, generally, change more quickly and more effectively. This set of solutions is otherwise known as the transverse information system.

Chapter 2

The Transverse Information System

How much time does a subject area need to get organized, gain visibility and become established in everybody's eyes as an obvious fact? Let us take the case of service-oriented architectures, which we shall deal with in more detail in Chapter 4. The subject first came to our attention at the start of the new millennium, at a time when web services were gaining in popularity. However, it was not until the end of 2006 that a consensus was reached and the babel of voices disputing the point of these architectures fell silent. Today the subject has established itself in its own right. Events no longer deal with the appropriateness of service-oriented architectures, but with the methods for implementing them. According to *La Tribune*, which devoted a whole page to this issue in January 2007, the process takes 7 years.

Meanwhile, another subject is quietly emerging on the horizon. It combines a group of subjects that are sometimes dealt with individually but which, together, make up the core of what could be termed the transverse information system. Service-oriented architectures are also part of this core, as are company data management, transversal business process optimization, and information exchange management.

Now that functional silos have achieved an unprecedented level of computerization, this is where new ways of improving performance will be found. It is a way of increasing the added value of IT, rather than overhauling existing systems; or rather, it is a progressive overhaul of the information system which involves capitalizing on the company's information assets and computerized assets.

The transverse information system fits between the business domains and, as such, acquires its own individual characteristics. It is not a revolution, but rather the culmination of a patient structure that took root a few years ago.

2.1. A regular increase in power

2.1.1. *A field lying fallow*

Some parts of the information system are in a surprising state. Driven by an insatiable appetite for certain subjects, companies unashamedly admit to deficiencies in areas that were formerly treated with disdain. The same is true for in-between areas, which are devoted to the exchange of information between domains, between functional silos.

For a long time there was no transverse technology between applications, other than pure infrastructure components, which were almost assimilated into the pipeline. We are referring to the much-vaunted middleware, which adds no real business value, and which has therefore fallen on hard times. In some cases, exchanges were designed and implemented on the basis of the interfaced application. No mediation software was installed. In others, companies implemented or used an exchange concentrator, which acted as a transfer platform for files on a daily basis, without performing any business role.

The point of assigning business functions to middleware was not apparent and was even generally discouraged. The decision-makers who had mixed business exchanges and rules were kicking themselves for this. Their exchange solution had become a hotchpotch that could not be untangled, a commodity accommodating business functions like patches that were easier to place in the middle than in their respective applications.

In the light of these unfortunate experiences, it was clear to everyone that inter-application integration was a technical area unsuitable for playing the smallest role from a business point of view. This was true until a new category of solution appeared, totally dedicated to standardizing data exchange: EAI (enterprise application integration). The subject won its spurs and seemed to be the perfect way to plan the exchange area both technically and functionally, transversely to the whole information system.

First trialed from 1999 to 2005 as a solution for organizing transversality, EAI was a convincing success. Some companies have been creating exchange bases for several years and have made them available throughout the whole information system. Others, despite sometimes having firm ambitions, have rolled out these solutions on a restricted basis to one or two projects. Finally, others are only just starting the necessary work to fit out this area of their information system.

Subsequently, the term EAI has been subsumed into service-oriented architectures. We think that the gradual disappearance of the term actually bears witness to the emergence of a transverse information system, which includes inter-application integration as one of its basic building blocks. It was EAI that legitimized this transverse information system which we still discreetly call middleware (when referring to the most technical aspect) or exchange area (when we are talking in terms of planning).

2.1.2. *A metaphor for the city*

Organizing the exchange area is a planning subject that is both functional and technical, one which we shall illustrate with a well-known metaphor, that of town planning. As we shall see, the state of affairs is… edifying!

Imagine a town where all the main buildings have already been built, where each part of the town is well defined but where, on the other hand, the road, rail and waterways network, which provides the links between the buildings and the sections of the town, is not very well organized. The water, gas and electricity supplies are not correctly divided or correctly distributed between all the inhabitants. Some transport links are not extensive enough and some journey times are excessively long. As a consequence, passengers waste precious time, resulting in delayed meetings or late goods deliveries. The network does not have sufficient resources to cope with all the vehicles. The city can't live without an efficient infrastructure network.

A parallel can easily be drawn with information systems. The buildings are the applications and the sections of the town are the functional domains. Water, gas and electricity are the shared resources that we shall call the company's master data, business services or transversal business processes. These resources are assets, which are processed using a far from perfect system. How many customer databases or products are duplicated inconsistently in the information systems of companies of any size?

Nevertheless, this type of situation, which would apparently create havoc in the city, is accepted much more readily with information systems. This is why there is still a great deal of work to be done to equip the information system with this network, which is not only capable of efficiently fulfilling the functional requirements that arise from the optimized management of information assets, but which can also cope with a limitless increase in data volumes, and ultimately build this common, shared infrastructure, which is a much sought-after goal.

2.1.3. *The middle empire*

The transverse information system is taking a long time to construct, since it is rarely credited with the business dimension that justifies investment. This dimension is, however, an inherent quality of shared resources. Data, services and processes are functional resources, deliberately geared towards the company's business, and which make up the core of the information system. By optimizing them you bring IT and the business unit closer together and optimize the alignment between them.

The basis of this work consists of optimizing information exchanges. Organizing these exchanges actually hides the type of applications that could bring real value. When organizing master data, for example, the distribution of standardized data to all potential users is a real textbook case. Whether you create a centralized database or not, the exchange cannot be separated from the creation of the data and its distribution.

Normally, with "traditional" exchange methods, you would pinpoint the applications that contained master data, and would distribute them to the applications that required synchronization. Innovation comes into play at this point, spawning technologies dedicated to managing reference data. Why should company data have to be stored in applications that divide them up? Why not store them in an intermediate, transverse, shared area from where they can be distributed to those who want them? You could put them in the middle.

Another example is business processes. A product restocking process between a warehouse and the retail outlets describes a set of activity sequences which are carried out partly within the applications and partly in the form of a set of exchanges between these applications. This transversal process has a business angle between the applications and therefore between the domains. Responsibility for these processes lies in the middle.

In the past, each of these subjects could form the starting point for an EAI project. The point of putting the platform in the middle, in the exchange area, was to limit its impact on the organization of the information system. The data remained tucked away in the applications, the shared business services formed a range of isolated components and transversal processes remained marginalized (about 5% of projects). Generally the assets remained where they were. Thinking has, however, evolved since then. Shared and combined, information assets are gradually moving towards an exchange area which, far from remaining on the periphery, has now become central.

2.1.4. *Towards convergence*

Each of the information assets mentioned is involved in this reorganization. Let us start with processes. The importance of transversal processes – in terms of improving performance, linking the value chain, and opening up to partners – is hardly disputed any more. Long neglected, transversal processes harbour great potential for creating value. They are not enclosed in a single application but run between several applications and can be seen by everybody. They lead to data exchanges that must be optimized.

Keeping duplicate business services in several applications generates the risk of inconsistency. Combining and sharing them increases their overall homogenity and the information system's ability to align. By centralizing developments and changes, and by creating applications built on transverse services, roll out time is reduced and the global flexibility of the system increases.

The same applies to master data. Leaving it in applications has a detrimental effect when it comes to seizing business opportunities (how do you create a complex product quickly if all the data is scattered and duplicated?) and slows down the application of changes (for the same reasons). Centralizing the system improves the overall quality of the data and enables the business to cope better with, for example, time-to-market issues.

Data, services, processes: by their nature these assets provide an obvious link between the business unit and IT. Managing them properly contributes to the overall flexibility and upgradeability of the information system and ensures its sustainable development. New requirements from the business units can be processed quickly, with controled complexity. To understand this properly, let us put ourselves in the opposite position. If inadequate management of these assets leads to missed opportunities, where then is the contribution to value creation? Good management of these assets and their associated exchanges is therefore no longer an option but a necessity. At a time when IT must support growth, it stands to reason that not doing anything risks failing in this objective. Rather than being a nervous obsession, the organization of data, services, processes and exchanges reveals an awareness that growth levers cannot be exploited without implementing innovations, which organize the company's information assets.

By localizing data, services and processes in the middle area, you have to allow for certain impacts on the use and location of these information assets. Their transversal, shared nature requires the revision of certain rules and methods, as well as technologies. The criticality of a centralized system becomes important. The more value-added business functions it incorporates, the more its resources must be available everywhere and the less it can afford any weaknesses. Tolerance of breakdowns, management of activity peaks and quality of service are assured by systems that demonstrate a very high level of performance.

This is why the transverse information system marks the emergence of a new information system, which requires specific work if it is to allow the company to grasp opportunities and gain a competitive edge.

This environment is being created gradually and some rules are therefore still undefined. IT departments are presented with a relatively blank page upon which they have total creative freedom. Some centers of gravity of the information system have been modified, as have certain areas of responsibility for the assets. A new system of governance must be formulated.

2.2. Optimizing business unit assets

With a view to safeguarding investments and supporting value creation, some companies organize all or part of their transverse information system and they do this whether they have an explicit awareness of this system or whether they are acting more "intuitively". By doing so they are wending their way through a platform logic which, on the one hand, can speed up the course of major information system projects, but which can also perpetuate the whole information system. We have labeled these new platforms and innovative solutions "new information system solutions" (NISS). They raise the value of the information system, by placing it within a logic to create value for the business unit and to support the performance of the company.

How are these solutions innovative? Because they enable the reuse and combination of the information system and, consequently, ensure its productive implementation and homogenity. The previous part emphasized the organizational methods that would guarantee consistent co-ordination of the new solutions. You also know in technical terms how these solutions can be obtained: by using a model focussed on the business unit, reusability, sharing and combining the components, deleting the code and assigning increased space for parameter setting and configuration, graphic displays, user autonomy in relation to the solution; so that certain modifications no longer have to pass through IT. The ability of the solutions to manage all these aspects becomes a predominant factor in the choice of a particular solution.

The transverse information system combines autonomous but interdependent domains that are put together to describe the much needed *lingua franca* of the information system. These domains are as follows:

– standardization then centralization of the company's master data (MDM or master data management), which opens up the way to optimized management of information, is a stable base on which the whole of the system may rest;

– identification and then display of shared, reusable services (service-oriented architecture) creates function frameworks and, using implementation methods based more on combining components than on the production of code, ensures that development cycles are shorter because of new software implementation methods;

– activation of transversal business processes and optimized management of the company's business processes (BPM or business process management) also reduces development cycles by means of an implementation method based more on setting parameters. It also introduces a much greater potential to upgrade the rolled-out processes, and enables specific features and local autonomous factors to be better accounted for.

Information asset	Service provided	Results obtained
Data	Homogenity of the IS Quality of the data	Reduction in product time-to-market Better knowledge of customers Increased flexibility and alignment capacity Rationalization of IS complexity
Services	Combining Reusing and sharing assets	Reduction in application development cycles Business flexibility and IS upgradeability
Process	Business user autonomy Better visibility for the activity Standardization of processes while taking specific local features into account	Creation of value by means of transversal processes Reduction in development cycles Increased flexibility and alignment capacities Improvement in the business unit/IT relationship

Table 2.1. *Benefits of business asset management*

These subjects are not independent. They complement each other. For example, you can combine the construction of a service architecture and a process management platform to reduce the flexibility benefit. Even if each one of the subjects can be addressed separately and staggered in time, all of these domains bring the business unit and IT closer together and improve operational alignment.

All the major players in the market are present in this global positioning, theoretically safeguarding the investment made. We say theoretically, because the level of maturity of certain players in this sector still requires a case-by-case investigation, which is more a demonstration of weakness than of strength. Choosing the platform of one or another of these market players almost becomes a question of culture and sensitivity in approaching a software publisher. To a lesser extent, this choice constitutes a decision to balance the application portfolio.

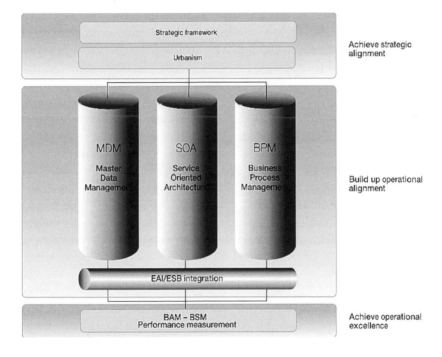

Figure 2.1. *Organization of the transverse information system*

By doing this, all the objectives of the transverse information system are met:

– Company performance is improved.

– New solutions are implemented that manage information assets better and make it easier to compile and create competitive, winning business models. For example, better controled product reference data will reduce the time-to-market of new products.

– Adaptability and alignment are improved.

– These solutions give priority to parameter setting and combination, to the detriment of new implementations and code generation. Projects are handled by evaluating the scope of the main changes, in order to lessen their impact and by reusing existing components. This option to reuse components homogenizes the information system and the behavior of the teams brought in to work on it.

– Complexity is rationalized.

– Centralizing the management of assets makes them easier to control and more future-proof. Furthermore, the complexity of the information system is better understood. On the other hand, the complexity of the information system increases. In fact, the purpose of these new solutions is to share information resources, particularly to improve process performance. Therefore, the increase in demand for the assets must be managed and control of information movement must be improved, which requires more robust, more complex and better dimensioned architectures.

– Operating indicators are measured.

– The assets are available at any time with the expected quality of service. They are also subject to utilization, which can and must be justified at any time. Management reports will certify the performance of the created solution and the fact that the service commitments have been honored.

These four benefits are not achieved by separate but by combined actions. The big bang is no longer possible. Planning must be pragmatic and performed section-by-section. Each major NISS project is an opportunity to urbanize a section of the information system.

2.3. The impact on the IT department agenda

Given the type of questions for which they provide an answer, there is every reason to assume that NISS are on IT managers running lists. But this is not always the case. A study carried out with 01 IT Department in 2006 revealed that service-oriented architecture or master data management topics, were perceived to be more of a concern for information system architects (which they are to say the least). However, it is very easy to show that this is not so.

2.3.1. *A question of governance*

The subject of information system governance has determined some of the actions of IT managers in the past few years. Defining governance goes beyond the remit of this book. We even failed to find an obvious definition in the excellent book by Frédéric Georgel, which examines this subject in detail. In that particular publication, governance is sometimes described by its objectives, sometimes by its methods but never for what it is. Therefore, during our study, we asked contributors to give us their own definition. Their replies speak for themselves.

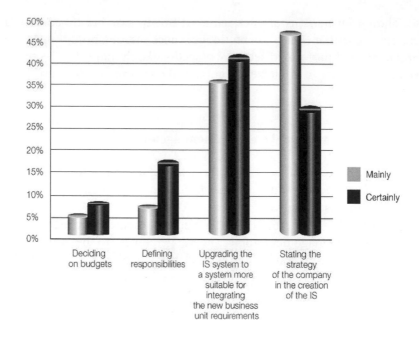

Figure 2.2. *A definition of governance*

As you can see, the overriding opinion is that governance is not so much about responsibilities and budgets as organizing IT, so that it is geared to the business units and the company's strategy. The aim behind organizing resources better is to achieve greater strategic and operational alignment. By resources we mean people, but also resources such as information assets. The topic of NISS is completely in line with the expectations of IT managers. It is even one of the main contributions of governance.

2.3.2. Redefined priorities

When asked about their opinion concerning the issues involved with governance, the consulted IT departments gave a variety of different answers. Nevertheless, a predominant trend emerged among 50% of the respondents: the main governance issue is better alignment of the information system with the business unit.

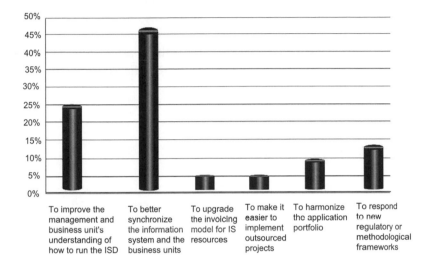

Figure 2.3. *Governance issues*

Considering the previous results, this verdict may seem logical because it is linked; however, when these two pieces of information are read together they show how much the context of IS governance has changed since it started. It is no longer about effectively coping with the increase in regulatory constraints. It is no longer about how to organize sourcing and outsourcing. From now on, organization will have to be based on a strong objective: establishing a continuous, enhanced link between what the business units want and the IT solution.

By organization we are not just referring to people and how they collaborate with each other but rather all resources. This includes technological solutions that can provide answers, which will strengthen this link and make it more free-flowing. The new information system solutions meet this need perfectly.

The emergence of the transverse information system provides an environment which does not require businesses to break up functional assemblies that have been created, sometimes at great cost, but, on the contrary, allows them to collaborate with these assemblies better on the one hand, and to make them work more efficiently on the other hand.

2.3.3. Supporting the NISS investment

Since the emergence of governance procedures, there has been a gradual change in the positioning of managers responsible for IT investment decisions. Having once been mainly responsible for implementing IT solutions and operating the system, the IT department is becoming with increasing frequency a partner of business unit managers and general managers in terms of investment choices.

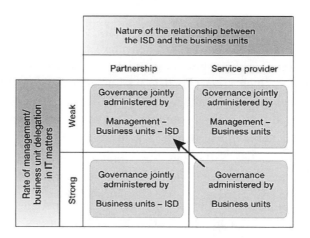

Figure 2.4. *The changing role of the IT department*

As a contributor to profitable growth, the IT department must provide solutions for major business unit issues. As the owner of the evaluated innovation, the IT department must promote the components it thinks best able to provide the answers, then find the means to incorporate them into the existing system at low cost and with minimal impact.

The business units must be given proof that value has been created, whereas IT must be given proof that progress has been made in organizing the information system.

The principles of sustainable development lie in the link between the business unit and IT. The whole information system benefits from this link.

With the new information system solutions, the IT department has this triple lever. The advantage and disadvantage of these solutions are that they provide structure. They are not chosen for their impact but for their ability to organize the transverse information system over time – a subject that will become increasingly important between now and 2010, whether we like it or not. Companies who have taken this into consideration will have prepared their growth levers by then.

The means of determining the results and impact of implementing the NISS are set out in Chapter 11.

2.3.4. *Organizing transversality*

Data, services and processes are theoretically useful and can be used by everybody. They constitute transversality points at company level. For new projects and for running applications, transversal teams dedicated to managing assets are gradually being set up.

It is often more effective to anticipate this change and to ensure that the organization is in place before the technology is rolled out.

A distribution sector company appointed one of its project managers to head up this branch of IS. This decision is testament to a thought process that is already well advanced: middleware, which was previously a technical infrastructure idea, is giving way to the transversal information system, which focuses on the business unit.

Thus, when organization work starts on this vast construction site, one of the first and best actions to implement is to entrust it to a person officially nominated as responsible, rather than letting roles and responsibilities be vaguely assigned while waiting for the results of the study or until a consensus emerges.

This question of transversality is not merely a fanciful concept invented by consultants. A considerably large number of companies have approached it in the past by creating competence centers, a solution that is still popular and which we shall deal with in Chapter 10.

The IT department panel consulted in our study gave a clear answer to the question of transversality. In 755 of cases, it is about establishing a better model for collaboration between the business unit and IT.

How? By incorporating various temporary or permanent profiles in these structures, from the business expert to the operations engineer, via the assistant project manager and the technical expert.

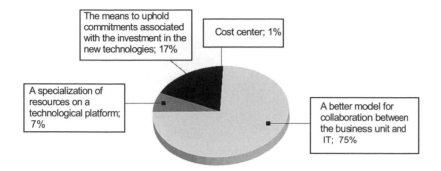

Figure 2.5. *The purpose of transverse structures*

In this logic, the competency center is everything but a development factory. It ensures that the information assets are used properly and guarantees efficient governance of the solution over time.

Whilst in some cases the transverse structure may, ultimately, be gradually watered down into other teams, this cannot be the case with NISS. Since the information assets are transverse, the responsibilities must also remain transverse. The questions do not relate so much to the setting up of a competency center but to the responsibility entrusted in such an entity.

This explains why responsible transversality is not the dominant trend that organizations are pursuing. In spite of all the interest in this question, 27% of IT departments cannot or do not yet wish to set up transverse teams. On the other hand, 47% of them say that they are giving the question serious thought.

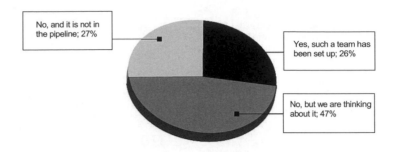

Figure 2.6. *The desire to set up transverse teams*

It is therefore still a little too early to say whether a revolution is underway and that the arrival of NISS will have a significant impact on the organization of IT departments. However, the implementation of NISS, solutions that are able to ensure better alignment to the business unit over time, cannot be restricted to technology. The organization must work towards effective co-ordination. This is probably why, in feasibility studies, we have seen a great increase in requests for recommendations regarding organization, prior to choices being made. The 47% who are thinking about it have asked themselves this type of question. Furthermore, if the successful implementation of NISS depends on the establishment of transverse responsibilities, it is likely that a pragmatic decision will be made in its favor.

The transverse information system is a domain which is becoming organized, but which has not yet gained universal visibility. It is a blank page, which each IT department has plenty of freedom to fill in. It is the opportunity to try out solutions that are much trickier to construct due to their impact on the existing system, which lies within a functional silo. In the following pages we provide numerous examples drawn from our own experience. They illustrate the answers found, sometimes with our help, by businesses of all sizes and in all activity sectors, in terms of the integration of NISS and their contribution towards the effective governance of information systems.

Chapter 3

Master Data

Information represents a real asset for a company. As manufacturing wanes, this asset becomes more important, this is occurring in our economies where the service sector is gaining ground.

Information is a valuable asset, whatever form it is in, from the database or a unit, to non-structured information or a document. If it is well organized, information makes decision-making more reliable and even enables opportunities to be detected proactively.

The wider this asset base, the more difficult it is to administer, at least without appropriate management. Housing stock, share portfolios, collections of any kind – all these require a minimum of organization if they are not to lose energy and value.

It is difficult to imagine a stamp collector leaving his precious stamps out of his sacrosanct albums on the edge of a shelf. And it is not only a question of being careful.

As unlikely as it may seem, without an album, without a register kept from day to day, without a portfolio to refer to, a collector could easily buy a duplicate.

It is the same with a company's information. Data that constitutes the very foundation of the information system, which is always increasing, which should represent a permanent center of attention, is still managed today with a staggering lack of thought. As the amount of information increases, the company even gives the impression of being helpless faced with this explosion.

3.1. An unclaimed asset

3.1.1. *An eloquent study*

In a survey carried out by Microsoft/01 DSI with the help of Unilog Management at the beginning of 2007, only 11% of people surveyed showed that they had some sort of control over the management of their information assets.

For the remaining 89%, this gap has nothing to do with the quality of the existing infrastructure but rather with data management: creating and modifying it, accessing it, ensuring that regulations are complied with, etc.

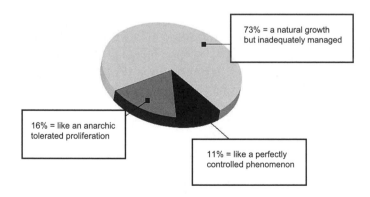

73% = a natural growth but inadequately managed

16% = like an anarchic tolerated proliferation

11% = like a perfectly controlled phenomenon

Figure 3.1. *Perception of the growth of information (source: Microsoft)*

In the detailed replies, the worst off seem to be large companies.

It is a phenomenon that is, no doubt, due to a more consistent amount of data on the one hand but also to the existence of information silos, indicating gaps as far as transversality is concerned.

Some 21% of companies with more than 500 employees even go as far as considering the growth in the volume of their data as an "anarchic proliferation". Moreover, only 21% of companies with fewer than 250 employees think that they have perfect control over this growth.

This assessment is not always perceived as serious, nor shared within the company. Sometimes it is necessary to untangle a complex chain of causality to realize that an unfortunate decision has been made owing to a lack of high-quality data or data that is not sufficiently synchronized.

Sometimes people focus on the performance of processes, whereas this performance cannot be achieved and maintained on a permanent basis without quality data. The cost to businesses of low-quality data has been estimated at more than $600 billion a year in the USA.[1]

Data is the foundation stone of the information system. Would you think of living in a house with shaky foundations? While it is admittedly possible, it will turn out to be more expensive, less comfortable and, undoubtedly, more risky in the end.

1. Source: the Data Warehouse Institute (TDWI), "Data quality and the bottom line: achieving business success through a commitment to high quality data", *Data Quality Report*, TDWI, 2002.

3.1.2. *Reference data*

Nevertheless, the means exist, even if it is true that as far as they are concerned, certain inequalities still prevail. In fact, not all of them provide all types of information with the same coverage yet. Structured data management has thus made significant progress over the last few years.

In particular, reference data management is emerging as a domain where technology, methods and organization converge towards industrial solutions that are likely to significantly improve performance.

Reference data describes real-world entities (customers, products, suppliers and even others) within the company's environment, which are considered to be invariants because of the limited number of modifications that affect them.

This is information that structures the company's activity. The content of this information is not modified during a transaction:

– some will be common to a large number of companies, such as customers, suppliers, employees, the organization and its structure, the company's range of products and/or services, its geographical location and the geographical structure;

– other information will be completely specific or linked to the business unit or sector of the business, such as the database for microprocessor tests in the semi-conductor sector, or the molecule database in the pharmacy division (the latter could be considered a raw material database, which it is frequently).

Reference data is used at a number of points in the information system, as shown in Figure 3.2.

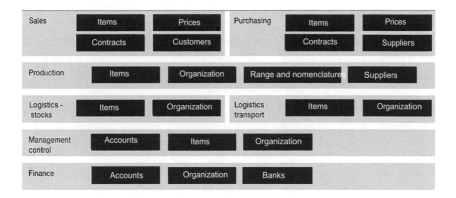

Figure 3.2. *Reference data and its duplication*

The characteristics of reference data may change without undermining its nature or its uniqueness. Three major types of data that concern us can be identified here.

3.1.2.1. *Master data*

This is normally the *main business unit objects* (*business unit core*) *of a function domain*. This data is at the heart of the information system and is used by the principal applications, in which it is tagged several times: customer, item, supplier, etc.

3.1.2.2. *Constituent data*

This is data which will be used as attributes for master data. It contains several attributes itself: addresses, bank details, bank ID, etc.

3.1.2.3. *Parameter data*

This consists of *tables of values* or *nomenclatures*, such as postcodes, currency codes, IATA codes, etc. Essentially, it is the most shared data and for this reason it must merit special attention.

Each of the three data types is complementary and connected with the others, as shown in Figure 3.3.

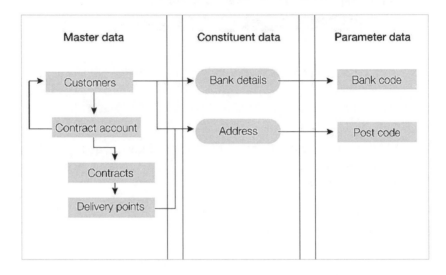

Figure 3.3. *Connection of the types of data*

The management of reference data must comply with the three following principles:

– the option to identify what the source that authenticates a certain amount of transverse reference data is;

– sharing the administration of this reference data by installing tools suitable to manage it;

– making this reference data available to different consumers and distributing it in a co-ordinated manner.

As each player, both internal and external, uses his own IT tools, this data is provided to be consumed by the different applications authorized to use it. For this reason you will note that reference data is normally present at several points of the information system, whether synchronization mechanisms have been put in place or not. This is so that the reference data becomes the preferred data.

3.1.3. *The issues involved in good reference data management*

Reference data is necessary both on an operational and a strategic level and, ideally, it is always the same data but processed and used differently. Managing it badly, only taking a part of it into account or using poor-quality data leads to incomplete or incorrect decisions being made with harmful consequences for the company, its image and its development. Mediocre data quality disrupts a company's day to day business, incurring additional operation costs and dissatisfaction with the whole ecosystem (customers, suppliers, staff, etc.).

There is a great deal at stake when managing reference data, both from the business unit and the information system point of view. We shall mention the main ones here and we shall refer you to works that deal with this subject for more information:

– *Business process performance*: reduces business cycle times associated with reference data or reference processes; improves and making processes more reliable thanks to accessible, high-quality reference data; and reduces processing times and costs associated with modifying reference data, passing on data modifications to all the applications using this data.

– *Making analyses and decision-making more reliable*: avoids duplicated data, incorrect or incomplete data, non-compliant data, etc.

has a 360° viewpoint, i.e. a unified, consistent view of reference data; and reinforces decision-making processes.

– *Regulatory obligations*: track modifications and manage versions of reference data to meet regulatory constraints.

3.1.4. *Structuring data management*

Efficient data management requires consideration of principles specific to this area and decisions concerning the allocation of roles and responsibilities for these principles. They describe the life cycle of the data from the definition of the semantic model, "what data describes the company and its ecosystem and what terminology shall we agree on to describe it?" to the ways of tracking and auditing the data, "what use has been made of this data since it was created and who has used it?".

3.1.4.1. *Definition of a semantic model*

"Let's call a cat a cat": this famous French expression (which in English equates to "let's call a spade a spade") leaves no room for doubt, the reason being that you will only find one definition of "this small pet mammal with soft fur, [...] triangular ears and retractable claws [...]" in the dictionary. A dictionary is a goldmine because it brings everybody round to the same way of thinking. Furthermore, although there are several published in France alone, the semantics of the terms are identical from one dictionary to another or, in any case, should be, since they are determined by a central body, the French Academy.

This goldmine does not exist in most companies, perhaps because very few of them have agreed to appoint an "Academy" responsible for making the semantics agree. Worse still, if it does exist, it has often been initiated by the IT department to meet the needs of function departments. In other words, they can consider themselves lucky if this dictionary exists and is not gathering dust at the bottom of a cupboard. Still from the 01 DSI/Microsoft study, the "lack of willingness on the part of the management", the only people ultimately authorized to set up a transversal system, is one of the major obstacles to rolling out a data management procedure.

Why not create an Academy for all companies from now on? Some standardization initiatives exist throughout the world but their purpose is mainly to make communication between companies possible. The company is a king within its walls. It can rewrite the world if that is what it wants. The search for performance explains it and justifies it. But there is an imbalance when, internally, the function departments speak different languages. Each one describes the world differently within its silo and there is no dictionary to reconcile them. It is at this very moment that you reach the limits of autonomy. It becomes possible for one term to describe two completely different entities semantically.

There is a famous example of this situation. It's called "missile launching". During simulations carried out by the American army, the missiles launched missed their target by a considerable amount and were engulfed by the waves. The reason given, outrageously, was that the different army corps hadn't used the idea of a mile in the same way. In one case the calculations had been done by taking a land mile and in others a nautical mile.

This example is significant enough. It shows how a small difference in meaning can trigger major catastrophes. It shows how the absence of a semantic model is likely to destroy value. Consequently it is difficult to find efficient data management by letting this idea go. It even appears to be a vital pre-requisite and the necessary time must be devoted to define it, all the more so since there are a number of data modeling workshops on the market with the right tools to carry out the procedure (the Mega Suite, Corporate Modeler by Casewise, Aris by IDS Scheer, PowerAMC, etc.).

3.1.4.2. *Metadata*

When you buy a product, you find a lot of information on the label that describes the product and tells you particularly about its composition, whatever the product and whatever you are going to use it for. It's the same with data management. It doesn't matter what you are going to use the information for, it is described by more or less standardized information which enables it to be managed: metadata. Metadata is data about data and its context. It provides the necessary information for monitoring, processing and acknowledging user rights, data archiving and storage.

In what way is metadata useful for managing data?:

– it improves the governance of data thanks to a precise definition of the data, the associated rules and the links that this data has with other data and with the functions that use it;

– it makes administering proof easier when responding to compliance and security constraints; and

– it authorizes the management of information assets (security, quality) by specifying the sensitivity of each piece of information, by assigning indicators to measure data performance and quality by eventually increasing the value of the information.

In the same way as a semantic model, a meticulous, sound definition of metadata is a key factor for success when drawing up a data management strategy. Metadata completes the semantic model and sets the foundations for the information system, at least partially and for a certain time.

3.1.4.3. *The process manager*

Once the model has been defined, it is important to create two types of processes to deal with reference data management:

– data creation processes; and

– data distribution processes.

The purpose of the first is to have the data created by the different business units involved in its life cycle. This is done either by exchanging data between users up until the information is stored in the repository or by using an already centralized console. In all cases these processes require a human activity.

The second ones, on the other hand, are highly automated. Once the data has been created, it must be distributed to all the applications that use it. An orchestrator, if necessary an SOA, is likely to play this role (see Chapter 4) sending the information:

– either in push mode, with the application integrating the new data as it goes along;

– or in pull mode, where the application is notified of the arrival of a new piece of data and goes to fetch it when it is available to integrate it.

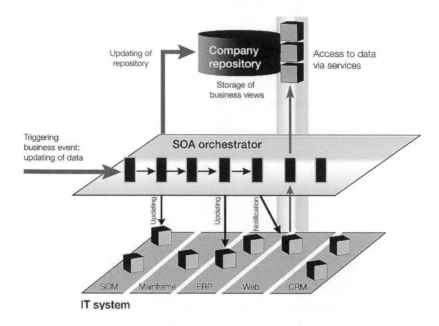

Figure 3.4. *Creation and distribution of reference data*

The type of repository (centralized or virtual) will be discussed in the following pages, in particular by relating experiences. In all cases, this repository must be accessible via data access services and not directly.

Finally, it is important that the creation and distribution processes are clearly defined and maintained, because they will set the overall synchronization rhythm of the information system. Some compromises may be found. They will depend on the rhythm of the alignment requirements. Implementing these processes will thus bring flexibility to the business unit, whereas the solutions will bring flexibility to the information system.

3.1.4.4. *Data quality management*

Data quality management is the last stone in our building, a stone that is a little different. Unlike the compilation of semantic models and metadata, which act almost as invariants, improving data quality is a continuous procedure.

Specific solutions for dealing with data quality management are gradually emerging. They are used to answer a number of questions in addition to those already mentioned, using preparatory work on the data and repeated actions that can maintain the required quality over time.

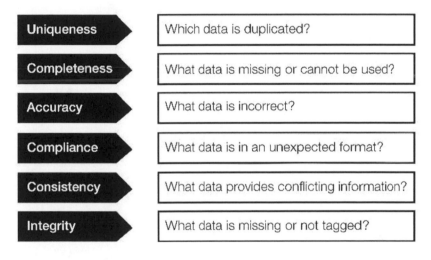

Figure 3.5. *Data quality criteria*

Procedures for evaluating, improving or monitoring quality are normally equipped with DQM (data quality management) software suites which enable the following stages:

– data profiling, where the data is analyzed to find errors, inconsistencies, data redundancy and incomplete information;

– data cleansing, which corrects, standardizes and verifies data;

– data integration which reconciles, merges and associates semantically linked data;

– data augmentation, which improves the data by using internal and external sources, and removes duplicates; and

– data monitoring, which monitors and checks the integrity of data over time.

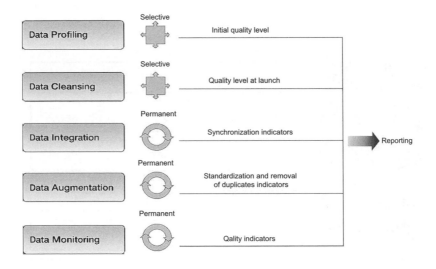

Figure 3.6. *Data quality procedure*

In this market, current developers normally come from the decision analysis environment, illustrating the gateway between the operation and the decision that efficient data management enables:

– Informatica, Informatica Data Explorer and Informatica Data Quality;

– BusinessObjects (Oracle), Data Quality XI (ex-FirstLogic);

– DataFlux, Data Quality Integration Solution;

– IBM, WebSphere Information Server (formerly Ascential).

3.1.5. *Transverse solutions for reference data*

Ensuring the consistency of reference data between all the environments of an information system has always been a difficult exercise. Suffice it to say that the branches of a company often work independently of the parent company, thus brushing aside opportunities for synergy or economy of scale. Mergers and acquisitions also pose great problems as far as reference data consistency is concerned, just as company splits do (deregulation or anti-trust for example).

If at a technical level companies manage to integrate the new software solutions from an acquisition, they find it difficult to integrate the management processes because of basic incompatibilities between the processes themselves as well as the data models.

The advantage of creating one point of truth for reference data has been clearly highlighted since 2005 and there are many of us, IT players, who have become aware of this. But if this role has been clearly established, the responsibility, on the other hand, has not been uniformly appreciated. As proof of this we shall show you the replies broken down, as shown in the Microsoft/01 DSI study (see Figure 3.7).

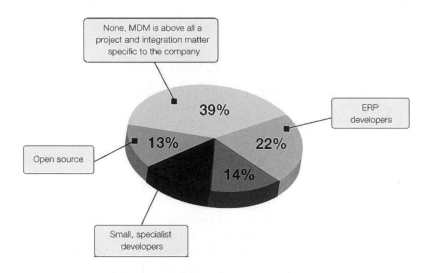

Figure 3.7. *Responsibility in reference data management (source: Microsoft)*

If you abstract the only non-technological reply ("a project and integration matter specific to the company"), the even distribution of replies on technological offers does not show any leadership and no responsibility is clearly apparent. ERP developers appear to have a slight advantage over the others (22%), but this perception must immediately be demolished. In fact, according to Franck Régnier-Pécastaing, our Master Data Management Manager: "reference data cannot be supported just by an integrated software package. It will always have certain attributes missing and so could not be a real piece of reference data that can be consumed by all." At management software package level, this involves customization, both in its internal structure and in its communication with the outside, activities that consume time and energy, at the time and on an ongoing basis.

Since responsibility for the data does not seem to be able to be borne natively by the applications, the cursor is transferred mechanically to the transverse information system – open source developers, small specialist developers, infrastructure suppliers – end to end, these categories refer to mediation solutions that can share data and share its creation, modification and distribution processes, all concepts inherent in the transverse information system.

These solutions create and co-ordinate centralized or virtual repositories, within a more global master data management procedure.

3.2. Master data management: centralization

Within the data management process, the setting up of a centralized, transversal repository is the area which has advanced the most in the last few years. These technologies have been combined under the acronym MDM, master data management.

Several implementations in businesses of all sizes bear witness to the importance attached to this basic NISS area.

3.2.1. *Master data management*

MDM is a method of processing data that pools all master data within a repository.

This will be used as a model and a single source of truth when creating and updating data in the various applications involved. *This repository is a pre-requisite.*

Far from being attached to an existing business application and still less unique, this repository is located within the transverse information system.

Specifically, this repository contains all the objects essential to the life of the company and describes the links between them: customer, supplier and partner reference numbers, etc.

Thanks to this layer, which is normally associated with control and validation devices, the objects are modified consistently and duplication is avoided. Ultimately this device aims to guarantee business data quality in the production phase.

In general terms, a reference data management solution:

– defines the roles and individual access rights for each stage in the data management process;

– provides data cleansing services to compare records and remove duplicates;

– offers collaboration capacity to co-ordinate decisions for reconciling and rationalizing reference data;

– is responsible for detecting changes, synchronizing and replicating data in order to pass on any modification that has taken place in the repository.

However, it calls for:

– a manager to be defined for each reference data category (customers, products, suppliers, organizational structures, etc.). This manager will ensure the quality and updating of the data in all systems, processes and for all people who use this shared resource;

– reference data in all areas to be extracted from the various operational, transaction and analysis systems to load them into repositories for each area or into a central hub;

– data quality standards to be applied to obtain a set of clean data (particularly when removing duplicates from the records);

– reference data reconciliation and rationalization rules to be defined. The aim is to obtain an optimum list or hierarchy for each area that is comprehensible to all users whether they are individuals or applications; and

– the rules and methods for synchronizing repositories or the hub with operational and reporting systems to be defined in order to guarantee that all systems use the right data all the time (same value, same version).

3.2.2. *Two choices of architecture*

In these centralized architectures, the choice of data storage may follow two different methods:

– The purpose of a globalizing repository is to *manage models that collect together all the dimensions of a concept within the same object* (for example, the customer seen from both the marketing and logistics point of view, etc.). An example is a chart of accounts that includes the attributes defined by management and those defined by accounting.

– A shared repository *manages small models shared by several IS entities* (for example, the customer with a minimum number of attributes: name, address, number). You could implement this concept for the customer with a common, shared repository and more complex models suitable for each function area: scoring indicators for marketing, address information for the delivery department, preferences for the website, etc.

3.2.3. *A customer database in industry*

In its transformation plan, a major international company has identified thirteen master databases to improve the quality of data at group level. Strategically, the customer database has been identified as the first one to be created. The aim is to gear the company firmly towards its customers rather than its products. Quality control and better synchronization of operations are the two major requirements.

The project was supported by a software package for customer databases: IBM WebSphere Customer Center. However, the company decided that an MDM application must be able to cover several types of database, and thus WCC must comply with the databases used or the organization, in addition to specialist solutions for product data management which is extremely specific (for the half-finished product database for example).

At the end of the project, the main benefits were checked in the standardization procedure initiated by the database procedure and project resources were simplified and shared. To sustain these benefits over time, this company set up an organization responsible for defining the rules and monitoring projects following the database organization. The organization extends from the strategic level (Governance Committee) to the operational level (Data Referential Foundation). It is responsible for data, and is in charge of rules but also for applying them properly. The business units are very heavily involved in the procedure.

The iterative approach is seen as the key factor for success. The projects progress at a measured pace but are consistent with an overall governance vision. The first project (the customer database) has the advantage of being the most visible, sensitive to the business units while enabling the solution to be implemented in a structured way. Thus, the database was created first, followed by a data quality manager.

Amongst the difficulties encountered we shall mention that initially not enough account was taken of the existing systems, the link processes with the legacy systems were constrained by their specific features. It is vital to assess the existing systems in order to define a reasonable, structured level of ambition.

The involvement of the business units depends on the value the database projects may provide for them. However, this value is difficult to demonstrate because database projects are essentially projects which support business processes and applications but do not appear directly in the business units. The value generated is therefore indirect.

Thus, if data is the foundation of the building and if the object is openly to achieve an increase in the value of the data, it is in the processes that you will best manage to prove the value created: creation and distribution processes certainly but also and above all the performance of the company's operational processes. Quality can be measured but indirectly: you could probably manage to estimate the cost of bad decisions associated with low-quality data or the cost of missed opportunities. The following example, referring to the time to market for new products, proves this.

3.2.4. *Volume retailer databases*

A company in the volume retailing sector wants to improve its merchant database management. This covers all the product master data but also suppliers and contracts.

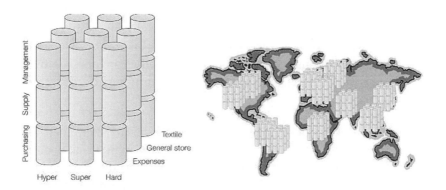

Figure 3.8. *Merchant databases*

Although it is very sensitive, this data does not have all the necessary flexibility and upgradeability; in fact, the information system development logic was first aligned to the business unit, causing the juxtaposition of applications and technologies that were sometimes redundant.

The processes for creating and managing data normally describe inter-application paths, which, taking into consideration the large number created, turned out to be more and more unmanageable and a source of inconsistencies, i.e. the same information entered at several different points with very little control of errors. In spite of this acknowledgement, when this company merged with another company in its sector and their respective information systems were joined, there was an opportunity to put the subject of reference data at the top of the IT department priority list.

This is a recurrent factor in NISS investment. Improving what already exists is often not the best way of convincing budget holders. Logically and legitimately, providing a significant response to a business issue is the way to trigger a budget allocation. Here it was also a question of reducing the time taken to get a new product on the shelves. The positive effects on certain existing processes and on the planning of the information system are thus not directly sought after but are benefits brought about by these solutions, by good management of information assets and by effective governance over time. You must know how to grasp this starting point to extract the entire value from the NISS investment.

To come back to our subject, the group obviously examined the "merchant database" subject to reduce the heavy management costs (0.2–0.4% of turnover per year) that the merger did not reduce automatically. Several projects were initiated to control the whole repository chain: pre-repository, opening up the information system to partners, modeling the product sheet, a manual process for enhancing information and control, monitoring indicators, error management, etc. A significant structuring project will in any case only see the light of day by sponsoring at several levels.

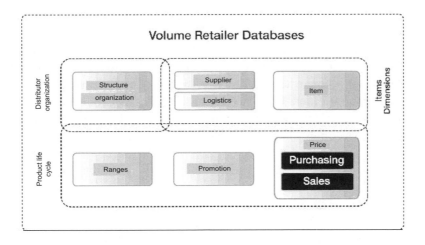

Figure 3.9. *Structure of merchant databases*

This is also part of the NISS investment – the option to have flexible resources often involves major projects and a large amount of structuring. We shall return later to platform logic; it is a generic, accelerating set in the end but one which you must take time to create properly. The initial projects are connected to this platform. Thus, this business relied on an initial successful example to subsequently implement its repository procedure globally. Moreover, this success preceded most of the projects, as well as the setting up of the repository competence center, and enabled the dynamics to be initiated in each country.

In a way, an NISS platform is constantly changing. An NISS project is never really finished but the quality of the solution created will be judged on its ability to integrate new functions, new data and new projects quickly.

When we talk about platforms we are not just talking about the technological solution. Chapter 2 showed the importance of the organization and governance of the solution. In our case, a competence center was constructed at the same time as the repositories. Effective change management is also an integral part of the success of the procedure because several categories of personnel are involved in implementing this type of solution. The business processes involved with referencing suppliers and items, purchases and creating data have been revised to be more effective. They have been documented, roles and responsibilities have been described and each business concept has been explained in a glossary.

Generally, even if the technical complexity of the construction is not to be underestimated (and the example above can be used to show its scope), change management is one of the main pitfalls to be avoided if you really want to see the procedure through to a successful conclusion. We shall come back to this subject in Chapter 10.

3.2.5. *The state of the market*

As the master data management market is growing strongly, all types of developers are trying to gain a foothold. We shall see that these operations take place in two main directions: "business to technology" or "technology to business".

The most notable developers on the French market are:

– IBM: WebSphere WPC for product data, WebSphere WCC for customer data (these two products are due to merge in 2008);

– SAP with SAP MDM, a product that came about as a result of a buyout; and

– Orchestra Networks with the EBX.Platform solution for all types of master data management requirements.

Other developers are serious challengers providing effective solutions:

– Oracle has several customer or product orientated solutions: CDH and UCM Siebel for customer data management, Product Data

Hub, PIM DH and UPM for product data, as well as an analytical MDM solution: Hyperion system 9 MDM;

– TIBCO offers TIBCO CIM;

– we shall also note the arrival of Microsoft in the MDM race as a result of the buyout of MDM Stratature. Its aim is to integrate Stratature into Office Business Applications, then to offer a packaged consistent range (the solution will not be operational until the middle of 2009).

Although the range of specialist solutions for specific business issues (product, customer) will continue to evolve, the main market developers will adapt their solutions to offer complete coverage.

3.2.6. *A rollout process, substantial projects*

Everybody acknowledges the importance of good master data management as a vital factor in a stable information system. However, there are not many IT departments who are committed to moving into such areas. There is a real-time lag between realizing the importance of the area and implementing it. We find ourselves in a familiar situation. The added value to the business unit remains difficult to define and consequently there is no budget to make this project a real priority. We must add to this something that we have seen in all our examples, which is that this type of project may turn out to be of an immense size, which will involve making it a real business project. Without this, and even with a budget raised by the IT department, the involvement of business units will be difficult to obtain and the objectives will not be achieved.

Remember the key phrase of the former liege man of SAP, Shai Agassi: "Think big, start small." Extremely effective even if a little obvious, in any case, always valid. To be effective, the MDM procedure needs to be implemented gradually to achieve the objective of being a unique master database for a large scale business. No business can afford to reorganize all its master data in one fell swoop.

This is even at odds with the NISS approach which aims above all to be based on existing strengths. But of course, when it is the foundations that are affected, projects turn out to be complex and unwieldy and the building may shake on its foundations. The important thing is that it does not collapse. The important thing then will be to find quick interim gains, for example, a basic reporting system on already consolidated reference data. However, for all that, these solutions risk giving the illusion that the objective has been achieved, whereas MDM is only used for basic reporting, i.e. that the investment to be granted to achieve the actual objectives remains substantial:

– an MDM project is both a business project and an infrastructure project;

– without control of the reference data, an MDM solution will not be enough to cope with the management of reference data completely.

3.3. Enterprise information integration: federation

3.3.1. *Virtual dynamic views*

It is not only concepts of physically centralized master data that are emerging but also virtual directory concepts. These architectures are known by the acronym EII, which stands for enterprise information integration. These solutions will be used as the basis for defining a set of pointers towards the actual location of the reference data. Physically, the data does not migrate towards the central truth point. It is almost a question of creating a directory that potential consumers will interrogate to draw the required information from it.

The application that physically contains the master data will actually continue to play its part as a referral agent: the data distribution flows thus travel in the opposite direction to that adopted in centralized master data frameworks.

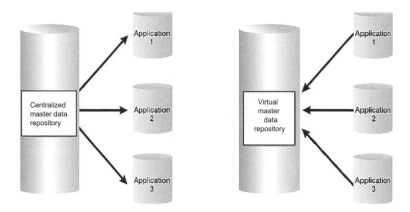

Figure 3.10. *Contrast between the exchange trajectories
depending on the type of master data*

You cannot take the application's role as a referring agent away
when creating and updating data. Consequently, trying to give the EII
a sense of responsibility as you would an MDM will not shift
responsibility but duplicate it. And when two people are appointed to
the same position, you would be right to worry about situations you
can't get out of or even catastrophic situations.

3.3.2. Gestica: dynamic views for large-scale businesses

Gestica is a social security and pension fund manager for the
agricultural sector. It came into being as a result of the separation of
several units but only achieved total independence a few years ago. Its
information system is organized around certain applications, each with
a grain of truth to describe a member or a company.

When Web applications intended for members were being
implemented and the customer relation management solution was
gradually put into place, Gestica became aware of the necessity to
share the interrogation of existing applications. The technological

choice was to display the Web services from legacy applications, thus initializing a service-oriented architecture.

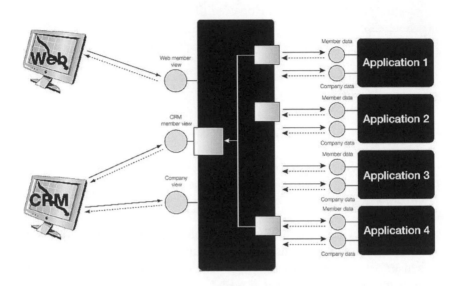

Figure 3.11. *The establishment of virtual data views*

At the center of this system is the virtual master data, provided in this architecture not by a dedicated EII tool but by a service bus (see Chapter 6). This displays the services consumed by the multiple channels provided to use the data. The bus acts as a hub towards which the data converges to create independent views of the physical location of the data.

This model also has a cache concept. When a request is made from one of the front ends, the type of the following requests depends on the type of this first request. For example, when the first action is consulting general information on a member, it is likely that the second action will be, at a 90% probability, checking this member's benefits history. Boosted by this knowledge, any request referring to obtaining general information may also return information on the history of benefits. This data will not be recreated for the user but displayed subsequently if this user requests it. The data bus is used like a data cache.

In this way you avoid interrogating the business applications twice. However, you run the risk of transporting data which will not be subsequently used. It is all a matter of compromise.

This type of project is not as extensive as a centralized master data management procedure, even if it is only because of the lesser impact on existing systems. On the other hand, it normally saves a great deal of thought about the management of reference data and seems to be more of a tactical solution. However, we should moderate our comments. In Gestica's case, constraints at several levels (existing IS, regulations, etc.) prevented a centralized master database from being created. Setting up a virtual master database brought about the expected responses.

3.3.3. *The state of the market*

The data integration market is less dynamic and has fewer solutions than the centralization market. However, in this market there are products supplied by some of the best known players in the industry:

– BEA: Aqualogic Data Services,

– Composite Software; Composite Information Server,

– IBM: WebSphere Federation Server; and

– SAP (formerly Business Objects): Data Federator.

3.4. Between centralization and federation

3.4.1. *Two very different models*

MDM and EII represent very different, complementary solutions. MDM aims to *harmonize* and *distribute* the reference data corresponding to the only truth accepted in the company. EII *does not harmonize* (no data reconciliation) and the data displayed by the tools is recreated unchanged from its source without necessarily corresponding to a single truth. EII is a data bus which aims to use a determined set of applications. To build the virtual model for the target applications you can use data from several master databases, as well as transactional data from other sources.

The main objective of the centralized master databases is harmonization and the quality of the data which complies with the unified model, which is shared by all of the applications using the data in question. However, the virtual master database excludes quality processes from data transformation. The logical model shown to target applications meets their needs and not the needs of a unique, shared vision. Every creation or updating process which relies on such a solution turns out to be very complicated to define, mainly because of the management of concurrent access. Consequently, you can understand that such an architecture is more geared towards consumption of data than production of data. In short, from a solution point of view, the tools are still too unsophisticated for the engine to claim to be allocated to the control of reference data.

Normally, such an architecture corresponds to localized, specific requirements, particularly as part of decision-making architecture. EIIs are also more and more frequently being integrated into reporting tools for decision-making solutions or into ETLs. They enable the implementation of specific cubes to be bypassed within the datamart for rarely used indicators and/or those that call up little information. You will also find EIIs integrated into portal applications and, normally, less and less frequently sold on their own.

3.4.2. *A balance to be found*

It is unusual for the innovation pendulum to swing definitely towards new technology. If it extends the capacities of an area into a request for innovation, the reply received only rarely cancels and replaces existing solutions. Web services have not wiped the range of technologies that have existed for several decades from the map. How many applications developed in Cobol or PacBase are still there in our information systems? While a new technology provides solutions, it is not necessarily the answer to everything. After some months or years of practical use, you will see the limitations it is necessary to bypass, potentially opening the way for new innovations.

It is not unusual to note that these limitations did not exist in the previous models. The best example is, perhaps, the replacement of the client/server with the thin client Web model, what Alain Lefebvre called the "universal client server" in a major pendulum movement. The limitations of Web ergonomics have not really been resolved over time. They have been bypassed at best and the pendulum has again swung in the opposite direction. The appearance of the fat client model, inbetween the lightweight Web and the sophisticated client/server, marks where the pendulum stops somewhere between the two extremities.

It is the same with data management. The balance between centralization in a third-party master database and federation using virtual views must be defined. It is specific to each business and, if we are tempted to declare it, specific to each project. New adjustments must be permanently *found*.

In *L'EAI au service de l'entreprise évolutive* which was published in 2003, we gave an example of synchronizing customer data. The architecture created provided a compromise between centralization and federation:

– the most frequently used data was centralized in a master database with pointers to the least requested data;

– the applications were still depositories for this. The frequently used data could be updated from the master database, in return for sometimes complex arbitration procedures.

What has changed since 2003? Obviously the arrival of tools dedicated to managing data on the one hand, then the awareness of the importance of suitable organization on the other hand.

3.5. Data governance

According to the analysis and advisory firm the Gartner Group, *data governance* is made up of a *collection of good practices* that consider information to be a company resource in its own right. This resource must be managed with *precise rules, clearly established processes, responsibilities* and *circulated within organizations* using their *technological standards*.

3.5.1. *Extent of data governance*

More practically, data governance is everything that enables all the data quality and security dimensions to be managed perfectly. It therefore denotes all the processes that guarantee the quality, availability, security and regulatory compliance of data.

The aims of data governance are similar to the already known but not always well practiced objectives of data administration. Unlike data that is used by a limited number of applications, transverse reference data requires a rigorous governance procedure. The following problems must be avoided in particular:

– loss of traceability of model content, a piece of information is detected in a model but you no longer know its meaning or whether it is legitimate, etc.;

– divergence in modeling the same object, when several different models represent the same object, which leads to an increase in the amount of implementation software (one program for each type of model) and therefore has a detrimental effect on maintenance, documentation and support;

– divergence of values, where the same object has different values depending on the applications; and

– poor data quality (duplicates, completeness, etc.).

It is generally accepted that companies with an effective plan in this area are always able to produce more accurate, complete, consistent data on their activities in all their departments.

3.5.2. *Three significant central themes*

The advantages of rolling out a data governance program throughout the company are numerous and diverse, just like the challenges involved in implementing a firm framework.

3.5.2.1. *Strategy*

Strategy defines the *objectives* of the company at data level. It tends to pursue a *long-term vision*. It aims to improve the intrinsic values and use of the data in order to increase the data value. This is done mainly by applying a data quality policy.

Data governance must tend towards increasing the value of the data. It must be considered outside the specific constraints of a business area. In this it meets the requirements of the transverse, independent character of data processes. It is a quality control framework that aims to evaluate, manage, use, optimize, check, maintain and protect a company's data.

3.5.2.2. *Security*

General security rules must be defined for all types of data and therefore, in particular for reference data, in order to guarantee the level of security required to protect against legal, financial or image consequences.

3.5.2.3. *Regulatory compliance*

Regulatory constraints result from a legal, national or international framework. Certain bodies are responsible for checking that the company is in compliance with the regulatory framework (CNIL, CRE, AMF, SGDN, etc.). By extension, non-legal constraints, freely accepted by the company, may also be included in this category (for example an environmental observance charter or a charter of human rights for grading by sustainable development agencies).

These regulatory constraints normally affect reference data, as well as master data management processes (creation, modification, deletion and distribution). For example, the CNIL constraints for "individual" clients and their rights to access and correct data held by the company, or otherwise CRE constraints for "commercially sensitive information".

Setting up a master database centralizes data management as well as audibility from the point of view of internal control departments (that use internal control and audit business units and tools) and external departments (various authorities).

3.5.3. *A dedicated organization*

In order to perpetuate the actions carried out on reference data, some companies have set up an organization that you could call a master data management committee or a central master data co-ordination unit. It is responsible for defining the transverse rules, organizations and tools. Depending on the requests made by the projects, it makes decisions and issues recommendations on the way to proceed. Ideally this will be a mixed structure that includes business and IT profiles.

This structure has several resources which it has itself potentially created to carry out its actions:

– semantic data dictionary;

– metadata descriptions (models);

– data quality monitoring indicators; and

– data tracing and audits.

The priority is to capitalize on the identified reference data semantics and models. To do this you could plan to create a directory by using the leading market modeling tools. Nevertheless, it could also be very useful to think about monitoring data quality by considering implementing a DQM tool that will generate reports on the quality criteria used.

The presence of a sponsor is critical. By providing the means (resources and personnel), the sponsor gives visibility, legitimacy and credibility to a still innovative and, in this regard, potentially fragile procedure.

3.6. Towards information management

In addition, effective management of structured data is vital but the information is not only restricted to structured data. If we were being just a touch provocative, we could say that master data management is almost marginal compared with the management of documentary information, the phenomenal amount of information to be tracked down on the "invisible Web", the importance of monitoring the competition, the economy and the strategy. One figure alone sums up the situation: 80% of information handled by companies is not structured.

The management of non-structured data is normally addressed specifically and addressed by implementing other categories of solutions called enterprise content management or ECM. ECM incorporates specific areas such as electronic document management, paperless technologies or even archiving topics (including the amounts of information involved). You can thus see projects emerging where structured information management is mixed with non-structured information management.

This is the case with projects that monitor the implementation of certain large integrated software package modules, such as SAP. Thus, PLM (product lifecycle management) solutions that can be likened to product repositories can cope with the two systems to provide a global management system for product data. The fact remains that experts agree to acknowledge the difficulty in dealing head-on with the two types of information and readily recommend staggering the construction by gradually activating the groups of functionalities depending on priorities.

Few companies are yet adopting a centralized management strategy for information capital at group level. Even so, exchange standards are emerging that open up semantic analysis possibilities with a great deal of added value for the business unit in terms of the company's information capital.

3.7. Bibliography

LEFEBVRE, A., *Intranet Client Serveur Universel*, Eyrolles, 1999.

Chapter 4

Service-Oriented Architectures

Ideas, even the most simple ones, are like springs. Torrents of new ideas gush out of them which over time, given sufficient interest and willingness, will become a strong current, first of all of thoughts, energy and ultimately liquid assets. This applies to service-oriented architectures (SOAs), a major topic based on a very simple idea: aligning the IT system with the information system in order to increase their ability to adapt and align.

In itself, this is not a new idea. It was first mooted in the 1980s at the peak of the client-server wave. However, its development was hampered by a major technological constraint: the lack of interoperability between existing applications and technologies. At the time, this restriction did not seem to be a problem. Each information system could develop independently of its neighbors without affecting the company's performance. Following the emergence of integrated software packages (Enterprise Resource Planning – ERPs), the question of interoperability was no longer in the picture.

However, integrated software wasn't the answer to everything, and then the need for intersilo communication grew. At the same time, the emergence of Web services broke the interoperability barrier. SOAs could only make their real appearance when all these factors came together.

This reminds us of the example of the *Russian Ark*. After creating his film based on a single shot sequence, a wish that had become technically possible, Sokourov had to cope with the consequences of his discovery – an incredible number of questions about the use of the technology, the methods (how can one cameraman carry a steady-cam weighing 35 kg for almost 90 minutes?) and the organization (which team should be used to move around the museum corridors?), which had never entered his head. His intuition, his idea and his talent were only starting points on his road to becoming a pioneer.

The development of SOAs was very similar. As soon as the Berlin Wall fell, IT asked itself a multitude of questions which didn't yet have any answers. The subject went from just bubbling to white hot with a large number of technological, software, method and organizational innovations, a virgin territory which attracted numerous soldiers of fortune.

Although there were very few signs to indicate that soon many feature-length films would be filmed in a single shot sequence, we can now tell that the implementation of applications in services mode is booming. Everything pointed to the fact that they would become a dominant standard, from the players who had made substantial investments to the number of companies which, one after the other, expressed their interest in these architectures, and their search for effective levers to transform the information system. According to Gartner in 2008, in future, 80% of applications will be designed observing SOA standards. All these factors transformed this idea which was, on the face of it, very simple into the main IT environment stream, a long river which was not completely peaceful.

4.1. Basic impacts

In order to understand the issues and potential of SOAs, it is necessary to look into the reappraisals that they have caused in the IT environment. From the end of the application concept to the establishment of real interoperability, SOAs forces us to get used to new capabilities in order to master the new issues better.

4.1.1. *From application to service: the end of a reign?*

One of the issues of an SOA that is not very well appreciated is the reappraisal of the application concept, which has been a part of IT landscape from the very beginning and which can now be gradually separated from it. A service is a functional element which describes a function of the company: creating a customer, valuing stock, calculating a property loan are services, etc. The application, the monolithic turnkey block, may be seen as a group of functions, i.e. services, but linked in such a way that they are inseparable and difficult to access independently of each other. Therefore, the application, a technological unit, does not offer sufficient granularity to represent the company's business. In the traditional four-layer enterprise architecture model (processes, functions, applications, technologies), the application is the unit that embodies all the difficulties of going from the business to the IT department. There is no simple link from one to the other.

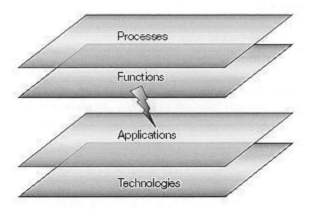

Figure 4.1. *From the function to the application: a link that is far from free-flowing*

Nevertheless, the ability to evolve from the model to reality is a vital condition for aligning the information system quickly. The service reconciles the two views: it is at the same time a business function *and* an application.

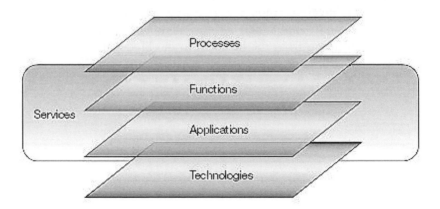

Figure 4.2. *The service, the link between the business unit and IT*

Note the announcements and movements of major software players such as Oracle and SAP: both companies are applying an SOA approach to their software package modules. However, both of them are probably the major suppliers of applications throughout the world and you could hardly suspect them of wanting to scuttle themselves. These vendors no longer consider the application or the module to be the central component of their architecture. It is the service that holds the key. Apart from this, it is all the services provided and the functional coverage offered that define the scope of their solutions. In the end the scope doesn't change much; it has increased in granularity and therefore alignment abilities.

By working at service levels a lower level of granularity is reached which favors targeted developments. Semiconductors, atomic energy, genetics – there is no shortage of examples where capacities and resources increase as we go down to units that get smaller and smaller. It is the same in IT.

On the other hand, the size of the service is not only smaller, but is left more to the discretion of the person who designs it. If the design is successful, all the services will represent the business of the company: the alignment of IT to business will be faster.

4.1.2. *The fall of the interoperability wall*

If the service is specialized, it also remains technological. Its main purpose is to create real interoperability between worlds that are not very used to talking to each other: His Majesty Java on the one hand, the Microsoft empire on the other, the PHP rebels in the undergrowth.

With Web services, there are, theoretically, no longer any limits or constraints to technologies or information systems communicating with each other, whatever they are, considering the standardization of services and their communication channels. This is why, in our opinion, it is risky to separate SOA and Web services. Without interoperability, can you seriously talk about alignment?

Interoperability is the technical constraint that has been removed. we can therefore think about business matters and concentrate on aspects with greater added value than the technical establishment of communication between communities that are separated by an insurmountable wall.

It must be admitted that Web services constitute the reference implementation for installing this type of architecture. However, not all applications introduce services and not all communications are yet based on Web service protocols. This isn't the case today and it is not very likely that it will be the case in future. The existing systems are too sizeable and it will take years to overhaul everything. Are SOAs the promise of a romantic idealist? Very fortunately, no. Integration solutions effectively bypass these limitations by ensuring ad hoc transition interoperability.

4.1.3. *A central domain with a far-reaching impact*

Far from being isolated, SOAs interact with a large number of other domains which either contain an SOA component or which are extended, enhanced or even redefined by the SOA.

The domains listed in Figure 4.2 are implicitly or explicitly linked to SOAs.

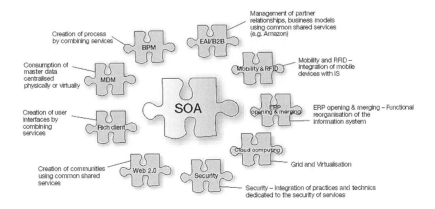

Figure 4.3. *SOAs: a key topic*

Let's look at these topics:

– *ERP opening and merging*: the major vendors are now applying an SOA approach to their software package modules intended for other applications or partners. Establishing a semantically common service model allows different software packages to be merged in order to facilitate the alignment of mixed information systems.

– *Master data management*: master data is consumed by candidate applications in the form of services, in order to customise access to data. These links are shown in more detail in Chapters 3 and 7.

– *Business process management*: service assembly describes the orchestrations that are fully automated or are fully automated or partly automated with human integration. The use of services by BPM platforms is just as much an enterprise architecture topic as a technological one.

– *Integrating company and partner applications (EAI/B2B)*: applications and partners communicate by exchanging information based on service invocation, activating an industrial business model.

– *Mobility and RFID*: communication between mobile devices (telephone, PDA, digital pen) and the central information system is carried out by exchanging information based on events and services. Using services ensures interoperability of all the devices whatever their level of heterogenity.[1]

– *Rich client and composite applications*: the rich client and server units are separated using communication based on the service invocation where the granularity enables differentiated management of the applications from the same screen.

– *Web 2.0*: the integration of application components provided by partners (mashups) within applications enables priority to be given to reusability and speeds up the development process while perpetuating and extending the Web business model.

– *Security*: a whole section of information system security as a discipline is now concerned with SOAs. Certain security protocols and authentication devices policies are peculiar to the world of Web services and companies require dedicated expertise in this field.

– *Cloud computing*: as a component with a finer granularity than the application, the service can be distributed ad infinitum, multiplying the number of physical components depending on the capacity requirements of then technical system to cope with any load balancing or fault tolerancy matters.

All of these topics spin a web at the center of which is a major topic: standardized communication and, in the center of this, the essential topic of interoperability. From a technological point of view, this assessment is drawn up by using Web service technology or service virtualization. It is an IT transformation.

Apart from this idea of interoperability, which is central, there is another vital idea emerging: getting away from the idea of application and moving towards the idea of service. This idea places SOAs at the center of the IS transformation. Because of this dual purpose, SOA is a major issue. SOAs are not about owning or managing projects. It is a

---

1. This is what is called commodization or commodification of the information system.

topic that brings business and IT together. With a subject such as this, organizational matters become essential. We shall deal with this in Chapter 10.

4.2. A major lever for a change in progress

It is easy to explain the extraordinarily seductive power that SOAs exert. Connecting the information system and the IT system, in other words interoperability, encompasses a vast range of topics: you don't normally need as many as this to be popular.

With such promises, such capacity, SOAs are setting themselves up as one of the main information and IT system transformation levers, particularly in:

– the support of business strategies and models particularly directed at the e-commerce channel;

– the improvement of the information system performance;

– a broader integration.

4.2.1. New business models

SOAs seem to be surfing on the wave of models spawned by the Internet economy and sometimes forgotten since. Technologies have not gone backwards, the use of the Internet has increased, more discreetly of course, and new concepts have emerged with Web 2.0 at their center. There is a new vitality in the development of e-services and the associated business models.

One of these models was incorporating the value chain to unify the relationship of the company's customers with the company's partners. This is the choice that one of our customers in the distant selling B2B industry made. For him, this involved an increase in the potential of his e-commerce sales channel:

– by increasing the number of online items from 80,000 to 1,000,000 by integrating from partner catalogs information flow;

– by using a unique customer banner to deal with orders provided both by our customer and by his partners;

– by offering real-time transparency of the delivery process by showing the customer the milestones of the delivery process.

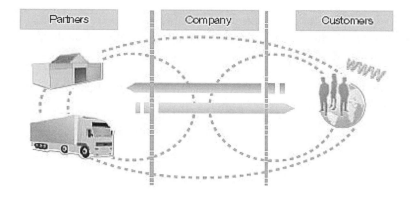

Figure 4.4. *Incorporation of the value chain*

The significant increase in the number of items transformed the company's business. Previously it used to stock 80% of all items sold. With the new model, it was no longer possible because of the related costs. It transformed itself into an added value intermediary. The wide range of its catalog will enable it to direct the customer to the best partner for a given item depending on criteria such as availability of the product, price or delivery details. The use of services also makes it possible to distribute the contents over different media. This is the case with the example above because they will share the partner catalogs or follow up orders whatever the channel used by the customer. On a wider scale, the examples of Amazon or eBay teach us that it is even possible to use services provided by other companies to create your own virtual shop or to insert your shop into a partner's site.

Internet retailer Amazon is the undisputed champion of all categories of SOAs. Any partner may use the services provided by Amazon to create their online store by delegating stock, logistics and order processes to the online seller. It is also possible to synchronize lists for the partners selling their products on the Amazon site. 150 services are thus accessible to the various sales channels:

– the Amazon.com website itself;

– the partners integrating data;

– the partners using the services;

– the applications developed by using the AWS (Amazon Web Services) platform.

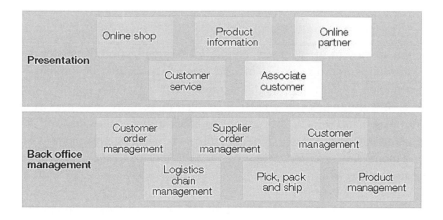

Figure 4.5. *Incorporation of the value chain*

What Amazon did was implement the display of services generally from the first stages of the design. Amazon's information system has been SOA-enabled for several years now and this decision was taken at a time when it was still possible to extend this procedure considerably basically without questioning past investments. But inevitably everyone is not Amazon, and for many companies the weight of the legacy systems prevents the deployment of the service on the scale of the whole information system. Beyond the service level there is a more traditional integration level, at data level, required take into account a larger number of scenarios.

Over time, Amazon itself became a supplier of technical solutions for companies that wanted to set up an online shop by using tried and tested, reusable technologies.

The use of SOAs will, of course, increase in line with the upsurge in interest of e-services and the second wave of e-commerce.

4.2.2. *More effective information systems*

4.2.2.1. *Access to master data*

As we saw in the previous chapter, the organization of master data is a vital building block in the organization of the transverse information system. Applications must not access data directly, both for architectural flexibility reasons as well as security reasons. On the contrary, priority will be given to decoupling solutions and the construction of a service model dedicated to accessing master data. This model has nothing to do with the architecture of the selected data (centralized or virtual).

The connection between MDM and SOA is particularly apparent in the data phase distribution, when data is distributed to the consuming applications. Access to data is set out in the form of services. Each application consumes the view intended for it. No direct link is set up: the master database remains independent of applications.

At the same time as it physically separates the two levels, this solution links data and services by setting up an organized data access model. Just as the data is available to the whole company, the service model that allows access to it can also be standardized for all requirements. It is a permanent, stable enterprise service model.

4.2.2.2. *Increased functional consistency*

Reusing a service that has previously been performed for different requirements is an attractive prospect for the benefits that can be foreseen: new requirements can be taken into account faster and uniformly, with reduced maintenance costs, increased functional homogenity and fewer redundancies.

Figures 4.6 and 4.7 show the benefits of this shared system.

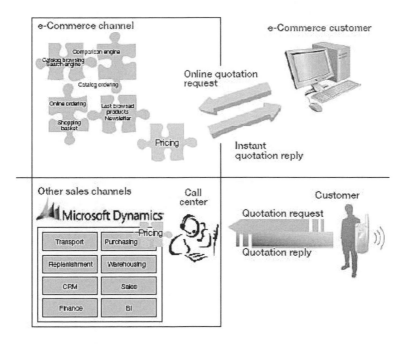

Figure 4.6. *Sharing services*

If a customer contacts the company's call center to find out about prices or the availability of a product in the catalog, he must get the same results as if he searches for it himself on the company's website. However, the central site and the website both implement their own pricing engine. Since the results also depend on the customer's ranking, you can see that if the customer data is duplicated, there could be inconsistencies in the results between the two channels. The idea is to use a single pricing engine, which is located, as here, in the ERP.

The pricing engine is set up in the form of a service to the whole information system. When a customer uses the website to find out a price, the request is transfered to the ERP, as if by a light reflection effect. The result is returned to the user as if the processes were located at website level.

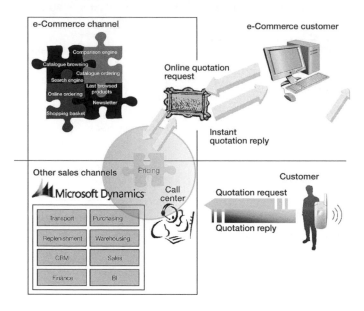

Figure 4.7. *Shared service*

Consequently, this principle also entails the appropriate dimensioning of the architectures involved. The same service is called up by all the channels that use it. If the service is provided by the ERP, this creates a new flood of requests coming from the Web. Where before the service only had to cater to direct users, it now has to manage a load of back doors – a whole new surge. This point applies to all legacy systems: thus, in this part we shall address the opening up of mainframe systems to the outside world by providing services based on web services standards and using a mediation bus.

In addition, this principle does not easily fit certain real situations. In the English-speaking world, the "not invented here" syndrome carries a lot of weight. So as not to lose authority over its project scope, a team will not see any problem in revising a service which already exists somewhere else for its own requirements. With the development of enterprise architecture concepts, you can imagine that these considerations will become more and more accepted.

For all these reasons, as attractive as they may appear, sharing services is not the main lever that encourages companies to proceed along the SOA path. It is a target that will probably be achieved when all the methods are fully developed, and when the company has gained the necessary maturity to think in service mode. For the time being, different strategies are first of all being drawn up which will not prevent the creation of substantial added value, however, are based on a well defined scope, according to a movement that will start on the periphery of the information systems and will gradually come closer to the center.

4.2.2.3. *Managing multi-channel exchanges*

Rather than focussing on the periphery, let's talk about transversality. It isn't just by chance that SOAs have replaced EAI integration technologies in literature and discussions. It is first of all because SOAs have become an inter-application integration topic, which enables information flows to be conveyed both internally and externally. The management of multi-channel access in the back-office (Figure 4.8) as well as in the front-office is one of the favorite options in this area.

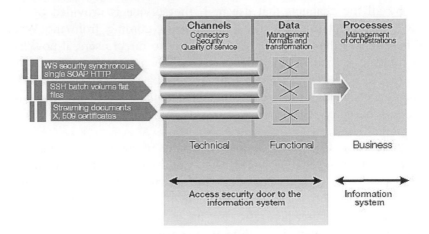

Figure 4.8. *Management of multi-channel access*

The idea is simple. It is a question of making it easy for a partner to connect to our information system to exchange data. The example above is taken from a case where the data is documentary and enclosed in metadata. We can also provide examples where this is master data, particularly product data that is passing through.

The aim is to provide a standardized connection model for partners, regardless of the data format or the transport and security protocols used. The partner is not required to have exchange systems. Access services to the information system can be used and an input/output security door to standardize the differences. Thus, the data is prepared for sending to a single business process.

4.2.3. *A more integrated information system*

The SOA model is about to become a dominant model for businesses of all sizes, in all sectors. However, all the opportunities that it creates and all the structuring that it involves are far from being understood. Consequently, you run the risk of seeing the proliferation of initiatives claiming to be SOAs when in fact they only have a distant relationship.

As a key topic that generates several others, SOAs provide CIOs of international groups with the opportunity to position themselves as providers of value, for their local units and their subsidiaries. There is still time to organize business, organizational, methodological and technological aspects from the start and to create appropriate bases.

The purpose of these will be:

− to make people aware of the added value, the risks, the opportunities and the constraints inherent in SOAs and all the associated domains;

− to organize the international implementation and roll out of applications;

− to promote standardized business models;

− to export the standards, practices and technological components, to maintain and safeguard construction in the long term; and

− to serve resource centers, and to provide services that can be shared and distributed to whole groups.

By adopting this type of operation before the overall adoption of these architectures, central CIOs will play a unifying, advisory role which is normally part of their remit. Here they are establishing a positive role, for themselves and avoiding the restraining effect that could be felt if this positioning were to take place too late. If organizational pitfalls are avoided, the whole information system will benefit from the general implementation of these architectures.

This type of general implementation is normally carried out by organizing an international working party made up of the players in several subsidiaries. This will avoid the often badly received "we have made something for you" attitude.

The participation of future users in the construction phases will ensure widespread use. This also presupposes that the construction is marked out, and the regular delivery of significant products is assured regularly.

4.3. A new experiment in the finance bank

4.3.1. *The context*

A large European bank implemented a SOA to deal with security management processes, from the front-office to the back-office.

There were two reasons for this:

– to implement a process management solution based on service invocation. "Processes are nothing without services and they are fundamental for the business." For this bank, the entire IS would have to be described by the business process; and

– to divide up the functions into services to achieve modularity. "The service approach is a question of procedure, not technology."

Both procedures are independent but connect naturally. With the implementation of service architectures and the use of Web services, calculation rules were centralized at the start of 2005.

Since then, this bank has been trying to adopt a more systematic approach to service architectures. It reviewed the 50 main business processes, then divided up the functions of these processes to compile a service map. It subsequently constructed a road map and pursued an iterative (bottom-up) approach, while bearing in mind the general plans drawn up during the initial planning procedure.

4.3.2. *The benefits*

The construction of a SOA has been noted to produce several advantages:

– Firstly, the ability to upgrade thanks to the service's decoupling ability. You can assemble two technological units (for example, two back-end systems) without risking a big bang, by going about it in small jumps, with no sudden changes and by avoiding tunnel effects. In the past, this bank had already been committed to displaying a service layer from Fortran programs and to calling up VMS services from a Sun platform. It thus created new applications from existing components.

– Secondly, reduced complexity. This bank felt that its systems were complicated, with a large proportion of specific code and major issues in terms of volumetrics. From the front-office to the back-office, this may create complex irregularities, especially if there is no transversal system to organize communication. The service aspect breaks up the complexity and the approach to resolving this complexity. Another example of this principle is mentioned in Chapter 7.

– Thirdly, increased reuse and factorization. The product catalog must serve all requirements. Thus the products are only referential in the static sense. In fact, new products are created by combining existing products. The product repository must provide all the product transactions to meet front-office and back-office requirements. When a product is changed (by the set of processes that changes the state of the object in its life cycle), the product repository must give all the methods to recalculate it.

What is at stake here is the consistency of the whole information system. With these architectures, it is easier to maintain services, and developments are faster.

4.3.3. *Pitfalls encountered*

When services are implemented they are not available to everybody immediately. How do you inform people about and share existing services? How do you prevent another department implementing them again unintentionally? One of the main difficulties noted is managing notification of the existence of services. Once more, without organization, technology cannot be rolled out in a controled manner. The role of the repository and a person dedicated to inform people about this repository seems vital to us for a successful roll out of these initiatives.

4.3.3.1. *Roles to be redefined*

The main pitfalls encountered are the major changes produced by these architectures, particularly in project management. Since some services have already been implemented by others, or are being implemented in other projects, a project no longer has exclusive resources. Connecting the different schedules becomes difficult to manage. In a way, a project manager may lose control of the project schedule; and there may be a number of personal difficulties, because how do you maintain a sense of responsibility in such a context? You need transverse coordination, where projects may become programs.

This scenario hardly occurs if you adopt an opportunistic approach to these architectures. However, if you are actually aiming to promote combining, reuse and sharing, then you will aim to adopt an industrial approach. This requires knowledge of the responsibilities of the managers. This is one of the reasons why transverse skills can no longer only be regarded as non-essential. They have not only become vital but also critical and for this reason must be experienced.

A service approach completely changes the way in which people work. For example, exception processing is not yet understood naturally. It can be used to identify IT process managers and to promote function/project manager pairs. Finally, from the developer's point of view, with each one concentrating on his services, you could fall into a Taylorism of horizontal and vertical work, where you lose the understanding of your job. That is another reason why transversality and communication are essential.

4.3.3.2. *Standards to be defined*

Common modeling standards and practices must be defined. If this is not done, a large part of future work will consist of changing formats, drifting away from the principle of shared services. The increase in the number of changes made will have an effect on system performance, and thus must be avoided if there is no need for them.

4.3.4. *Lessons learned*

Change management is an idea that cannot be separated from this type of approach. The greater the scope of the project, the more critical this phase will be to the acceptance of the new technology. We have already noted this, even if it is only through the redefinition of the work of the project manager or the developer. It isn't only the technological vector that may lead to the transplant being established or rejected. After some months of general implementation, you will note that services have increased in number without this deployment necessarily being controled. You will realize the need to carry out a full inventory, to establish taxonomies and a common semantic for the services. At the unit level you must find and establish the limitations of using each service.

Finally, contrary to what the marketing for SOAs would suggest, the Holy Grail of the process that you modify on the fly is not currently realiztic. On the other hand, the explicit side of the process enables you to understand the behavior better and, for example, to set indicators to measure performance and to inform about any malfunctions. Visibility is one of the main added value factors.

Finally, if the service actually enables you to get away from the concept of an application (as a defined function block), this is partially replaced by the idea of a business process. When you roll out an SOA, you no longer appoint application managers. From now on you appoint process managers.

4.4. Technologies and architecture

Amongst the large number of explorers who came to open up the unknown lands of SOAs were many software vendors from all over the place, of every nationality, with extremely different visions, abilities and talents. It consequently became inevitable that software vendors would supply a range of software solutions with a number of different functions, which could construct an SOA, based mainly but not solely on Web services.

Technically, this is why SOAs, which already existed in the 1990s at the time of second client server generation and object orientated approaches such as Corba, weren't actually developed until now. The arrival of Web services, a symbol of the convergence of players in the industry towards standards, broke down a barrier to interoperability which, as we have seen, is one of the foundations of the approach. The capacities of servers, memories and networks will now be able to deal with resource-hungry protocols such as those that are being used.

4.4.1. *Components of the technological offer*

From a functional point of view, a SOA rests on several additional functional, technological building blocks. Normally all of them use Web services in a minimal form as an implementation pivot for services, even if:

– they can manage a certain diversity of technologies, particularly in the lower layers;

– the idea of service is still independent of the idea of Web services at the modeling repository level.

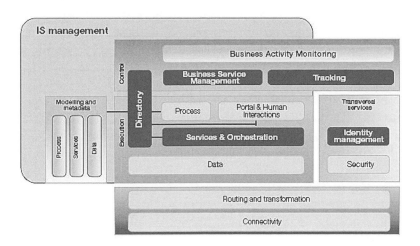

Figure 4.9. *Functional SOA architecture*

4.4.1.1. *Services repository*

The directory is a component that cannot be separated from SOAs. It is, however, regularly neglected. An example is necessary to fully understand its importance.

A large bank launched itself into service architectures at the turn of the century. Initially, its aim was to share services introduced by the customer relations manager, using this role like a reference customer data manager. As this experiment proved conclusive, it adopted SOAs on a larger scale and implemented this architecture model generally for all its applications so that, in 2005, more than 500 services were introduced and reused.

500 services in 4 years. You can intuitively understand the consequences of such an increase: redundant services and a mixture of business and technical services, dependences between services that

have become difficult to display. The architecture became extremely difficult to manage. The lack of control over the complexity caused by the SOA made the system even more complex; more complex to control and more complex to maintain. Old-fashioned organization and tools were allowed to remain on a base that aspired to industrialization to retain its real properties (alignment, flexibility and fast delivery).

It is easy to be wise after the event, however, you can guess intuitively what should have been done: the services categorized by metadata, modeled in a repository and their dependences modeled, and the repository usedto promote reuse in new projects.

This service repository ensures the consistency of the service platform at business level. Its structure and its metadata control the provision of new services. Each service belongs to one or more categories (also called taxonomies). More interesting still: the repository not only stores service descriptions, but can also be used as a register for defining all the security and architecture management policies. Thus, using the modeling tool, you can model service contracts by linking the service with the policies that you wish to see observed.

Finally you will find functionalities such as managing authorizations over all the referential metadata, notification systems in the event of modifications to or non-compliance with the rules, or even the documentation associated with each service. You will realize that companies that have put such a repository in place, at the beginning or while rolling out their service architectures, have been able to avoid the above problems. Since then the bank in question has also put in place a service repository, and is starting to take its architecture in hand again. It is never too late to do things properly.

4.4.1.2. *Relationship between repository and registry*

The repository is a service description tool. The registry is a component that has been present from the early stages of SOAs or, at the very least, Web services. You can therefore now differentiate between a service repository, a design time component used in the design phases then as a metadata manager, and the registry, a run-time component, because it is used in execution.

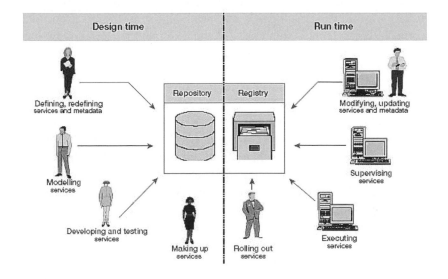

Figure 4.10. *Connection between the service repository and the service directory*

The repository plays its part upstream from the registry. Either it fills in functionalities that are not in the registry, because they are not in the Web services standards, or it communicates with the registry to maintain consistency between the model and the reality on the ground. The repository is even more wide-ranging than the Web services concept and the service concept.

In fact, the repository can be in the form of an information system modeling workshop, which is also able to model data, processes and exchanges, i.e. all the information assets. The repository may thus become the referral agent for the transverse information system.

4.4.1.3. *Enterprise service bus*

An enterprise service bus is a software component responsible for exchanging information between services. Comprising the low layer of a SOA, it provides functionalities such as secure information transport, transformation of data and content-based routing. It is based mainly on the use of standards and particularly on those set out when using Web services, which explains the dominant role played by these standards in the construction of an SOA. This, however, is not all.

The role of the bus is also to free problems associated with the technological heterogenity of the architecture's communicating component. Although the use of Web service protocols guarantees interoperability, not all the components of an SOA naturally observe these protocols. If these components cannot be upgraded quickly, you must be able to compile using their method of communicating; flat files, XML, database access, proprietary APIs, EDI protocols, etc. It is up to the ESB to manage these aspects.

Consequently it is becoming an essential component of the architecture's interoperability, by moving from one exchange protocol to another, by propagating security protocols, by transforming formats. Starting with this principle, the ESB is becoming a solution that is close to that offered by EAI (enterprise application integration) solutions. I say "was offered" because after all, does anyone still claim to be in this market these days? However, these solutions still exist. It is just their label that has changed. We shall come back to these points in Chapter 6 which deals with managing exchanges and information flows.

4.4.1.4. *The orchestrator*

The orchestrator has the privilege of combining the service calls according to a sequence which could equally be called a process. The orchestrator may also be responsible for the human interactions identified in the activity chain. In a way the orchestrator is a process execution solution. If it enables you to launch the construction on its way to the process by making the process and its monitoring actually visible, it is far from providing all the functions that may be desirable in such a context, for instance the task management. You would tend towards other solutions, additional ones in terms of architecture and in functionalities: business process management suites (BPMS). The next chapter will clear up all these misunderstandings.

4.4.1.5. *Security management*

Security is a hyped topic and the security of SOAs is a specific subject that must be addressed. Specific because it is surrounded by Web service protocols (WS-Security, SAML, etc.) where standardization and finalization also come into play.

In an SOA context, security covers several areas:

– encoding of messages;

– single sign-on and identity federation;

– the digital signature of messages;

– the propagation of security tokens; and

– trace history for all service invocations.

In an SOA context, which works by assembly and integration, it is important to be able to propagate security information regardless of the protocol used or the scope of the application.

For example, when a user's work station is made up of several services, each one accessing different applications, the user does not have to enter more than one password. The mapping between application passwords is handled automatically.

Also, when a process orchestrates services, and if these services access several different applications, in order for the process to run smoothly it must include the ability to manage multiple identifications and the large number of different protocols used. Without excellent security management, the whole operation of this type of architecture suffers.

Knowing this you can better understand why several major names of the IT industry have fallen victim to a frenzy of buyouts over the last two years. They had to acquire the most promising young newcomers in order to put forward an offer that could cover the whole range of SOA security functions.

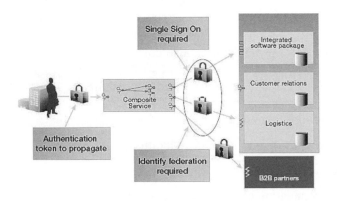

Figure 4.11. *SOA and security*

4.4.1.6. *SOA management*

If the SOA simplifies certain complexities in the information system, it creates others which must be mastered. When components are shared, it is vital that they work properly. Without this the whole performance of the company will be adversely affected. When services are introduced to partners, they must never prevent the partner from making a sale on this channel. It is vital to measure the services performance in real-time. This is what SOA management solutions are for. Their job is to monitor, analyze, alert and optimize in real-time.

Their main task is to manage service contracts and service levels (service level agreements or SLAs). The policies defined at repository level are linked to services and compliance with them is monitored in real-time by the SOA management solution.

You can make sure, for example, that the time taken to manage a transaction is less than 0.2 seconds, and/or that a service can respond to 50 requests a second. This policy may be conditional (the condition may vary depending on whether the partner is gold or silver) and may be modified dynamically.

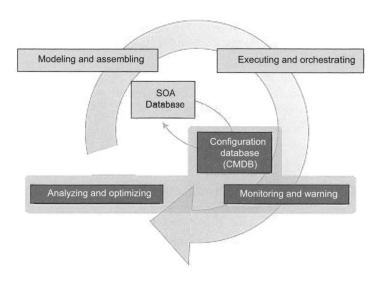

Figure 4.12. *Range of SOA management functions in the SOA cycle*

If service levels are not reached, the user receives a warning message. Performance indicators display the level of system performance and trace the dependencies between services. Should the system slow down, it is possible to navigate between these dependencies to find the link that is adversely affecting the performance of the chain.

Put this way, a solution like this seems vital to the construction of an efficient SOA. And yet, compared with blocks such as the enterprise service bus or the orchestrator, SOA management solutions still fall short. Due to their lack of awareness, companies do not see the point of such solutions at first sight. Furthermore their cost, at a time when companies are starting to show an interest in this type of architecture, remains a stumbling block to their rapid adoption.

Some of these functionalities can be provided by the service bus. This is the case with BEA Systems (Oracle Corporation). Other players on the market, pure players who offer their solution to famous names (such as Microsoft) with SOA Software, or suppliers with a global presence which have made their way by a series of buyouts (Progress, Oracle), offer a standalone solution which is separate from other components.

All of these factors are presented in more detail in Chapter 9, which deals with solutions for measuring real-time performance and operational excellence.

4.4.2. eBay: intangible architecture principles

The online auction site eBay recently presented its technical architecture and the technical choices that enabled them to achieve record availability and manage a prodigious increase in capacity while keeping maintenance and development costs at a reasonable level. SOAs featured at the heart of this construction.

The following design choices were implemented:

– The first choice, the intangible SOA design mode, is well on the way to becoming the most vital. It consists of dividing up the site functionalities into separate function blocks in order to limit the side effects and achieve a stable state. This point is developed in Chapter 7.

– The second, horizontal clustering (15,000 invocations rolled out simultaneously in 8 data centers), limits the database load (no stored procedures).

– The third is that the site is absolutely stateless, in that no service retains any context (things have come a long way since object-based architectures).

– Finally, no distributed transactions are used. Distributed architectures have been a constant restriction ever since they started. More than ten years after the advent of XA technology, the subject of distributing transactions between several systems is still as sensitive as ever. SOAs have not brought about a miracle solution. The difficulty is still the same since it is a question of integrating a variable number of different applications. eBay banned the use of XA in its architecture.

4.4.3. *The technological offer: the state of the market*

There are two major categories of players in the SOA market:

– the key players in the industry (IBM, Microsoft, Oracle, SAP), who are global suppliers capable of covering all of the described scope using complete platforms; and

– the traditional pure players (Tibco, Software AG and Progress Software), dedicated to one or more technological components, whose inferior functional coverage is compensated for by their increased specialization in the module that they offer.

In the French SOA market, these specialists can often be counted on the fingers of one hand, whereas a few years ago there were dozens. As well as being a sign of the times and an indication of the industry's increased maturity, it is also a sign of the importance of the SOA market. A number of buyouts have taken place already, which obviously affect the major offers on the market.

In fact, it is obvious that these buyouts will not quickly result in a real platform in the short term. In terms of functional redundancies between components and difficulty in assembling them: there is much work to be done on planning and architecture before the reality can exceed the vision.

As far as demand is concerned, in France, as in the rest of Europe, there are not many companies that have invested heavily in SOA transformation projects. This will come, but for the time being, a number of companies have preferred to make gradual, repeated, low-risk investments. This does not mean that the pure player is systematically preferred to the major players, but rather that few projects provide the opportunity to roll out a whole platform.

In the field we are asked to identify the modules required in the short term, then in the medium term depending on the opportunities. This has led to the establishment of SOA maturity models which are used as shown below (see Figure 4.13). As for major projects, there is no doubt that they will end up being widely implemented. For the time being, companies who have invested in them generally play differentiating cards. These are strategic projects where success is critical. We shall introduce them in Chapter 7.

The demand is definitely taking shape and the offer is also being created. The major vendors are still in the technological maturation phase of their platform offer. Taking account of the demand, the race that is taking place before our eyes is explained mainly by frantic competition between major vendors. It will be won by the one who is able to provide the first most complete, consistent, homogenous platform and, of course, the most innovative and efficient in the effort it asks to companies to use them.

4.4.4. *The maturity model*

In 2005 Sonic Software, HP/Systinet, Amberpoint and Bearing Point published a document containing the SOA maturity model. It describes the way in which a company must organize its construction to achieve a mature model. As an example, the building block at the top of the model is optimized business services.

This maturity model principle is thriving. It is now being implemented generally in a number of IT industry areas. It is a CMMi (capability maturity model integration) legacy which, globally, certifies the level of implementation achieved by an IT design department in its software development processes. CMMi comprises 5 levels: the higher the level, the more mature it is.

How can these principles be transposed to the world of SOAs? This exercise may be interesting but lacks pragmatism. We prefer the expression of a maturity model contextualized for each business. Although it has departed a little from its original purpose, using this model enables a company to outline the way in which it will be able to increase its SOA skills.

Figure 4.13 shows one of the models made during a mission in the retail sector.

Many people see SOAs as a first-choice driving force to rethink information systems. The predominant place taken recently by enterprise architects in and around SOA projects bears witness to this willingness to combine modeling and construction, to distance themselves slightly while remaining pragmatic, and to invest in lasting, future-proof structures.

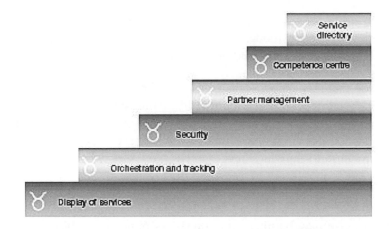

Figure 4.13. *Example of a maturity model applied to SOAs*

4.5. Flexibility is an event? Yes, agent!

The reorganization of all or part of a system involving all business services is carried out in the same way as the reorganization of the company's master data. It is a question of identifying, constructing and using the components. Once the services are created, the company has at its disposal a capitalization of assets that it can maintain and upgrade as it wishes, at low cost, with increased reactivity. The initial small idea, therefore, has already become a large river due to all of its benefits. And what if SOAs were not already victims of their size? Also what if, in a world that is progressing at a faster and faster pace, this innovation was not already about to be caught up and overtaken by others?

In an article published in the June 2007 edition of *IT-Experts*, Mathieu Poujol, an analyst with Pierre Audoin Consultants and a noted market watcher, predicted the advent of an SOA 2.0 as a result of the arrival of agent-oriented technologies. Before him, a Gartner analyst, together with an Oracle manager, had also done the same with the emergence this time of event-driven architectures (EDAs).

Agents or events, it doesn't matter, but it is interesting to note that several initiatives are already being presented, in some cases with the help of analysts, as the means of overcoming an already apparent limitation of the SOA model.

So as not to sink into a discussion of experts, we suggest a metaphor, found in the "Future Events" section of *Le Monde*, under the heading "Transformed into a computer, the cell will analyze its own health: making computers with living cells". This is a project that Kobi Benenson, an Israeli biologist and computer expert, is carrying out at the Center for Biological Systems at Harvard University in the United States. In a few years' time billions of biological computers could give valuable information on how cells in the human body are working by detecting individual pathological cells.

SOA and its variations can be compared with what Mr Benenson is trying to achieve:

– In an SOA world, the cell would display the service that the medical services would interrogate to determine the existence of a pathology.

– In a world that integrate event management, the cell itself would broadcast the first alarm signals as soon as the pathology is detected. You can imagine how much time would be saved in detecting problems, as well as the ability to treat the problems as soon as possible with the least amount of damage.

– Finally, in an agent-driven world, the cells would take the corrective action to contain the illness themselves and would also take corrective action themselves as far as this was possible. They would manage the first incident level themselves, while warning the medical services to take the appropriate action as soon as possible. In the end, more time is saved in detecting and solving problems, and some problems may even be solved without external human action.

This is the main feature of agent-driven technologies: programming objectives which, to a certain extent, come close to expert systems. The maturity of these technologies is increasing. If you gave the SOA a maturity score of 1, you would give a score of 0.95 to event-driven technologies and a score of 0.85 to agent-based technologies. So why mention them here?

The best way of using them is to include them within an SOA, and make them benefit from the SOA current maturity. It is also the best way to use event management-based technologies. Services, events, agents, these concepts are not exclusive. The technologies complement and enhance the initial solution by providing it with completely new flexibility and alignment abilities to cope with situations that would previously have needed interminable algorithms, just by using simple configurations, and to deal with unforeseen situations effectively. These extensions are actually the logic of the current transformation and do not distort the model in any way. In this regard you could say, without fear of contradiction, that we are witnessing the birth of a new version of SOAs.

It is still a little too soon to know whether the event or the agent will, in future, make up the assets in full or whether they will be integrated as properties of existing assets. We would be tempted to go for the second option but the field is wide open. In the events domain, Progress and TIBCO are leading the field with dedicated solutions integrated into their platform. The agents domain is, for the time being, dominated by less illustrious solutions developed by promising specialist companies (for instance, the French company Oslo Software, whose software suite is entirely dedicated to this technology).

Chapter 5

Business Process Management

Business processes occupy a vital place in the company. Some are critical, others are necessary, while others still are only of minor interest to decision makers. However, all business processes, regardless of their business or strategic importance, have a strong influence on the performance of the company; because they are not only value creators for the business, but are also cost drivers. Whether it is an industrial production line, recruitment, sales or even purchasing, all these activities, as soon as they are broken down into sub-activities performed by different players, become business processes.

However, are all these business processes valued correctly in the company? In their traditional organization and managerial customs, companies are still struggling to acknowledge that their business processes are vital tools for improving performance management, competitiveness and profitability. And it is no surprise that they realize that the information system also has its limits when representing business processes. There business processes are, fragmented, distributed between various business applications, when in fact they work best when kept together.

Who hasn't suffered the pernicious effects of this deficiency? Who in operations hasn't had the information in time to complete his job under the right conditions? Which manager has not been able to see his sales process? Which IT manager hasn't wasted his energy on a game of follow-my-leader between the business requirements and the capabilities of his information system?

Managing business processes like a new strategic department is becoming a priority for many companies. And yet the importance of IT in process issues has put the information system and its limitations under the spotlight. How can these business processes be brought together when they are found in little pieces, some in a front-office application, some in an accounting ERP, others in an invoicing system? When the company starts to ask itself these questions, it is time for it to turn to a business process management (BPM) system.

5.1. From managing business processes to BPM

5.1.1. *An example of the business process*

To familiarize ourselves with the business process concept, let's take four common examples.

5.1.1.1. *From recruitment to promotion: HR processes*

Our first steps in a company normally take us to a manager or an HR manager's office for a job interview. We know that we are entering the company's much talked-about recruitment process. After the first interview, another will follow, then another one until the company is sure about which candidate to hire.

Now here we are, a new recruit in this wonderful company, having successfully passed all the stages in the recruitment process. We have met an HR manager, an operations manager, his superior, then returned to the human resources floor for a last interview with the department head.

But we have not necessarily finished with human resources. This is because throughout our long career in the company, we shall be involved to a greater or lesser extent in various processes. These include our annual progress review, the formulation of our training plan, the calculation and payment of our salary, not to mention the numerous administrative tasks, which involve us. We are at the center of the HR department's business processes.

5.1.1.2. Purchasing: the first vital process

To be able to work we need an office and all the supplies in it: a computer, pens, pads, a land-line telephone, a calendar, etc. To meet the basic needs of its employees, the company must regularly purchase supplies from all sorts of suppliers: office suppliers, computer suppliers, telecom suppliers, etc. And to meet its own business requirements the range of its suppliers widens still further: raw material suppliers, carriers, ISPs, accommodation providers, service providers, etc. Whoever the suppliers are, and whatever goods they are supplying, a purchase normally breaks down as follows: a purchase requisition is issued, a purchaser places the order with the supplier, the supplier delivers the goods to a recipient who confirms delivery to the supplier and sends them to where they have to go. The supplier may then invoice for the order. This is broadly the purchasing business process, the first stages of which are illustrated in Figure 5.1.

5.1.1.3. Selling: the second vital process

A company's main purpose is to sell its products or its services to its customers. In companies which have other companies as customers, a large number of sales are made using invitations to tender. In fact, when selling does not involve products in a catalog, it refers to projects which involve a set of products and services to be supplied to the customer.

The response to an invitation to tender is normally broken down as follows: when the invitation to tender is issued, the invited supplier must first of all decide if he wants to reply to the invitation. This first stage is often called "Go/No Go". If the supplier agrees to take part in the tender process, a reply team is assembled. It is responsible for compiling a response which will be sent to the customer before the deadline. The specifications are then analyzed so that a suitable solution can then be devised.

Once this solution is defined, the sales price is calculated depending on a certain number of criteria: the cost of the solution, the required profit, the risk, the commercial strategy adopted for the customer, etc. Depending on the size of the dossier, i.e. its sales price, it must be validated by the management before being sent to the customer, which gives rise to one of the most traditional approval workflows.

When all these factors are finalized, the bid is drafted, references, technical appendices and the projected project team's CVs are added and then worded in terms designed to attract the customer and interest him in the dossier. The bid may then be sent to the customer. Subsequently the customer has to start analyzing the bids from the different candidates – after the tender bid process comes the supplier selection process.

5.1.1.4. *Developing the service: meeting customer requirements*

The services world is in the ascendant: telecom services, Internet services, banking services, personal services, our consumer society is quickly opening up to this new generation of products.

Providing a service for a customer is not always a trivial matter. When we take out an ADSL subscription, we can expect not only broadband Internet access but also telecom and digital TV services. Furthermore this range of multimedia services is increasing a little more each year: personalized video, TV recorder, free international phone calls, etc. To be competitive, an ADSL supplier must be able to have the line and all the services activated and running quickly, ensure impeccable quality of service, or at least a level of service better than that of its competitors, and offer effective, available customer support.

Thus, in optimum conditions, customer satisfaction goes through three major processes for this sector: the service activation process, called provisioning; the maintenance of service quality process, including, amongst other things, detection and resolution of breakdowns in the telecom infrastructure, as quickly as possible; and finally the processing of customer calls, called ticketing.

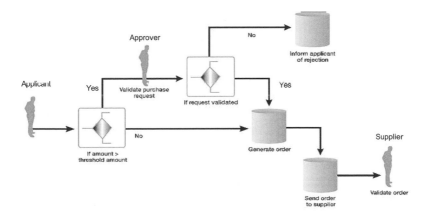

Figure 5.1. *Extract of a purchasing process*

5.1.2. *The company and its business processes*

5.1.2.1. *Processes: dynamic business unit representation*

Business processes are everywhere in a company. But what is a business process? It is a logical sequence of well established activities with a specific business objective. The recruitment process, for example, is composed of all the activities necessary for appointing new employees: including writing a description of the post, drafting the job advertisement, making interview appointments, conducting successive interviews, compiling an application folder, making decisions, checking references, etc. In fact, all this can be broken down into processes. To do this it is necessary for the activity to be represented dynamically, i.e. over time and to list all the actions or tasks necessary for the activity.

A company's business is underpinned by its activities: R&D, production, marketing, sales, purchasing. To these activities, called the core of the business, can be added support or business activities inherent in the operation of a company: human resources, IT, financial administration, legal, general services. The business may be completely described by processes, as soon as someone sets out what must be achieved to execute it. A consultancy practice business, for example, offers consultancy projects to its customers. The practice's first objective, therefore, is to sell this sort of service to its customers. To achieve this objective the practice must achieve other essential objectives. It must identify potential customers. This is the job of the sales and marketing department: tt must also develop its consultancy offer – the role of marketing and, if necessary, R&D; it must make itself known and recognized on the consultancy market – the role of the communication department; it must have competent consultants in sufficient supply to meet demand, which is up to the HR department. To achieve all these objectives, who does what, how, where and when? Such considerations boil down to thinking about the processes implemented to achieve the objectives in question.

5.1.2.2. *The importance of business processes*

But why should we be interested in business processes? The reason is that these processes provide many answers to the issues and problems facing companies. They ensure, for example, that customers are provided with their services as quickly as possible, a differentiating factor for a telecom supplier. They provide traceability for the transactions made in a banking transaction, an absolute regulatory requirement for financial institutions. They ensure that practices and procedures are standardized, a well-known issue for major international groups. They improve the quality of products and services. They optimize productivity significantly and definitely increase customer satisfaction.

Would managing business processes therefore be a remedy for all the ills of the company? Of course not, but ISO 9001 quality standards show that the process approach is definitely a formidable improvement and optimization lever for the company.

To convince yourself of that, you only have to look at the decisive progress made by industrial production during the last century. Everything began with a simple but extremely effective principle: the production line, the heart of the production process.

A business process approach consists of applying a business improvement procedure to all processes or, at least, the most important ones, by setting out to implement processes end-to-end rather than performing each activity one at a time.

To make a comparison with the world of athletics, let us take the example of a relay race. You do not necessarily win this type of race by lining up the four best sprinters in the world. Major championships have provided numerous examples that prove this point. In order to win a relay, it is vital to pass the baton properly. A relay race is a process which links four sprinting activities with a baton handover. The process can only be executed perfectly if it is optimized end-to-end, i.e. if the baton handovers are as effective as the sprints themselves.

5.1.2.3. *Business processes in the traditional organization of the business*

Returning to the business world, where are business processes located? Or rather the question should be: where are they not located? Each job, each department, each site works according to a set of processes, explicit or otherwise. Some processes are specific to a company division. They only involve resources that are internal to the organization.

On the other hand, other processes involve several units: the recruitment process, for example, generally involves not only the candidates but also HR managers and operations managers who do not belong to the HR department. They may even involve external resources, such as recruitment consultancies responsible for pre-selecting candidates.

In other words, business processes are transverse to the company's divisions, whether they are functional, sectorial or geographical, as shown in Figure 5.2. As such, in order to work they have to cross the organizational frontiers that exist between all these divisions.

And yet, by its nature, a frontier is not open to all. Moreover, whereas the organizational units of the company are never hermetically sealed, their frontiers may, however, constitute major obstacles to the proper operation of processes.

Using business processes as a company improvement lever sometimes resembles an assault course. This is because the company is not historically organized around its business processes, which may act as a brake preventing them from being implemented or achieving their objectives.

The process approach therefore comes up against the traditional divisions of the company along three major lines: departments (HR, sales, purchasing, production, etc.), sectors (product and service lines) and geography (countries, regions, sites, etc.). Innovation by processes is thus not only a question of technology, it is also a question of managing the company, the organization and the strategy.

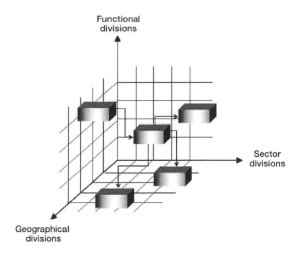

Figure 5.2. *The process dimension in the organization of the business*

5.1.2.4. *Managing business processes*

Given the seal of approval by the ISO standardizing quality procedure and made popular by business process reengineering initiatives, a BPM approach has developed and is growing each year. This approach is based on three fundamental principles:

– adding a process dimension to the company's organization;

– continuous business process improvement; and

– intensive use of information technologies.

Adding a process dimension to the organizational structure of a company boils down to defining responsibilities for each process. Major business processes will therefore have their own director and their own functional and technical experts. For transverse business processes, managers may be appointed for each division.

While organization by processes is not absolutely necessary for adopting the process approach, it is generally an influential condition for its success. The reason for this is simple: since the processes are transverse to other organizational dimensions, the improvement in the end-to-end process (i.e. in its entirety and its complexity) will be all the easier if the company has a suitable managerial structure.

Continuous improvement of business processes fits in perfectly with the quality procedure. To make this possible, it is necessary to know the smallest details of the business processes and to be able to measure their performance. The management of business processes therefore follows a typical continuous improvement cycle: analyzing, executing, measuring.

Finally, the intensive use of information technologies is justified by the place of information in the processes, as we shall see later in this chapter.

5.1.3. *The issues involved in managing business processes*

Managing business processes is admittedly an onerous project. But before launching into such an ambitious task, it is better to find out in advance how relevant the approach is. Management by business processes provides good reasons for reassuring decision makers. Its relevance is unquestionable because of the savings it makes. It is even probable that in a few years time, it will no longer be a question of relevance but rather one of necessity.

Among the various gains, let us mention those most evident: effectiveness and efficiency, productivity, performance, control, visibility and compliance, so many critical criteria for profitability and company competitiveness.

5.1.3.1. *Effectiveness and efficiency*

Although they are similar in their etymology, effectiveness and efficiency are subtly different. The first indicates the rate of success, while the second considers the relationship between a result and the effort put in to achieve it. A salesman is effective is he sells a lot. He is efficient if he does this at the lowest cost, in other words if a few minutes of his time are enough to clinch the sale. What sales department would not dream of having such a salesman on their team!

Efficiency and effectiveness are two key business process performance indicators. Effectiveness shows the value created by the process, efficiency the costs incurred. How do you increase both of them at the same time? By ensuring that the work done throughout the process is optimal, i.e. there is no time and energy wasted. Tasks without added value such as IT entries, redundant tasks due to bad organization or unsuitable tools, a lack of co-ordination, a lack of clarity in processes, these are the enemies of efficiency. As for effectiveness, it is not usually innate but rather it improves and gathers pace. Effectiveness goes alongside rigor, organization, collaboration and quality, as many factors that accompany good control of business processes.

5.1.3.2. *Productivity and performance*

Productivity is a recurrent obsession with managers. The reason for this is because it is normally synonymous with growth and results. In a number of sectors it goes hand in hand with performance. By performance we mean speed of production, not the overall performance of the company, which includes all the criteria mentioned in this chapter. To be competitive, you must always produce with increasing speed. However, so as not to be someone like Charlie Chaplin, swallowed up by the gears of the machine, it is important to control the production process from end to end, whether it is traditional industrial production, or production of services or even distribution.

An example that we all know is that of Internet and telecom providers. It was more than ten years ago that this sector exploded and the sun does not seem to be setting on it yet. The reason for this is simple. Its growth is based entirely on the innovation of multimedia technologies, which are only just starting. Directed at everybody, these supply offers interest millions of customers in France and billions throughout the world. The demand therefore requires large-scale productivity, while the pressure of competition in this market demands total customer satisfaction. This is done by activating services in record time, as well as maintaining the most effective after-sales service.

But the processes brought into play when activating these customer services are far from being basic. An activation process must spread through a labyrinth of dedicated systems, each one releasing the service subscribed to, the broadband ADSL line, the customer account, the e-mail account, the mobile account, digital television, national and international telephone services, digital ranges, video on demand, etc.; without taking into account the customer's technical eligibility based on his geographical location! This is why processes called provisioning, which are responsible for allocating and activating all these services, have been the focus of major rationalization and optimization projects by all the major telecom operators, with one simple aim: to meet the productivity and performance requirements of the market in spite of the complexity of the infrastructures to be set up.

5.1.3.3. *Control and transparency*

How can you manage effectively if you cannot see or control the group's activities or the work of each individual? This unthinkable situation is, however, a common reality in business. Even today, a number of managers deplore the obvious lack of visibility, overall as well as detailed, of their activity. The reason for this is organization, of course, but also the information system which, although it has all the necessary information, very often cannot reproduce it in a way that it can be used by managers.

Let us take an example that occurs more often than you would think. In large groups, the process of replying to invitations to tender is normally tracked by branches, countries, divisions or even sites. Because of this, it is not unusual for one of these groups to unknowingly submit several replies to the same invitation to tender, all of them noticeably different, which may have unfortunate consequences: disqualification of the invitation to tender, loss of credibility with the customer, being entered on the customer's black list, etc.

There again, good control of their business processes will enable managers to ensure end-to-end control of their activities and their staff. Knowing who does what, when, how and why, is exactly the visibility managers need to complete their tasks.

5.1.3.4. Compliance

Economic globalization has brought with it a new wave of regulations. Today, businesses are not only subject to national regulations, they must also comply with European and American directives etc. Banking businesses, for example, are very heavily constrained by an ever increasing number of regulations. There are so many regulations that they monopolize a very large number of IT projects carried out in banks. From Sarbanes-Oxley and Bâle II to SEPA and MiFID, each new set of regulations brings its own set of constraints: traceability of transactions over the long term, security and reliability, inter-bank exchange rules, obligation to perform transactions in the best interests of the customer, etc.

The compliance of a business activity with a particular set of regulations necessarily includes the compliance of its processes. The breakdown of work provided by the process approach makes it easier to make any activity comply.

5.1.3.5. Standardization

Standardization aims to standardize practices within the company and its business units. It is important for the management to be able to refer to a work base common to all the units that are under its responsibility. Processes are therefore ideal candidates for standardization because they describe operating procedures and define how to work.

5.1.4. *Business processes and managing information*

5.1.4.1. *Information and management*

BPM initiatives that have emerged over the last few years rely heavily on information technologies. Why? First of all because the management of processes is based primarily on an in-depth knowledge of these processes. It is therefore necessary to describe them by documenting them, while ensuring that the documentation evolves with the processes themselves.

The best way of describing business processes is to model them. Logical diagrams, where each activity is represented by a box connected to others by arrows (indicating precedence), are now common in functional divisions that are trying to represent their business and therefore their business processes.

Knowledge of business processes often requires a considerable amount of information. Business processes are modeled in accordance with several abstraction levels. Each activity must be documented in detail, the players, their organizations and the relationships that link them must not be forgotten, just like the business rules that govern the processes and the infrastructure used to support them.

Several models are also often necessary for a complete description of a set of processes. Various, varied logical (activity) diagrams, state diagrams, flow charts, mapping of all processes and infrastructure, etc.

Similarly, measuring the execution of processes often produces a large amount of data: end-to-end execution time, execution time for each stage, error rates, execution statistics by division, by player, purely business indicators: sales volumes, turnover, profitability rates, etc.

Just like any management activity, process management therefore relies heavily on IT. As we shall soon see, this need has led to a boom in specialist software packages for modeling and business process monitoring.

5.1.4.2. *The role of information in processes*

The second reason that justifies the predominant role of IT in the management of processes is the place of information in business processes. A process is a logical sequence of activities.

This sequence cannot proceed without a stage-to-stage transmission of information, from activity to activity, from task to task: information is the oil that greases the processes wheels. BPM is very interested in this dynamic, which enables a set of activities to be carried out together to serve a common objective. This explains why information is at the heart of the issues.

To illustrate this, let us take a look at common malfunctions in business processes. An order could not be delivered within the timescale because the delivery order was not received by the delivery man. The delivery order was not issued in time because the purchase order was not received. The purchase order had not been issued because delivery information was missing or because the person responsible for processing it was absent, and so on.

A number of breaks in business processes are due to bad circulation of information. How many times do you hear an employee complain that he doesn't have all the information he needs for his work? Or a manager complain that he is often informed too late to make the right decisions at the right time? For a business process to run properly, information must pass through at the right time, in the right format and with the right content.

5.1.4.3. *Information: the raw material of business processes*

In some cases, business processes handle nothing but information. This is the case in the services sector. In the banking world, exchanges are intangible because they are mainly financial flows. On top of the information used by the process to determine what stages to follow, we need to add the business objects: customers (via their account for example), transactions, products, services, etc.

More generally, business process information describes the objects, physical or otherwise, which are handled within the processes. These could be anything from an application file in the recruitment process or a tender offer in a tendered sales process, to an order or an invoice in a purchasing process, etc.

5.1.5. *The company, processes and ISs*

To summarize, business processes are valuable tools, which enable the business to improve both in carrying out its business – with significant gains in terms of quality, performance, effectiveness, efficiency, compliance and in its management – with increased visibility and control over the processes and the activities involved, thus increasing reactivity and anticipation.

In its traditional configuration, the business is not, or is only marginally, organized around its processes. Logically then, it is the same for the information system, which is normally inherited from the organization of the company itself.

However, BPM involves a great deal of information management: process models and associated documentation, use of process execution data and business objects, and data monitoring.

The process dimension must therefore be embodied at all levels of the business. If it already exists at operational level in a large number of cases, it is at this level that the process concept is the most common

– it must definitely reach the upper tier of management by inserting itself into the organizational structure of the company at the same level as functions, sectors and geography; as well as the lower tier; and the information system, which is generally organized by non-transverse applications.

This is the purpose of BPM: to increase the value of business processes, both at managerial and IT level, and to prioritize them in line with their importance in the operation of the company and its results.

5.2. Understanding BPM

5.2.1. *BPM stands for business process management*

5.2.1.1. *Managing business processes between the business unit and IT*

BPM is an approach which centers on the management of information circulating within the process. It is based on the following basic principles:

– a continuous improvement strategy based on a modeling, automation and business process monitoring cycle;

– process organization, defining the roles, responsibilities and skills necessary to implement, execute and control processes;

– a methodology used to equip the process step in accordance with the continuous improvement and process organization cycle; and

– software tools providing the information system with a business process layer.

BPM is therefore a response to the process management issue, tackled both from the business and IT points of view. It is not only a quality procedure, a management method or a technological inspiration but rather all three at once.

5.2.1.2. *BPM: three confusing letters*

In the 20 years that it has been with us, we have to conclude that BPM has been the source of a great deal of confusion: acronyms, homonyms, uncertain definition, application fields that are sometimes minimalist and sometimes excessive. Why is it so confusing? Why does BPM appear to be so complex, so indistinct?

Firstly it is because the acronym BPM has several meanings. Apart from BPM, the most common are business process modeling and business performance management. In addition, the IT market has spawned services associated with BPM, such as business activity monitoring (BAM). We also talk about business process analysis (BPA), business process improvement (BPI) and business process outsourcing (BPO), as well as business process monitoring (BPM), business process automation (BPA), business process execution (BPE), process performance management (PPM) and many others! This proliferation of acronyms relating to business process issues has made it more difficult to understand an approach that is, by nature, already complicated.

A second source of confusion is the BPM market, which is populated with a myriad of developers, analysts, consultants and integrators. Since the acronym is used more often than the full name, the BPM market refers to all the software systems dealing with one of the BPMs and others of that ilk mentioned above. This is without mentioning players in the IT market in its broadest sense who are saddled with the term BPM, faced with the importance, which has been attached to, and which will continue to be attached to, the business process approach.

5.2.1.3. *BPM: at the crossroad of process initiatives*

BPM was initially an approach promulgated by the IT world to take account of the business process dimension within information systems. In the tradition of the business process re-engineering initiative instigated by Michael Hammer and James Champy, BPM was born out of the necessity to inform people about all the business process players, whether they were human or applications. Thus, BPM was very quickly supported by human workflow technologies used to automate the transmission of tasks between users, in accordance with a process logic. But the complexity of this communication between humans and applications meant that workflow developers were devoting their time to humans, while inter-application initiatives were increasing at the same time, the most famous of which was EAI (Enterprise Application Integration). In this same period, i.e. at the end of the 1990s and the turn of the century, ISO 9000 standards also evolved towards business processes by placing them at the heart of the quality process.

Workflow technologies and EAI technologies were not the only ones to shift towards a process-based approach at the turn of the century. Integrated management software packages (ERP) normally offered their users a wide range of business processes. The rules engines, which were intrinsically very close to business processes, also played a part in forging this new business process era, not forgetting the modeling programs which, to accompany the boom in business process reengineering, tended towards methods suitable for describing processes.

All this work, although obviously complementary, continued to advance, each in its respective domain. It is only recently that we saw the emergence of the first truly integrated solutions for all process issues. These solutions went under the name of BPMS for business process management suite (or sometimes BPM system).

BPM as we know it today is the culmination of a merger of process-orientated technologies. However, it is also the result of thinking around business processes, supported by BPR and quality procedures.

Because of its privileged position between management, business unit and information system, BPM thinks of itself as an integrating system:

– not only of technologies, combining all of these things into processes and rule engines;

– but also of the organization between management, operators and IT, offering convincing solutions for collaboration between these three groups.

5.2.2. *Continuous process improvement*

With BPM it is not a question of redefining business processes entirely, as was the case with business process reengineering. Just the opposite in fact, it is a question of developing a favorable environment in which to improve them gradually.

This improvement follows a threefold cycle: describing, executing, measuring. The description of processes uses a modeling approach. Executing them is more precisely about automating their information part within the information system. Measuring and, more generally, monitoring, is done based on the results of the execution.

To ensure continuous improvement, BPM takes advantage of the fact that business processes can be broken down into component parts. Thus processes can be considered in sections and optimization points can normally be isolated, thus making gradual improvement easier.

Let us take a simple example with the purchasing process. Imagine that in our company this process is suffering from goods taking too long to arrive. By analyzing the purchasing process as used in the company, we note in particular that the order is still being sent to the supplier by post, whereas the supplier has the means to process orders electronically.

Another thing that slows the process down is an approval workflow that too often blocks the issue of a purchase requisition. These two causes of delay are unconnected and it is therefore not necessary (and often not appropriate) to try to resolve them at the same time.

Dealing with these two problems separately, the first is resolved by automating the sending of the order, and the second by revising the approval sub-process. In other words, when step-by-step improvement is available, it must be used as far as possible.

5.2.3. *A process layer in the information system*

5.2.3.1. *From ERP to BPM*

Managing business processes at the information system level is not the exclusive preserve of BPM. Since the process concept is inherent in the running of activities, business processes have quickly been represented in business applications. Most ERPs include an extensive process repository, which allows users to manage information via these processes. However, it is not a question of BPM here.

Since the process dimension is therefore not specific to BPM, where is the innovation? It is in the layer separation principle, the crux of IT architectures. In fact although ERPs effectively integrate business processes, there is no denying that they impose an additional boundary on such processes, that of the software package itself. The contribution of BPM is to dedicate a software layer in the information system to execute processes separately from the execution of the invoked activities. In other words, the essential principle of BPM is to separate the how (the process) from the what (the participating activities).

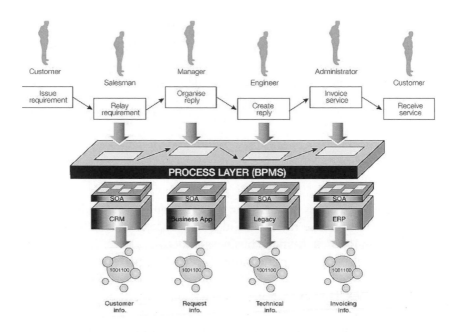

Figure 5.3. *The process layer in the IS*

BPM therefore brings something new, a separate, complete module of the transverse information system, which is able to orchestrate users and applications in accordance with a process logic, as illustrated in Figure 5.3.

5.2.3.2. *BPM: the process dimension only*

A frequently confusing feature of BPM is the type of information that BMP solutions cover. Does BPM only process electronic documents, as was the case with one of its antecedents, the document workflow, or otherwise structured data like another of its predecessors, EAI?

The answer to this question is that BPM takes absolutely no account of the degree of structuring of the information, whether it is low for documents, or high for database data. The purpose of BPM is to free business processes from information system boundaries.

However, to date there are two major boundaries that have a great impact on the IS architecture and its use. The application boundary on the one hand, a problem addressed by EAI at first, then the SOA, and data structure boundaries on the other hand, given that the worlds of GED and business databases are still far apart.

As an integrating technology, BPM does not therefore show any preference between applications, nor between data sources.

The same question is asked about the degree of process automation. Is BPM the new name of a workflow or EAI? The answer is that neither are. BPM includes both of them and integrates all processes whether they are largely manual, like collaborative processes, or fully automated like banking transactions.

Thus, as the following figure shows, BPM is located solely on the process dimension. We call it BPM as soon as the information system has been provided with a separate business process execution layer, which is transverse to business applications and to the data sources involved.

This layer orchestrates the players in a process that is in accordance with the imposed logic. Let us add that at the IS level, human players are represented by user interfaces, which are themselves applications.

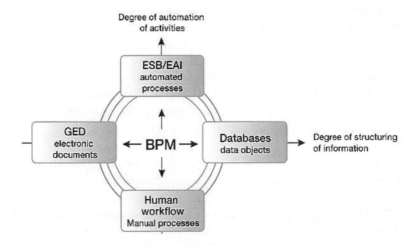

Figure 5.4. *BPM: automating and structuring information*

5.2.4. *Process layer contributions*

BPM docs not only contribute to the beneficial effects of managing the business processes that we mentioned before. This is because BPM brings a major development to the information system, just like SOA or MDM, disciplines that are studied in other chapters of this book. At the information system level, BPM provides three essential assets:

– a significant improvement in the alignment between the business unit and IT;

– a major opportunity for continuous change; and

– a high level of participation in the globalization of the information system.

5.2.4.1. *Aligning the information system to the business unit*

The alignment of the information system to the business unit is one of the great challenges of IT innovation. How can business users be supported effectively in their daily work? As the old adage goes, "Birds of a feather flock together". Why do business users want nothing to do with the superb IT creations that their IT departments proudly offer them? Because these applications bear no resemblance to them. Because they force users to get lost in a maze of screens, user guides, surprise buttons without ever satisfying them completely. *Birds of a feather flock together*. It is mimicry that is needed here. The information system must work like people, no longer by application as it has done so well up till now, but rather by processes and activities.

It is certainly not a question of destroying all these valuable applications that are vital for managing information, but on the other hand it is a question of organizing such applications in accordance with business processes and business services. BPM is involved with process orientation, SOA with service orientation.

5.2.4.2. *Flexibility faced with constant change*

In a socio-economic world that is moving faster and faster, change becomes the norm. Companies integrate mergers and acquisitions more and more into their life cycle, markets get bigger and increase in number, there are more and more competitors and they are even fiercer than before. Within a company reorganization becomes commonplace, while careers are increasingly shorter as the 21st century has ushered in generations who are more and more mobile. Change is everywhere, with direct impact on the business unit and its processes. Companies must face up to it. The best strategy is to turn each constraint into a strength. It has to be flexible, i.e. prepared for constant change.

Flexibility is inherent to the essential principle of BPM – separating the how from the what, the process from the activity. But how does this separation promote flexibility? Any change causes a shock wave, either weak or strong. To absorb this shock wave it is preferable to create a flexible structure, where each floor has a certain freedom of movement in relation to its neighbours. It is this physical law of flexibility that has been taken up again by the layer architecture frequently found in information technologies. The creation of Web applications, for example, has gone through this transformation – separating the presentation of the logic and data storage has ensured that the impact of functional changes and technological replacements are kept to a minimum.

Once more, BPM has not invented anything. It is only applying a tried and tested, very effective principle to reduce the effects of change; because when the business unit changes, the how and the what, do not necessarily change in the same way. It may mean that the process has to be changed without altering the activities involved as, for example, modifying business rules. On the contrary, an activity may find itself completely changed after a reorganization without having a major effect on the process. The separation between process and activity dimensions caused by BPM thus prevents the change spreading to where it is not meant to be.

5.2.4.3. *Reviving the company unit in the IS*

If a customer had the magic power to walk into the information system of some of its major suppliers, they could not be blamed for thinking that they had been transported into a hall of mirrors at a fair. They would see as many images of themselves as applications in the system, and if it occurred to them to follow the track of a business process, they would find themselves in the ghost train straight away! Of course, this metaphor of the information system is somewhat exaggerated. Nevertheless it imaginatively underlines the mixed nature of large information systems, which has become almost natural. This division can be explained in many ways, and can be justified. But do we have to resign ourselves to it? Each customer is unique. they should not be managed separately in each of the applications that are useful to them. A process should not get lost in the dark tunnels of the inter-application environment, or crash into the swing doors of applications just like the ghost train when it trundles into a new part of the haunted castle.

BPM enables the company to take back control of its business processes as they are in the information system, thus inviting the company to undertake the globalization of the system. As distributed and decentralized as it may be, the company forms a whole. It has a unique, global identity. As do each of its customers, suppliers and partners. Thus, for the information to be as useful as possible to the company, it is logical that it also acquires this unique, global identity.

5.3. The business process from the IS perspective

5.3.1. *Processes seen from an IT angle*

What does a business process look like when seen from the information system? A process is a sequence of activities co-ordinated in accordance with a predefined logic. When each activity is completed, the process goes past a stage. However, these ideas of processes, activities and stages can be defined based on a, more or less, strong degree of abstraction. The information system, like a good, self-respecting machine, only understands the specific, the rational, the categorical. At its level, the business process is therefore a completely detailed structure, made up of tasks which are basic activities, transitions, which link the tasks, and rules, which impose a business logic on everything. Tasks are performed by players. These players may be users of the system, therefore human players, or applications since the task is then automated. In a word, a process interacts with its environment using the event or events that are likely to trigger it.

Let us take as an example the first task of the order process. The applicant creates his purchase requisition by filling in the form provided for this purpose. Once the requisition has been recorded, the system automatically performs the following task, which is to send it to an approver responsible for validating it. The process-triggering event here is the manual creation of a purchase requisition, although it could also be an automatic creation triggered by another process, stock management for example, integrating an automatic restocking request.

Thus, processes have very different aspects depending on whether they are seen by the business unit or by IT. The business unit uses a macroscopic level of description where the implementation logic does not matter much. The essential thing is to represent the organization brought into play, the rules in force, the possible scenarios, so many factors essential for the business units control of processes. IT uses a detailed – not to say microscopic – description level, where the human player becomes a task form accessible from a basket, and where he is on an equal footing with the application services and the data objects handled.

BPM deals with these two levels of process description and all the intermediate levels. Would there be intermediate levels? Of course, because to prevent the breakdown of the macroscopic business process, into an implementable process from changing into a real descent into hell, it is better to go about it in gradual refinements, specifying more functional elements each time, and going into technical considerations little by little. To our knowledge there is currently no standard method for precisely determining the number of description levels in business processes. Everything depends on what you are trying to represent and the people who will use the process models. The essential thing is to ensure that its readers understand it regardless of the abstraction level. When this readership is the information system, the description must be categorical and rigorous.

5.3.2. *BPMS architectures*

As we mentioned before, as far as the information system is concerned, BPM consists of a process management layer. This layer is inserted between the interaction with the users layer, populated with Web interfaces and other thin or fat clients and the application layer where the information resides. But what is the process layer? This layer must contain everything necessary for managing processes, for analyzing them in the initial stages, executing them and then analyzing them after the process is completed.

5.3.2.1. *Modeling business processes*

What we call the initial analysis of business processes refers to the structure of processes. This starts with defining them, declaring them at system level. This is the modeling domain of the business processes, business process modeling. Process modeling is supported by a software market, whose leaders are the Aris platforms produced by IDS Scheer, Mega or Casewise.

Not to be confused with design software, these tools include a modeling repository where each object has its own existence: for example, a customer player is associated with a single object, whatever diagram represents him. If the object is modified, it is modified on all the diagrams at the same time. Modeling is thus consistent and the diagrams are no longer drawn on loose sheets.

In the last few years, the modeling sector has expanded, integrating especially simulation functions. It is now possible in this way to check the accuracy of a model on the one hand, and a modification's affect on a process on the other hand.

Finally it must be noted that modeling software is not normally restricted just to business processes. Since the trend favors enterprise architecture and more accurately the architecture supported by modeling, that is to say model-driven architecture, the issue is global and applies to the whole structure of the company.

5.3.2.2. *Performing business processes*

Executing business processes is historically the domain of BPMS (BPM Suites or BPM Systems) platforms. Increasingly, these platforms are tending to reunite the three BPM cycle phases of modeling, execution and, monitoring. As things stand at the moment, let us just say that this convergence is a work in progress.

In order to determine the architecture of a BPMS platform properly, we shall return to the process assets for the information system – tasks, transitions subjected to rules, human players, i.e. the users, applications responsible for automatic tasks, and finally, events that represent the interactions of a process with its execution environment.

At the heart of the BPMS is the process engine, which is better known as the workflow engine. Its role is to orchestrate tasks that go under the name of services when the BPMS changes into an SOA. Just like a good conductor, it invites its musicians to join the symphony at the right time in accordance with the score. Essentially, it decides who does what, when and how. The process engine collects events, particularly those involved in triggering a process. It applies a logic drawn up by a set of rules. This logic enables it to determine what tasks to perform, depending on the context of the execution – therefore events – and which are the performers. He then assigns these tasks to players, users or applications.

The BPMS architecture results from:

– a process or workflow engine;

– a rule manager or rule engine;

– a user interface manager for human players; and

– an application interface manager for automated tasks.

You will then understand the state of the BPMS market better. You will find human workflows, document workflows from the GED environment, integration suites (formerly EAI but now known as ESB), rule engines and portals. Here once again, BPM demonstrates its integrating nature.

All these markets have rubbed shoulders with each other for a long time, each one dealing with a part of the BPM issue. Although still recent, the convergence has finally been initiated under the aegis of BPM and BPMS.

The major trend is towards complete BPMS, integrating all the sections of process architecture, which has become established by means of successive buyouts. This is the case with TIBCOs iProcess, BEAs Aqualogic or even Software AGs WebMethod platforms. Apart from the process engine, these include a portal, a rule engine and an ESB. Other developers concentrate more on the high end of BPM, like Pega Systems or Lombardi, which offers a process engine – inherited from a rule engine for Pega systems, a workflow engine for Lombardi – and a user interface. These platforms can nevertheless interface with an ESB, according to SOA standards, or directly with applications for a simple integration via a set of connectors. Therefore the BPMS market, although it is not yet fully consolidated, will henceforth offer sufficiently mature solutions to ensure the execution of business processes.

5.3.2.3. *Monitoring business processes*

Monitoring business processes is the domain of BAM (business activity monitoring) solutions. Chapter 9 is dedicated to this approach. We shall therefore not dwell on it here. Following the example of modeling solutions, BAM solutions are not restricted to the process dimension but offer global coverage of business monitoring.

Figure 5.5 summarizes the components of a complete BPMS architecture.

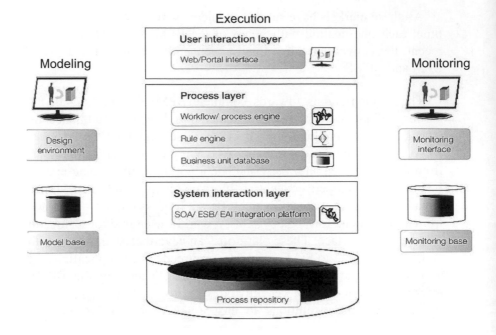

Figure 5.5. *BPM architecture*

5.3.2.4. *Towards a process repository*

Although the intention of BPMS developers is to provide their customers with a complete process layer comprised of all the modeling, execution and monitoring services, their offerings have not yet achieved the necessary maturity to do this. In fact, one missing component is currently needed in order to tie together the three parts of BPM: a process repository common to modeling, execution and monitoring. No BPM offering currently provides such a repository, in spite of the efforts to connect them, particularly in order to automatically change analysis models into execution models. Nevertheless, once this undoubtedly major issue has been overcome,

BPM will enjoy the consistency that it still lacks between its three key challenges: the modeling, executing and monitoring of business processes.

5.3.3. *Which BPM for which processes?*

IIow do you measure the suitability of a BPM procedure for a given business process? Given that processes are inherent in any shared work, the BPM approach has the effect of making them explicit, on the one hand, in the organization of the company, and on the other hand, at the information system level.

However, BPM is a large-scale procedure. As such, for the return on investment not just to be theoretical, it is necessary to tread carefully when choosing the right business processes for the procedure. How do you choose?

A simple answer would be to say that any business process is suitable for the procedure. This is true if you do not think about the necessary investment, particularly in the initial stages. For a more appropriate answer, it is necessary to distinguish between modeling, automation and monitoring.

A business process is suitable for modeling if it is important to document it and keep this documentation. Most business processes are therefore suitable for modeling. However, it is clear that a simple process, which is not transverse to the organization and which changes little, will find excellent ways of being documented in Word and PowerPoint. The second point of modeling is to serve as a point of entry for automation.

As far as automation is concerned, the key criteria are standardization and traceability. In fact, automation will be all the more beneficial if the business process is executed frequently. The fact that activities are automatic or human should not be a consideration at this level. Although today's BPMS market is still split in two – with platforms that are inherited from the workflow for largely human processes and, conversely, platforms inherited from application integration for largely automated processes – you must not lose sight of the fact that a process which is largely human today may become largely automated tomorrow, thanks mainly to the BPM approach.

Consequently, a process that can be standardized, i.e. sufficiently repetitive for a standard execution framework to be defined, is an ideal candidate for BPM.

Traceability is also a key factor that justifies a BPM procedure. In fact, by automating the distribution of tasks and the execution of rules, it becomes possible to precisely trace the activity generated by a business process. A process, such as a tender offer, does not normally have a very high degree of standardization, because each invitation to tender is specific and requires equally specific compilation.

However, the control of this process, which is critical not only for the sales function but also for the operators responsible for future contingencies, goes through a detailed examination of who does what, when, how and why. This is why this process is an excellent candidate for BPM.

As for monitoring, the necessity for a BPM approach is justified in the need for visibility in real-time, for strong reactivity and control of large volumes. Monitoring, an active part of business activity monitoring, also dealt with in this book, meets an innate managerial need and in fact accompanies any BPM undertaking.

It is nevertheless important to note that BPM projects do not necessarily contain the three problems all at the same time. A BAM project can be implemented without processes being orchestrated by a BPMS platform. A BPMS platform can also be implemented without thorough modeling of processes. Process modeling can be done without automating or monitoring processes.

5.4. BPM promises and prospects

5.4.1. *BPM: as simple as clicking a mouse*

Let's admit it: the promise that BPM is as simple as clicking a mouse is yet to be kept! There are a large number of brochures from developers boasting about the ease with which you can implement a BPM project with their solution. The promise made by these developers is the option to model processes, implement the associated execution layer, then monitor them in a completely unified environment. This is a return to the idea of model-driven architecture. However, today, convergence between the three process issues has not yet been completed and no solution on the market can actually claim to control all the aspects of the BPM issue completely.

This does not necessarily mean that it is too early to embark on a BPM procedure and acquire a BPM platform, but you will have to bear in mind that, as with any IT project, IT consultants and integrators remain the best means of ensuring a permanent implementation. Whereas developers introduce software packages, consultants bring methodologies and expertise, while integrators have this vital ability to transform a software package into a solution that meets the specific requirements of each company.

5.4.2. *BPM standards: still some way to go*

Transverse technologies such as SOA and BPM come with their own set of standards. The reason for this, in light of the communication and collaboration issue, is that the first prerequisite is to have a common language. We have seen that BPM technologies have come from markets that have been separate for a long time. The convergence of these technologies to obtain a standardized process layer therefore includes this common language, which the different components of a BPM suite will share, to describe, execute and monitor processes. This language is called BPEL (business process execution language). Even if there is still some way to go before

BPEL can deal with the complexity of business processes completely, including human interactions, service calls, event management, rules and data, all BPM developers have firmly committed themselves to the BPEL standardization route.

In addition, BPM also likes to think of itself as an integrator of the business unit and IT environments by offering a modeling approach. BPEL offers a modeling process called execution, i.e. it can be interpreted by a process execution engine. Consequently, the content and level of detail of this model will prove to be too technical for the business units whose preoccupation is to find common ground to obtain a consensus of models that can be understood by all interested parties. To meet this need, a standard level higher than BPEL has been established in the last few years: BPMN (business process modeling notation). This standard must also be enhanced to cover all the modeling requirements of business processes, but there too, most developers have become aware of the importance of using a common language in order to make it easier to pick up and use the tools.

The future undoubtedly belongs to a systematic modeling approach, known as model-driven architecture. To achieve this result, i.e. the automatic transformation of process business models into execution models, we may expect to see a reconciliation between or even a merger of BPMN and BPEL.

5.4.3. *BPM and portal: a vision geared towards the user*

A technology that we have not mentioned very much in this chapter is the user interface, which at present is predominantly supported by the portal. And yet BPM and portal are very close, so close that sometimes they are confused. The most complete BPMS platforms on the current market all offer a portal module (TIBCO, BEA, WebMethods, etc.) to manage the complexity of the interaction between users and the process layer.

This reconciliation is not incongruous, given the place that human beings occupy within business processes: operators and managers are still today in sole command and computerized automation has some way to go before it can replace them. This integration of portal and process layer also reminds us that the end user – the business user – remains the kingpin of the system, and that the process dimension must be integrated into a wider work environment suitable for all requirements.

5.5. Conclusion: the place of BPM in the company and in the IS

These days the need for customized management of business processes is an accepted fact in many companies, mainly large and very large companies. However, for most of them, companies that have chosen to manage by processes have found themselves faced with a painful fact – their current information systems are completely unable to monitor this procedure. The simple reason for this is that their systems lack the characteristic transversality of processes. The process layer, the real missing link between the operation of business units and traditional application systems, is at the heart of BPM.

BPM is neither a fad nor a revolution. It merely gives concrete expression to a new stage in the development of a company and its information system – one of collaboration via processes, of course. In future, the three letters BPM will perhaps disappear, defeated by the confusion of meanings or by innovations that are constantly being replaced by IT pioneers. But without doubt, the need for a process dimension in the organization of the company, as well as in the architecture of its information system, will remain a major, definitive change to which BPM will have made a very large contribution.

Chapter 6

Exchange Platforms

As we have already mentioned, there is no transverse information system that does not have specific resources to orchestrate this transversality. Distributing reference data, calling up shared services, orchestrating transverse processes: the whole transversality chain has a dedicated solution responsible for it: exchange platforms. They manage all information exchanges between silos. These flow managers are the center of what the Gartner Group calls the "company's nervous system".

6.1. The development of data exchanges

Since the end of the 1990s and the emergence of EAI (enterprise application integration) technologies, data exchanges have undergone several changes that prefigured the subjects dealt with in the previous chapters. In this part we shall give you a short history which will try to show how, in the IT industry, fads come and go and why there always remains a trace of them.

6.1.1. *EAI: the first wave of standardization*

At the end of the 1990s the concept of EAI appeared. These were platforms dedicated to managing exchanges between applications. In a world where Web services were barely emerging on the horizon, they offered a strong promise of interoperability, but not only that. Applications started to communicate as they went along and the whole company expected the promise of real-time to be fulfilled. The management of this communication was taken away from the applications and they were freed from this relatively indigestible load.

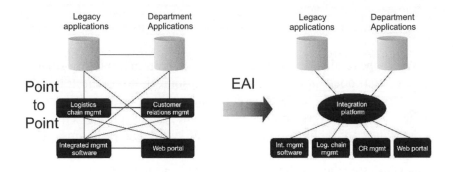

Figure 6.1. *From exchanges to EAI*

At a time when we are talking about transverse information systems, it is funny to note how much the perception of exchanges has changed, opening up the way to new areas. At one point, the management of inter-application gateways was more tolerated than experienced. It was an undervalued sub-project of the application function project it was attached to, with the interfaces often made by people to whom you did not particularly want to entrust other activities. They increased in number with the new projects and, with little documentation, created by outsourcers or people who have moved on, proved difficult to maintain, becoming extremely complex and inflexible. The EAI response not only provided the means to organize and standardize communication but also developed this area from a business unit point of view.

Previously this type of management had been performed at the level of files, vast containers of information where people were more concerned about the cover than the contents. With EAI, the fact that this could be done more systematically at single message level made it possible to manage the transmitted information from a functional and not only a technical point of view. Master data management (MDM), business process management (BPM) and even service-oriented architectures (SOAs) know what they owe to EAI in terms of achieving their potential and even finding their true place in the forefront.

Where are we after 10 years of practice? Some experiments have ended in the solution being implemented throughout the company. Others remained confined to tactical projects. Following mergers and acquisitions, some companies found they had two or even three EAIs that they intended to use for different applications, depending on the pattern of the project that they came up against. Others changed platforms over time or investigated doing this. Others are still choosing their first solution or have just implemented it. This market is still very active. Also, don't believe those who claim that EAI is a range of technologies that has never worked. Dozens of major projects, involving several thousand working days, have been successful. Those that failed or have been considered only partially successful without any real future must not only attribute this to the technology. Unsuitable methods, a failed change procedure and an underestimated learning curve are also factors that have led to a negative perception of the initiative.

6.1.2. *From data to process: a failed action?*

From 2000, i.e. very shortly after the appearance of the EAI market, developers tried to offer a business process manager in their solutions, and to integrate human activity into the flow of exchanges. Their reasoning was perfectly logical. Taken separately, each flow does not have a very high business content. However, put together in sequences, data flows become transversal business processes that describe the life cycles of the company's data. For example, the life cycle of a financial security, from its sale by a trader until its back-office settlement, describes a group of data flows linked as a function. With an EAI solution it is possible to represent this process graphically, to monitor its progress and to know precisely how far it has got and finally to be alerted in the event of an incident.

According to this principle, developers like Vitria, one of the pioneers of these systems, or TIBCO, through its buyout of InConcert, clearly took this direction. Was the market ready to follow them? The fact remains that, on the whole, companies largely considered EAI to be flow managers, strictly middleware, depositories for the information system's inner workings. The companies continue to do this, with all the value that standardizing methods and technologies can already bring to the subject of data exchange. But it was probably still a little too soon to follow the process direction and give priority to the emergence of a transverse information system. As a consequence, Vitria did not manage to establish itself on the French market in spite of all its efforts and InConcert became a toolbar with a strictly tactical use in the TIBCO solution.

By looking at the market you can also see that BPM solutions have become complete suites with a vast, specific functional coverage. The previous chapter proves this. They could not have developed as they have if they had stayed within integration solutions.

This was even felt by the BPM market: a large number of developers offering different solutions, all claiming to be representative of this market but with functional ranges that were, however, very different. The creation of BPM solution suites simplified the market by forcing developers to observe the relatively standardized functional model, which more easily shows each of the developer's comfort zones.

With hindsight, you cannot therefore regret this value adding separation. It is the sign of a precise, final definition of the roles of each module in the transverse information system architecture. As proof of this we mention the fact that during 2007 there was an upsurge in businesses creating their transverse information system based on an exchange bus coupled with an independent, specific process management solution. The range of products already showed a certain maturity. The demand will now fall in line.

6.1.3. *From data to service: the enterprise service bus*

As soon as the process wave passed, new eddies disturbed the decidedly troubled banks of the EAI market: ESBs. Forget Prion, now it's all about the enterprise service bus (ESB).

Although they actually appeared in 2003, these products came on to the market surrounded by the bright aura of a simple message: "The data exchange application integration model is finished. The future belongs to inter-application buses." These developers wanted to break with the traditional integration approach and were joyously proclaiming the "end of EAI", as if freeing companies from a restricting yoke.

Some revolutions are ill-advised. Banking on a massive use of standards and in particular Web service standards, these products struggled to meet all the existing scenarios, which an EAI dealt with relatively well and actually integrated all the diversity and heterogenity of IT systems. In addition, since the service displays a standardized interface (a contract), the use of the bus in principle led back to applications that were dogged by questions such as transformation or going over to the pivot format, all inconceivable topics for anyone working in the EAI environment who has mastered the concepts.

The market thus changed direction in order to eradicate this somewhat strange situation:

– on the one hand, you may think that ESB fans had gained the upper hand. The term "EAI" disappeared completely from the shelves and it is very difficult to find a solution openly claiming to be one, except perhaps at BEA, which was careful to provide a separate EAI and ESB whilst retaining the specific features of each solution;

– but in reality, the pure EAI players simply converted to ESB specialists. Was it a marketing miracle that consisted of fooling the world by going with the flow? It is a bit more complicated than that. In fact these developers products have adopted the principles which already made them ESB compliant and ripe for covering data integration such as Web service integration (which, don't forget, remains the reference implementation of service architectures). For these players, this progression was natural to such an extent that they didn't bother telling anybody about it. For them it was just a question of integrating an additional technology. In the end, their platforms already provided a high level of convergence and, in some cases, had done so for a long time.

Progress Software, with its subsidiary Sonic, which has since been reincorporated into the parent company, was one of the pioneers of this market. To date it remains one of the leaders. Its product can be likened just as much to an EAI as to an ESB. Finally, you could liken ESBs to EAIs dealing uniformly with two types of integration which, ultimately, does not observe the ESB principles as shown in the literature but, on the contrary, observes the requirements of companies for the good of all. The positive side is that EAI salesmen have finally been prompted to place greater value on market standards.

In the aftermath, the market saw a galaxy of players, such as Cape Clear or Fiorano, whose marketing boldly declared the end of EAI. Somewhat prematurely, as it turned out. Apart from Progress itself, these players struggled to get established, at least in France, where they remain on the fringes of the market.

The other integration players, big names in the industry and EAI pure players that have been around for several years, are generally still around in one form or another (WebMethods were bought out by Software AG) and are continuing to develop.

We still regularly carry out studies to determine the appropriateness of creating an exchange system. At the start of these projects, the question that our representatives ask themselves is not whether to choose between one EAI solution or SOA platform (our customers have waged war on acronyms). Instead, their questions related to the creation of a complete system, which could cope with all the exchange situations they may find themselves in, today or in the future, internally and with their partners. Their question is about the standardized equipping of what is called the "exchange area" in information system mapping.

6.1.4. *The convergence years: towards a global platform*

Companies that haven't standardized their exchange system normally use the same technology: a file exchange system that is more or less secure and more or less monitored.

The existing applications produce and consume these files themselves, normally causing an increase in the number of processes, an increase that generally leads to more or less pronounced redundancy. As nobody has actually centralized any knowledge of an exchange system similar to a file exchange system, it is often the case that over time the same information is extracted several times.

And yet the increase in inter-application flows makes the information system more inflexible over time. People are worried about touching gateways lest nothing works like it did before. Each modification, addition and update leads to long impact analyses in order to retrospectively control a complexity that is only rarely dealt with in the initial stages.

As we have already mentioned before, the arrival of EAI solutions had the effect of breaking a vicious circle and bringing organization into the exchange area. But not only that. These solutions changed the very nature of data transport. They usually work on an event-based, asynchronous data transport system, as they go along, in message mode. Little by little, with the continuing rollout of these platforms, the file, a dominant, globalizing unit, an information container, gave way to the message, common information, autonomous content. The distribution model, the planned batch, consequently also saw itself undermined. Of course, file mode exchanges haven't disappeared, the message mode has not become the only communication container, however, this is another story which we shall sum up in a few lines.

The important thing here is that through this explanation you will see the dual contribution of EAI solutions:

– *the IT dimension:* they help to organize the exchange area, to standardize data exchanges to benefit the general organization of the information system;

– *the business unit dimension:* they provide a different way of managing the cycle and timing of exchanges and may also speed up certain critical processes, benefiting the company's performance.

Because of this dual nature, we have noted that companies that use EAI were often linked to the telecommunications and finance sectors and the logistics function, which all benefit from improved performance as a result of the real-time data exchanges. We are referring to information systems where, moreover, information is presented in a quite intangible form and where the production system itself is not necessarily made up of tangible material assets.

We have also noticed that companies in other sectors sometimes had more difficulties encouraging investment. They were convinced of the basic point of organizing exchange systems but struggled to prove the value of the solution faced with the requirements expressed by the business units. If they could not prove the contribution of the innovation to the business unit, no budget was forthcoming. The negative verdict of the general management and/or the business unit managers was both inevitable and systematic. And it is true that if you only consider the IT dimension alone, it is very difficult to justify such an expense. Why break something that is already working more or less properly and replace it with these costly technologies? Is it necessary to rebuild the house while it is still standing, even if it is built on shaky foundations? How much money will that enable us to save? Or not lose?

We shall devote Chapter 11 to answering these questions but even if we know the levers, you have to admit that without proven value on the business unit side, we may soon give up. The organization of the information system and the planning actions are often brought about by an effective implementation of these technologies over the long term.

In the short term, the value of the proof is on the business unit side. Some companies have thus shied away from this type of investment for a long time, unfortunately delaying the construction of the first modules of their transverse information system.

Others have used these solutions in a restricted number of projects, then neglected them; not all the exchange requirements were covered. You can't blame them. EAIs meet a specific common exchange requirement in asynchronous mode, and yet the need to fit out the exchange area is much more global. The company not only wants to be able to cope with all the exchange situations, it also wants to be able to change from one exchange situation to another in time and as soon as the need arises.

In addition, it is not certain that this type of exchange is a panacea. In *EAI au service de l'entreprise évolutive*, we outlined a case where, on the contrary, management on-the-fly could create problem situations.

Rather than committing large sums to the development of compensation procedures, you could respond by slightly straining real-time. With hindsight, you would only use the on-the-fly procedure where it proved to be useful, and not as a general rule.

For this reason, during the study stage, we envisage the possibility of the exchange situations changing eventually, depending on the business unit requirements identified and the trends detected. Figure 6.2 shows the type of simulations we carry out.

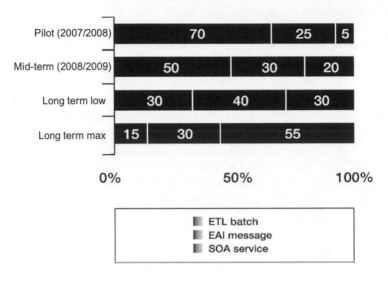

Figure 6.2. *Changes in exchange situations*

The situation shown here is quite generic: exchanges in service mode are still in the minority and reflect the situation commonly established in 2007 in most information systems. They will develop over time as the service requirements grow. Conversely, the file mode has a tendency to reduce, even if it keeps a significant proportion over time which is probably, eventually, incompressible. It is therefore the ability to manage the diversity of exchanges that will be a feature of an exchange system. However, the question is how do you build a complete platform from market solutions?

The ability to change from one exchange mode to another is critical to meet the company's alignment requirements. Let us continue with the example of this luxury goods company that wants to integrate the stocks of its 300 shops across the world more quickly:

– Initially, the exchange remains in file mode. The exchange platform is used to rationalize and accelerate the exchange process. By doing this, the performance of the process improves. By removing an obsolete technological link from the chain, access to the central stock data site is reduced from 48 to 24 hours.

– Secondly, the exchange changes into a services mode. The head office questions the shops by itself and obtains information in real-time. It can decide to obtain information from a given shop where previously it retrieved data from a regional group of shops.

– Why not change to services mode immediately? Because the applications do not support it. Due to their construction, the communication modes only allow for planned file production. The interrogation of the stock software in request/reply mode able to provide the tools for the service mode requires modification of the application itself.

You can also launch into an event or agent-based construction:

– with an event-based construction, the shops themselves warn of the risk of a stock shortage; or

– with an agent-based construction, restocking decisions can be made if certain rules are observed.

You could say that stock alert or automatic restocking are not recent functions. What has changed is the ability to construct the rules that establish these functionalities quickly and at low cost. In addition, this example explains particularly well the specific features of the models: in services mode decision-making is centralized, while in agent mode it highly localized.

However, this ability to use exchange software primarily to reorganize existing flows in the same way is widespread. It is a major modification to grounds for investment. Before, a new business unit issue was necessary: acceleration of the time to market, management of a process on-the-fly to obtain the grants necessary for software investment. Now it has become acceptable to rework an existing solution to improve the quality or the performance of the whole. It is a sign of acceptance of these solutions that they have ended up by gradually making a place for themselves in information systems. This is all the more remarkable given that the price of these solutions hasn't actually gone down in the last 10 years.

As the first module of the transverse information system, they also make up the foundations. From this the company can plan larger scale constructions.

6.1.5. *The exchange platform: mediator of imbalances*

The arrival of EAI and ESB brought about an awareness that contributed to the emergence of the concept of a transverse information system. By opening up the way to a type of standardized exchange, geared more towards common business unit data or towards functions, it has become more difficult to passively accept the scattering of certain data or the increase in functions to the same extent.

In fact, why would you want to organize exchanges if they themselves result from a lack of basic organization? This only leads to moving the points of complexity, not resolving them. It is thus necessary to tackle the roots of the problem.

We subsequently saw the emergence of SOA considerations within the integration area, the emergence of sustainable development concepts: if the information system was better organized, better planned, certain flows would have no cause to be there. Some of them only exist to "hide the misery" and find intermediate workarounds to more major problems. We have encountered this type of context during some of our roll outs. Our customers told us that, in their minds, implementing an EAI was only a temporary solution as they waited for the information system to be completely revamped.

For us who were completely convinced about the planning value of EAI, the blow was sometimes hard to take, but we had to admit that these decision-makers were absolutely right. If the services were correctly organized, some data exchanges would be obsolete. If the reference data was correctly made up, the related flows would not be perceived as synchronization flows but as business processes.

An acknowledgement was then required: the purpose of the exchange solution was to buffer existing imbalances in the information system.

The flow analysis for which the exchange platform is responsible is a good indicator of the quality of the information system. The better the information system is constructed, the more relevant and justified are the flows implemented in the integration solution. However, the more data is duplicated, the more services are redundant and the more you will find functionally useless flows in the exchange solution, although these will be technically necessary for proper organization.

In the first case, the exchange platform helps with controled planning of the transverse information system. In the second case it is like a carpet under which you have hidden a load of dust. The more time passes, the more the solution loses its flexibility. What is valid from a functional point of view is also valid from a technical point of view. Increasing the number of flows and transformation operations will have an effect on system performance. You have to know how to avoid these changes if there is no need for them.

For all these reasons it has finally become necessary to consider exchanges as a consequence of situations, a reflection of strengths and imbalances and as a solution likely to resolve the problems of organizing and planning the information system. Thus, it has been necessary to examine the organization of data, services and processes. Hence, exchange and integration platforms have become levers for an alignment and flexibility policy, rather than the expression of this policy itself.

6.2. Technologies and architectures

In order to standardize a domain, nothing works better than giving it a graphic dimension. A picture says a thousand words or, in any case, tens of thousands of lines of code.

6.2.1. *Architecture principles*

Figure 6.3 below shows the main principles of a simplified exchange and integration architecture, incorporating the following basic components:

– the application connectors or adapters;

– the message-orientated messaging system or MOM; and

– the message broker which is also, in some solutions, called the orchestrator of automated processes (called system-to-system).

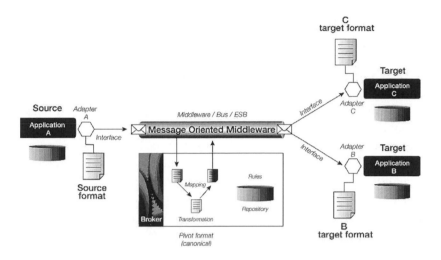

Figure 6.3. *Simplified EAI architecture*

In this situation, a source application (A) communicates data to two target applications (B and C). Application connectors provide direct communication with the applications. Between the connectors, the integration platform transforms source formats into destination formats. The message orientated middleware is the focal communication point.

6.2.1.1. *The application connectors*

The application connector is one of the main functionalities that came with the development of EAI solutions and which form one of their most obvious specific features. The purpose and strength of the application connectors is to collect or transmit information from or to an application, regardless of the technology on which this application is based. It is these connectors that smooth out to some extent the technological heterogenity of the information system. By hiding the most technical aspects of integration, these connectors were also responsible for elevating the flow designer/creator from an undervalued job, that of technician, to a more prestigious role encompassing the functional knowledge of exchanges.

The application connector can therefore communicate as well with a database, or a software package or a transaction monitor, as it can produce or read files. According to the architectures, you can decide to move data transformation activities or not. The connectors may offer specific functionalities, which have for a long time made these components strong differentiating factors among market developers, in addition to including them as important criteria for making decisions. Nowadays the quality and diversity of connectors remains a hot topic of debate, although the arrival of Web services has reduced the importance of this debate to a large extent.

Theoretically, application connectors should have lapsed into obsolescence with the general implementation of standardized exchanges based on Web service protocols. In practice, the heterogenity of technologies is an argument in favor of keeping application connectors. For this reason, the application connector cannot be dissociated from any integration solution, whatever it is. Some players have specialized in providing these connectors, the most well-known being iWay.

The main point of using these connectors is the introspection functionality that they have to demonstrate. Introspection enables application data models to be represented in their semantic rather than technical form. For example, if a customer's name is stored in an application under the esoteric label XCFGH (for whatever reason), it is the customer name information that has to be displayed to the EAI flow creator. In this way, and at the risk of repeating ourselves, flows are created at a semantic and not a technical level, which explains the increase in value of the flow manager function and the widespread enthusiasm for the EAI discipline.

6.2.1.2. *The mapper*

After connectors, the mapper is the second great contribution of EAI solutions to exchange management. This is a graphic component devoted to the data transformation phase and it is therefore used during exchange execution.

In practice, source and target formats are represented graphically on the two sides of the mapper's sections. They are application connectors which convey semantic information to the mapper about the formats. They are therefore easy to use: plotting the correspondences between the two formats, correspondences to which the transformation formulae are attached, with all the functions required for calculation operations, date management, calls to databases for transcoding, etc.

In the transformations you can use a pivot format that generally follows the structure of the company's master data. This is useful when transformations take place at the "extremities" of the exchange process. When the exchange is managed in the form of two half flows, using a pivot format is not so advantagous because the mapper is then able to make the transfer between the source format and the target format directly.

6.2.1.3. *Message-orientated messaging*

Communicating messages in asynchronous mode has only been made possible by the use of specific technologies – message-oriented middleware. Thanks to their asynchronous aspect, they have the great advantage of separating the EAI integration architecture completely. The applications do not exchange directly between themselves, and the message broker (see below) is no longer directly linked to the applications.

In this way, the applications do not have to manage the guarantee of delivery and the sole delivery of information sent, which takes a certain load off them. Once the data is published, the application can reallocate its resources to other operations. The platform is completely responsible for the exchange, thanks to the combination of connectors and the messaging system. The applications publish their messages, which are immediately picked up by the connector, which saves them and sends them to the messaging system.

In the same way, if the target applications are not available, messages are kept and will only be distributed when the applications are once more ready to communicate. The message-orientated messaging system is the component that assures the reliability of the platform. All the confidence that the company may place in its EAI is based on this component. This has to be an unfailing source of confidence. In fact, if the solution started losing messages, the distrust that would result from this would be difficult to allay.

6.2.1.4. *The message broker*

This component obviously plays an important role in all the integration architecture, since this is the component that will have the specific intelligence to manage exchanges:

– it will normally integrate the mapper and deal with transformations when they are not distributed at connector level, which remains the vast majority of project scenarios;

– it also provides routing functions, static routing based on fixed rules but also dynamic routing based on the content of the message or on parameters coming from requests to the routing repositories;

– ideally, it has functions associated with the management of transactions and, in particular, distributed XA transactions, with the mitigations that may still occur with this protocol, as we saw in Chapter 4;

– finally, it may incorporate functionalities associated with the security of information.

6.2.1.5. *The exchange repository*

Managing an integration platform, its functional and technical components, its development, implies being able to see their use, their distribution and their dependencies. This is the role of the exchange repository which functionally has the same role as the service repository shown in Chapter 4. It may be provided with the solution or require a specific tool from a market modeling workshop.

This repository maps inter-application exchanges, pivot formats and technical components used on the flows and, consequently, forms part of a link between the function part and the IT part. It may also keep and organize a part of the documentation of the different interfaces. In some cases, it may generate a first version of the functional and technical specification sets from filled-in elements.

6.2.2. *The approach: the first elements of transversality*

The advent of exchange technologies highlighted the requirements for transverse organization which had caused little concern up till then. The absence of a specific organization around the technology, however, certainly makes this less effective, even counter-productive.

This part will enable us to deal more easily with the process and organizational components dealt with in the following chapters. It highlights the specific requirements for the successful launch of transverse information system projects.

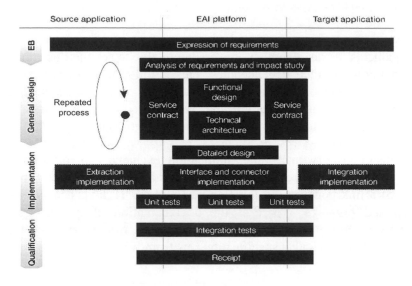

Figure 6.4. *The major lines of an EAI project procedure*

Generally, the procedure is just like the one seen in any standard project procedure. However, some points deserve to be highlighted.

6.2.2.1. *Needs analysis and impact study*

The creation of new flows or the modification of existing flows require a preliminary study to promote the effective reuse of repository components, or to identify the different impacts and side-effects.

6.2.2.2. *The interface/service contract*

The interface contract, also called the service contract, is the basic pivotal element of any inter-application integration procedure. It provides a bridge between the teams dealing with the applications to be integrated and the team responsible for the exchange platform. It is a contract, and therefore a mutual commitment, which cannot be modified unilaterally. It specifies the source and target formats, the pivots and other types of information such as the commitments made on the service levels to be provided.

If the application to be connected already has an interface level, EAI will use the functionalities of existing exchanges without requiring modifications, subject to all the information being available and there being an adapter for the application in question. Although this is the case with frequently used technologies, the adapter may be more difficult to find in the case of more "exotic" technologies. However, if the application to be connected does not have any interface technology (or if it has not yet been installed), the flow team may recommend the exchange mode to be implemented depending on the business unit requirements and the technical constraints.

The applications must provide an interface technology and undertake to observe a certain service level for communications with the exchange infrastructure. The flow team will draw up an interface contract stipulating each respective commitment (source or target, exchange infrastructure).

6.2.2.3. *Extraction implementation/integration implementation*

It falls to the source and target application teams to implement the means to extract or collect data, in the event that this operation cannot be automated by the connector set provided with the integration platform. In most cases, it is preferable for the exchange manager to be responsible for this operation but, taking into account the diversity of technologies and the specific requirements of each integration process, it is perfectly possible for a specific implementation to be provided for.

Whereas the team responsible for creating the flows is normally skilled in exchange technology, they does not have the necessary skill, for example, to produce files from an AS400 or update a CICS transaction. This is why application teams are generally responsible for this activity, since they are in the best position to control and reduce the impact on their applications or even to prioritize some lines of reuse.

6.2.3. *The framework*

The first industrial projects linked to inter-application exchange solutions highlighted some functional gaps in the products on the market – transcoding management, flow correlation, error repository, dynamic notification, monitoring functions, etc. Not only are these gaps almost the same whatever the product but, in addition, they have not really been filled in over the years, since developers have preferred to concentrate on other more popular functionalities.

6.2.3.1. *Managing transcoding*

The main, most significant functionality which is systematically absent from solution platforms is the management of transcoding. Transcoding, or cross-referencing, gives you an overall knowledge of the codes used by the different integrated solutions. It is used when data is transformed from the source format(s) to the target format(s).

For example, the "Platinum" code written in full will denote an excellent customer in a customer relations management application. At the level of the Web channel, which must integrate this data, the code adopted is, for example, code 1. The transformation of the string of characters, "Platinum" in its entirety to the value 1 is not the result of a written formula. It appears in a correspondence table stored in a database questioned by the EAI during the transformation process.

CRM application	Web site
Platinum ➡	1
Gold	2
Silver	3
...	...

Figure 6.5. *A transcoding table*

Using a correspondence table enables the multiplicity of scenarios that may occur to be managed. If you had to code each one of the formulae in the transformation tool, the solution would quickly become very difficult to maintain. But for all that, as strange as it may seem, the transcoding manager remains the major component that is missing from the market solutions.

6.2.3.2. *The error manager*

Another functionality to create yourself or to implement via a framework is error management. Any flow executed incorrectly may cause an error that is generic. The way each company manages this error is different. Some will want a user to be alerted of the problem, others will try to place the flow into an activity basket, while others will create a copy of the activity log and send it as an attachment to an operations manager. In addition, the ideal would be for an error code to be returned with the corresponding interpretation, the interpretation normally coming from an error repository, which is itself an extension of the functionalities initially provided.

The error manager is systematically created in the platform development phases, since it has to be used on all projects and by all flows.

6.2.3.3. *The flow monitor*

Tracking a piece of information that is constantly on the move may rapidly become a hopeless task. EAI solutions provide on a general basis, but not systematically, consoles for monitoring past or current exchanges. The operator can follow the flows that proceed correctly just as well as those that encounter problems. However, the generic nature of these consoles, supplied with the product, is not suited to the functional view of data flows that a company normally expects, and which calls for customized reporting. It is therefore normally necessary, at the very least, to customize the reporting layer to eliminate the most technical components, in favor of the components that definitely belong to the business unit. In other cases, the creation of complete, customized balanced scorecards may be justified depending on the requirements.

6.2.3.4. *Conclusion on frameworks*

In our opinion, all of the points tackled above emphasize the developer's relative lack of knowledge about the requirements of their customers. But for all that, once this deficiency has been identified, the next logical step is to make up for it. We have thus been forced, over time, to create these missing functionalities ourselves, first of all by expanding the solutions provided by the developers based on their own technologies. These were our first steps into the world of the EAI framework. Total uses a platform created on a WebMethods 6 base, OCP a Sun SeeBeyond 5.1 framework, Veolia Environnement, a Vitria framework, etc.

We were then forced to create a framework applicable to each of the market technologies (except Microsoft, for which we created specific accelerators for the BizTalk solution), based on standard technologies and Open Source tools. The aim was simple – to have a modular, expandable, open solution which could be connected to any integration product on the market, in a non-intrusive way, to offer accelerators to any new implementation of this type of platform. We called it a wide open framework.

Over time, we noticed that companies are sometimes reluctant to adopt one or other of our frameworks. They prefer to be surrounded by companies with an expertise in the subject, rather than companies that are able to offer them technical accelerators. Having thought we could offer added value and speed for future projects, this response initially surprised us. Then we understood what made our customers refuse to use our components.

The exchange platform is now perceived as a strategic tool, the heart of the transverse information system, itself the heart of the global information system. To entrust a part of this platform to a third-party installation which, even if it is in open source, contains an expertise that it is not necessarily easy to communicate, would amount to giving something away. You can't give a system strategic responsibility if you do not own it completely. Moreover, companies prefer to create a new framework all of their own, based on expertise that is theirs completely, rather than denying themselves access to a part of their platform, or operating as if this was the case.

6.2.4. *Change behavior: from now on a requirement*

Consequently, change behavior becomes an equally vital component of this type of construction. Companies need to control the platform that they create. It is a matter of their autonomy, as well as the desire not to repeat certain errors of the past, by permanently entrusting creation and maintenance to an outside company.

This choice could be made as long as the exchange platforms were not seen as central initiatives. Now that their strategic role has been recognized, these platforms must retain their legibility. This is also a way of taking the credit for the upgradeability and flexibility of the platform, in addition to knowing how to maintain it. As these two concepts are on the business unit's wavelength, it is logical that IT departments retain a great amount of responsibility, internally, over these constructions.

This knowledge is acquired from the initial projects. But for all that, they may still be implemented by outside companies who are experts in the area. That will enable the platform to be safeguarded and results to be obtained more rapidly, showing due respect to the state of the art, generally at a flat rate cost. Even so, internal IT teams get worried about becoming involved in the implementation of these projects, either in a supervisory capacity or a design and creation capacity, if the flat rate framework can be adjusted in this sense.

These teams may thus complete their training by gaining an understanding of the construction choices. They may also participate in the construction, without neglecting any aspect and particularly taking the credit for their framework. They must particularly ensure that the construction is carried out according to the rules, that the points of complexity are accurately indicated, in the same way as the adaptation of devices for maintaining the long-term flexibility of the platform and safeguarding the investment.

Sustainable development actions have become the criteria for choosing one service provider over another. The same is true for change behavior. Companies want to know how their service provider is going to guarantee a smooth baton handover once the platform has been constructed and the first pilots are operational.

6.3. Project typology

Rather than give more specific examples, we will proceed to give a brief description of the types of projects encountered to highlight the most significant situations.

6.3.1. *A universal access door to integrated software packages*

The main purpose of using an inter-application exchange platform is the joint implementation of an integrated management software package, whatever it is – a global package dedicated to managing customer relations, product manufacturing, human resources, managing financial processes, etc. Such an application is very often an important center of gravity for an information system. Any project that is rolled out inevitably provides the opportunity to manage dozens or even hundreds of incoming and outgoing flows. Such a volume in itself justifies the EAI investment to standardize the procedure.

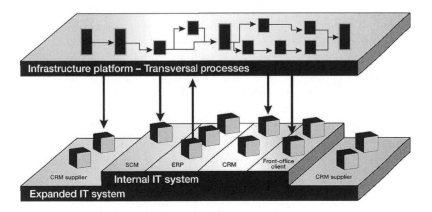

Figure 6.6. *Exchanges and integrated software packages*

Exchanges with the integrated software may relate to the distribution of master data. It is not unusual, for example, for a Siebel solution to act as a customer repository and for its information to authenticate the whole of the information system.

It is estimated that in about 60% of cases, an exchange solution is used to cover access projects for integrated software packages, which is a substantial proportion.

6.3.2. *The continuous creation of the company backbone*

Confining the exchange manager to "encircling" the software packages is certainly a widely adopted approach, although there are others which assign it a more prestigious role. This is the case when a company tries to gradually implement the use of the platform generally, application by application.

We can also cite the example of one of our customers in the industrial sector, in Switzerland, who had decided to launch the exchange solution on the range of interactions with its partners, mainly on protocols and EDI languages. Taking into consideration the end of hub support, they replaced it with an exchange platform, which was initially intended to cover the exchanges between partners on a constant basis, then to spread out gradually to the center of the information system.

Little by little, the solution was given the logistics flows, then the production flows, then other responsibilities such as synchronizing authorization flows in directories. In total more than 30 projects followed in succession over several years, creating a real backbone for company exchanges.

Although this use of exchange solutions is not the most widespread, it is generally the one that works the most effectively and is the most attractive. The platform is selected for its ability to cope with a large number of integration cases, not necessarily all envisaged at the time of purchase, whereas in the case of integrated software packages, the approach is generally less open. In addition, small and average-sized projects followed on repeatedly over time. Normally we avoid large-scale projects with their devastating tunnel effects, or we break them down into batches of a more reasonable size.

On the other hand, this approach is normally based on a flow management between two application modules and eliminates any idea of processes.

6.3.3. *Organizing transversal processes*

Even if the process approach has not been extensively rolled out in our part of the world, we have nevertheless encountered it on several occasions, each time with a real added value in the approach. Whether it is managing financial securities at Crédit Lyonnais or managing inspectors rounds at Veolia Environnement, the process approach gives the business unit indications that a strict flow management does not enable you to obtain. We can also cite logistics chain management processes (whatever the sector of activity) or provisioning processes at a telecommunications operator. For these processes, flows can only be analyzed starting from the time they are functionally correlated with each other.

It must be noted that these cases have been created using the process manager supplied with the platform, a manager, as we have already mentioned, with less perfected functions than current BPM solutions. However, these tools have proved to be perfectly suitable for the context of projects where it would have been too fraught to roll out a BPM suite. As nature abhors a vacuum, you will note that process managers will remain at two speeds to cover the different types of requirements met.

To illustrate this point, Chapter 7 will give specific examples of where the use of a process manager and a control solution bring a strong business dimension to an exchange management platform.

6.4. A common foundation

Data, services, processes: application and exchange integration solutions constitute the common foundations of the transverse information system. Whatever the name or the acronym given to them, they cannot be separated. At the same time they constitute one of the oldest modules, or the oldest recognized modules. Because of this they were the first to contribute to the development of mentalities and the preparation of the architectures that we design today. And so, to repeat the time-honoured expression, we can exclaim once and for all, and with a tear in our eye: "EAI is dead! Long live EAI!"

Chapter 7

Complex, Innovative Business Architectures

Taken separately, each of the NISSs provides a particular, specific service for the company and, at its level, contributes to the reorganization of the company's information assets and value creation. You will thus note the arrival in the field of substantial projects that take up several thousand or even several tens of thousands of working days, with the aim of reconstructing all or part of an information system or the accepted organization of the transverse information system. The size of the projects is such that it would be better to call them programs. Three significant cases, in three different business sectors, are described in this chapter. Before introducing them, we think it would be interesting to explain the connections between the subjects presented here, in several respects:

– to understand the added value inherent in combining topics;

– to present the construction principles of a complete NISS architecture.

7.1. Natural connections

7.1.1. *Reference architecture*

There is only one step, or rather linchpin, from the data to the process: the service, this much talked-about link that connects the function and the application. In the target NISS architectures it is quite simple, on paper, to show the links between the information assets within this service concept:

– the process puts into order the activities which, themselves, are implemented in the form of services to be performed;

– the business services perform the required activity, relying on services of finer granularity, following the already mentioned assembly logic;

– these services of fine granularity are particularly services for accessing master data.

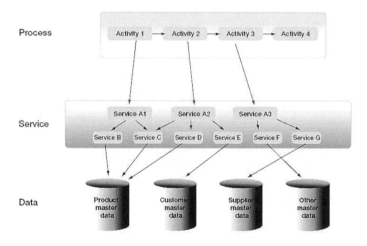

Figure 7.1. *From data to processes*

In this way, a type of navigation at information asset level is set up but it isn't the only point of the model. The application of simple but intangible construction rules will control the effective construction of this model:

– The data is the foundation stone of the information system. It may be modified but only marginally: the general architecture of the reference model, once set, is reasonably stable over time. In the same way, services represent the company's functions. The method may change but the function remains stable over time, which forms the service interface. Data and services are the invariables of the system. You will locate the most stable components there and, in particular, the business rules, which are rarely modified if at all, if it happens that some business rules become volatile over time, and that agility is needed, you may use rule management systems and create some variability points inside of your services. Business agility may then be managed without IT intervention on the services. See section 7.1.3 for more details.

– Processes and rules will make up the variable elements, the ones that will be affected by the change opportunities, in particular by outsourcing the business rules, which require regular or even frequent modifications. By using solutions that give priority to a graphic representation of the process, you give yourself the means to act selectively and precisely on the components that you wish to modify, whether this modification is carried out by the IT department or directly by the business users who will be given increasing autonomy.

The general logic is always the same: decoupling; isolation of assets complying unconditionally with the constructed model (data, services, processes); setting of preferred parameters rather than using code; moving functions that IT ultimately only uses for intermediation to the business which, paradoxically, will also help to bring the business closer to the IT. These are the main principles that must be included in the design and then the implementation of NISS architectures.

The following examples will convince you that, far from being theoretical concepts, these architectures control full-scale applications in real cases.

7.1.2. *Processes and services*

The SOA is a central architecture concept, a linchpin that plays a significant role in IT discussions as client/servers or the Internet wave would have done in their time. However, it has taken some time to emerge and decision makers are not yet fully aware of it. Perhaps this is because some of them think that they are only a repeat of concepts that they already know and, for the most part, have already been implemented. Others think it is tantamount to a strictly software engineering concept. This dimension actually exists and we shall develop it in Chapter 8 but it is really too simplistic. For these reasons, the SOA didn't initially interest the decision makers, who delegated this domain to their architects by asking them, in the best case scenario, to investigate the subject and create a prototype.

Thus companies were quicker at identifying technical services than business services. This is explained by the fact that it is normally the IT department that constructs an SOA and the technical department is a comfort zone. The services there are easier to identify. You can see immediately what can be shared.

You sometimes have bitter memories of talking about SOAs with a CIO. We remember the scathing "don't swear at me", which shows the contempt that some decision-makers poured the subject. Is it too technical an area? It is really the business that SOAs are aimed at. Identifying business services requires a higher level analysis, that can only be provided using enterprise architecture method. It's a more significant procedure, which takes longer to bear fruit, and where the IT department, if it is involved, feels less at ease.

The business process is uppermost in the decision maker's mind. This is what is given the right and the credit for providing flexibility and increased alignment between the business and IT. Growth is encouraged by improving business processes and business processes lay on services.

SOAs have a natural part to play in the orientation towards the business. If there are still a few technical services around here and there, the advantage of an SOA is to promote services that are semantically geared to the business and which introduce a group of functions that are generally identified in a business architecture.

People even talk about a service-oriented enterprise (SOE) to affirm the strength of this link between service and business. Identifying business services, as you have seen, is part of the enterprise architecture procedures, the same as those that work on the processes.

In short, processes are found to be service consumers. When the implementation of a process is orchestrated by a dedicated platform, any activity that makes up the process is likely to be a service. A business process is then led through a sequence of services. This is normally done between the business silos, between the function departments over the whole value chain of the extended business. The process is called transversal because, as the applications are normally linked to a business silo, none of them can be implemented on their own.

Just like SOA, business process management (BPM) has a place in the transverse information system. In all the experiences related throughout this chapter you will discover to what extent the two areas are linked. If SOAs form the new linchpin of the information system, it is the business process that forms the linchpin between the business and IT. This dual focus makes for a balanced construction.

7.1.3. *A new flexibility driver: complex event processing*

Even if SOA and BPM jointly increase flexibility and alignment capacities, new solutions and technologies are already emerging to provide even more performance in this direction.

CEP (complex event processing) solutions are slowly but surely taking their place in the information systems environment. They encourage decision-making in real-time, by analyzing the large number of events transmitted to them, by filtering and correlating them to identify behaviors and to deduce actions from them or suggestions for action to be taken by the user. They bring agility by managing volatile business rules within the services.

They are thus used in particular on the Internet in e-commerce or e-services application contexts. Specifically they are used to identify opportunities and threats based on an analysis of the behavior of the Internet user. For example:

– offering a new product to an Internet user in real-time during a visit to the site going by the way he is browsing, the products he has looked up or searched for, by the frequency of visits, by a history of his relationship with the company, etc.;

– detecting fraud in real-time at the moment it takes place, based on browsing and the type of transactions carried out.

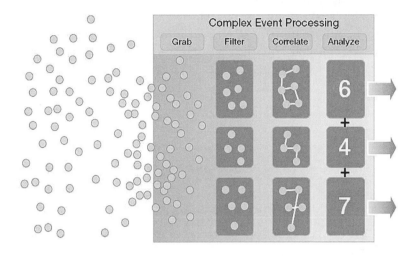

Figure 7.2. *The four CEP function levels*

These solutions are also used in air transport. By interpreting events transmitted from RFID chips in luggage, they enable a major European airline company to optimize the amount of time aircrafts are on the ground. The dynamic allocation of resources is also a CEP comfort zone. An excellent textbook case is the dynamic calculation of seat prices in transport, particularly air transport, depending on the number of seats occupied.

These cases are significant because decisions are taken automatically and in real-time. These solutions are not dealing with self-teaching software, but can recognize a previously known determinist behavior. Based on this, the use of statistical functions determines the probability of encountering an incident even before it has happened. In addition, these solutions cannot yet pick up all the events of the company. While waiting for an information system that has standardized event behavior on a large scale, these solutions can only recognize and interpret events that have been described to them previously.

The functional architecture of these solutions is based on several components: first of all, an event manager that can collect and correlate the information: next, an environment description in the form of objects or concepts. But the real heart of the system is an operation that is based on a simple model, the event-condition-rule model.

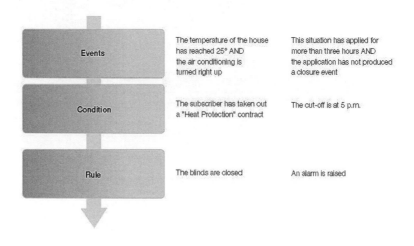

Figure 7.3. *The event-condition-rule model*

The implementation of a rule is itself likely to trigger an event, which will, in turn, trigger a rule in a causality to be controlled. There are not yet many vendors who market this type of solution. The two most obvious ones are currently TIBCO with Business Events and Progress Software with Apama. These two solutions are of excellent quality.

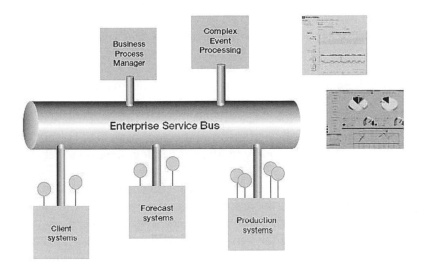

Figure 7.4. *Integration of CEP into NISS architectures*

Several qualities are attributed to CEP solutions, not least of which is constructing algorithms by using rules which are often simple and always isolated from each other. Previously these algorithms would have stood out mainly because of their length and their complexity (for more on this please see section 7.3.2).

In all cases, as a result of the types of process they enable, these solutions are intrinsically geared towards, and apply to critical business processes, for which traditional technologies cannot supply any simple answers.

7.2. An investigation into the distribution sector

7.2.1. *The issues: reorganizing the editorial production line*

In May 2007 we were commissioned by a company in the retail sector to help it decide how to revise its editorial management chain.

Historically, the tool that provided the relationship between this company and its customers has been the paper catalog. The arrival of the Internet led this company to offer its catalog items on a website.

With the affirmation of rich media content (audio, video, flash, etc.) and new products appearing more and more quickly, the editorial management chain proved to be less and less flexible. Provided by two applications using the same technical bases (one per channel), it was struggling to integrate specifically the new special features of the Web channel and required increased decoupling between the two channels.

7.2.2. *Mapping and modeling*

This project gave us the opportunity to highlight the transfer of a functional modeling procedure to an application architecture located on the transverse information system. The first stage was to understand the way the information system was organized by drawing a plan of what was on the different levels.

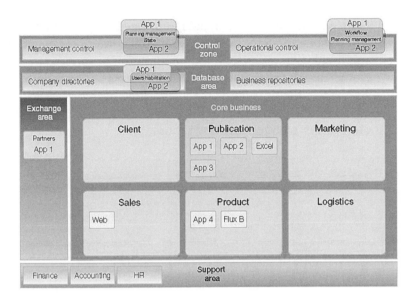

Figure 7.5. *Level occupation plan*

This illustration highlights the major function sets at the level of the area called the core business. The exchange area appears and you will note that it is one of the publication business applications (APP1) which is responsible for this, indicating a lack of organization at the transverse information system level. Generally you will note that all the transverse functions are inevitably provided by business applications.

We then listed all the services used by the editorial production chain. To do this we drew up an occupation plan of the function levels provided by the information system, then we focussed on the publication sub-system. Figure 7.6 lists all the function sets in this area, the services listed are for each set and indicate how these are dealt with from an application point of view.

This illustration shows how certain business services are duplicated in several applications and the benefit that it is possible to obtain by sharing them: a reduction in functional redundancies, applications will be able to specialize in their business core and the information system will be simplified. Some services, like the translation service, will be wholly shared and located outside the applications. This choice is justified by the fact that it is not at the heart of the business service: as a result it cannot be considered to be a constituent part of business applications dealing with product information.

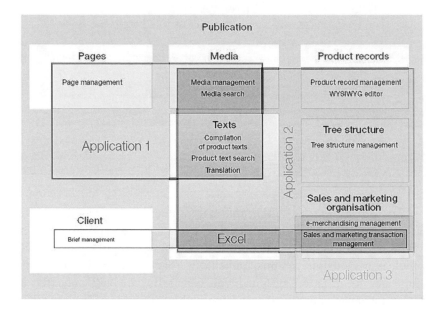

Figure 7.6. *Location of services*

From reading Figure 7.7 you will note an increase in the amount of master data and duplication of data.

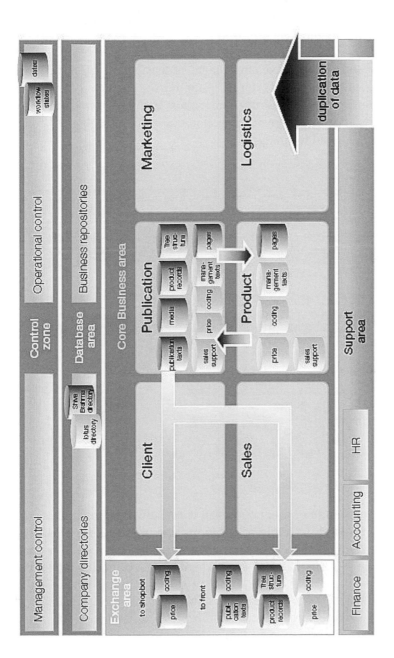

Figure 7.7. *Databases and exchanges*

The flows refer mainly to the partner exchange areas, and the product master data is synchronized.

Organization of the exchange area, redistribution of target core business functions and target non-core business functions, implementation of business repositories: a real IS program or, dare we say it, NISS. The target level occupation plan was strongly marked by these organizational techniques.

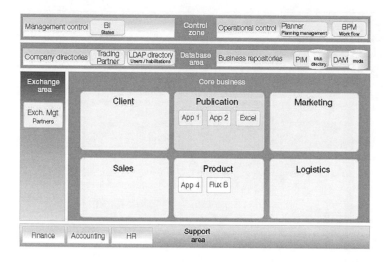

Figure 7.8. *Target level occupation plan*

The main feature of this target plan is to show how to organize the information system in terms of functions and applications; by listing the types of technologies likely to organize each of the areas. We shall mark out the route to take and show where budget priorities should be.

In conclusion, we have therefore constructed a target function and application architecture, which combines the components that make up a transverse information system.

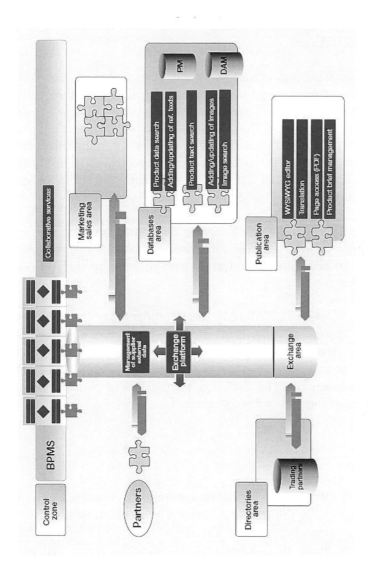

Figure 7.9. *Organization of the transverse information system*

In the target application architecture the main components of an NISS architecture are:

– a business process control platform, responsible for controling the execution of processes for making up the item data and product referencing;

– two types of master data: one storing the structured product data, in a dedicated PIM (product information management) application, and the other managing non-structured information in a digital asset management (DAM) application; and

– responsibility for data exchange by a specific exchange platform, which is not in the source information system, and which is responsible for providing the interface with partners, managed from a dedicated directory.

This architecture is strongly service-oriented. The processes themselves appear in the form of uniformly accessible services whatever the access channel that triggers them or calls upon them. Transverse services have been put in a shared area which the different consumers can access. The exchange manager is responsible for the mixed nature of formats and protocols.

7.2.3. *Keys for tomorrow*

This type of project is an opportunity to provide keys for tomorrow, and it is the decision maker's responsibility to take the direction that seems best to him. The aim of the initial stages of these projects is to make the decision-making process easier and more reliable through an increased understanding of the situation, by making visible what was initially invisible. The NISS study still requires such projects to be undertaken where the objective is both to make decision makers and players aware of the issues, benefits and impact of this type of solution and to construct a shared vision involving the greatest number of players. The subject of preliminary tasks is dealt with in more detail in Chapter 11. These tasks may then lead to implementation projects.

7.3. A project in the energy sector

Another project, another sector: this experience, centered on SOAs, shows how much the construction of NISS platforms applies to critical business issues.

7.3.1. *The issue: aligning the production and consumption of energy*

Electricity producers power stations are normally divided into three categories: nuclear, hydraulic and thermal. These three production methods have very different features:

– nuclear power stations are relatively cheap but also not very flexible. A power station reactor cannot be started up or stopped quickly;

– on the other hand, thermal power stations, using coal, are expensive but much more flexible;

– hydraulic power stations cost and flexibility is in the middle of the other two.

To optimize their production costs, the electricity producer must constantly base its thinking on a central indicator called the water value, which gives the relative price of the hydraulic system compared with the two other means of production. In this way, the company decides how to align and optimize its production structure in real-time.

This calculation only makes sense if it is aligned to actual or anticipated consumption. There is no point in overproducing. Electricity can't be stored. Electricity producers always have forecast data based on statistics, drawn up using a large number of variables. These algorithms are based on operational research techniques. They are modified regularly to integrate new variables. Each new modification has an effect on the data model and/or the evaluation rules.

We were chosen to help this producer create a more flexible, future-proof architecture. For several years a dedicated solution had been in place but this had a limited capacity for upgrading when integrating changes at the speed at which they took place. By change we mean here the regular integration of new parameters into the simulation calculations and the alignment of the whole system as quickly as possible. This type of rapid reconstitution can only be observed when the construction is based on foundations that can absorb change and reduce the duration of transitions between stable states.

7.3.2. *Looking for a stable state*

As we have already had the opportunity to draw it up, an NISS architecture is first of all constructed at business level, identifying services that are reusable but also stable over time because they are describing the company's business. Whereas the business is stable, expertise, on the other hand, advances. The service is permanent, but the way in which work is carried out may change. To be precise, we have tried to construct an architecture that can be upgraded, but which is built on stable components.

To achieve this we reconsidered the initial algorithm, a Fortran program, from the point of view of the functions it provides, in order to extract the business services. We then reconstructed this algorithm in the form of a set of services, which used a shared master database.

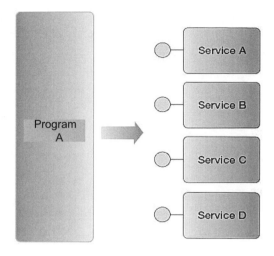

Figure 7.10. *From monolith to dressed stones*

From then on, any modification affecting a service has no effect on the adjacent services. Where with a single, large program it was necessary to analyze the impacts and to deal with complex side effects, the service model guarantees that the impact will be limited if it is correctly controlled in the initial stages.

7.3.3. *Interoperability*

Historically, the algorithm in question was defined by researchers using Fortran. At the other end of the chain, it was decided that the end user would benefit from new technologies, using a Microsoft fat client, with the aim of giving the user all the ergonomics and autonomy, with an efficient, modernized work station. All the Fortran services were provided with a Web services facade, which complied with the standardized protocols.

These services were assembled by business processes representing each one of the user's work situations, and each process called upon one or more services while it was running. The manager of these processes is the BEA platform, which uses Java technologies. The processes themselves are displayed in the form of services, which are made available to the user's work station, but also other channels such as Excel tables – to produce reports, or to external partners.

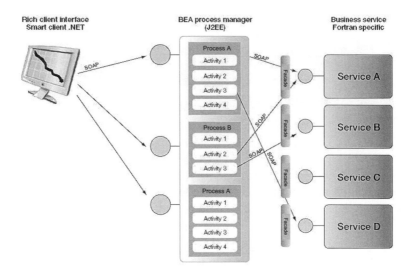

Figure 7.11. *Web services and interoperability*

The whole construction represents an interoperability model applied to critical processes for the business and shows how Web services actually enable the constraints specific to each technology to be removed.

7.3.4. *Upgradeability*

To make it easier to integrate new variables into simulation calculations, we had to develop an alignment method that stipulates precisely the existing textbook cases and how to deal with them, from the shared data model to the process and the balanced scorecard, including the services. This method explains how to evaluate the impact analysis and implement the various changes by ensuring that the overall consistency of the platform is maintained.

Technically, the development methods follow the principles set out in Chapter 8 in the presentation of the Brainsonic case.

7.3.5. *Conclusion*

A number of lessons have been learnt from these cases. The two main ones that we have highlighted here illustrate well the two complementary aspects of these architectures:

– the first, linked to the division of functions, applies to the construction of a service architecture that provides flexibility and upgradeability;

– the second, linked to interoperability, shows how Web services are required as a reference implementation when such constructions are being set up.

These two points are completely dependent on each other, and the vision would not be possible without suitable technology. The use of the technology is completely structured by the vision.

7.4. A program in retail banking

Even if we have kept on insisting on their iterative and integrating dimension, the NISS are not incompatible with a major project. As innovative as it is, the NISS response does not only apply to tactical contexts and still less to pilots or prototypes. In the actual case that we are going to talk about, we are no longer faced with a project, but with a program where the subdivisions have had to be developed over several years, with regular deliveries of different batches and the final completion scheduled for 2012. To make it easier to read we shall give this program the fictitious name of Allegro.

7.4.1. *The issue: reorganizing around business processes*

Implementing NISS is often an opportunity to respond to several of the issues already mentioned in these pages and the aim of Allegro is to respond to these: better performance, increased operational alignment, a desire for sustainable development on several levels. The following extract is taken from the program setup file:

> The retail bank has a new, young organization that is constantly changing, with tools that are not suitable for the transverse aspect that will now be necessary to deal with business procedures.

> Apart from this new organization, a patchwork of procedures between services or between individuals has been noted, as has a lack of documentation. With the large number of people about to retire there is a risk that a great deal of expertise will be lost.

> In addition, the activity is made more complex because of the large number and diversity of business procedures. An employee needs to access various applications and several employees may be called upon to deal with the same file. Added to this is the risk of losing information because of the number of paper exchanges between the front and the back office. Dealing with files is made considerably more difficult because of this. In addition, the activity demonstrates a certain lack of visibility, on the one hand for the progressing of files and on the other hand for global and individual performance. In spite of all this complexity, major service commitments between the front and back office must be observed.

What does this passage teach us? The need for transversality is accepted and perceived as specific but covered by ad hoc constructions. The need to retain expertise is coupled with a desire to standardize it, and therefore to find a consensus on the way in which business is carried out. The phasing out of documents shows how much the management of structured and non-structured information is converging towards complete platforms. In the end, the need for control is clearly recognized. It is in fact logical that with NISS a new need for monitoring is felt and should not be missed.

7.4.2. *The NISS layer cake*

To respond to the issues mentioned in this outline, a dedicated architecture has been constructed. We shall only show the aspects of the architecture associated with the management of structured information and the execution of banking procedures. The Allegro program does not aim to impose a big bang on the information system. On the contrary, it must come to a compromise with the existing applications and integrate with them so as to establish itself gradually, and replace some of them. In the short term, Allegro organizes the transverse information system. In the medium term it becomes the core of the information system. It is interesting to note that Allegro will eventually integrate all the retail bank's procedures, i.e. here about forty procedures. The first batch applies to the integration of four procedures chosen for their different characteristics in terms of integration. For example, certain procedures will be carried out completely by the business orchestrator, whereas others will continue to be dealt with by underlying business applications (the orchestrator will then only receive execution markers).

The program rests on three platforms:

– a collection platform, dedicated to capturing information in business applications. It populates the core of the program with information as it goes along;

– an orchestration platform, which carries out business procedures actively or passively, incorporates human activities and manages task baskets; and

– a real-time activity monitoring platform, which gives a picture of the current activity at any time and makes decision-making more reliable.

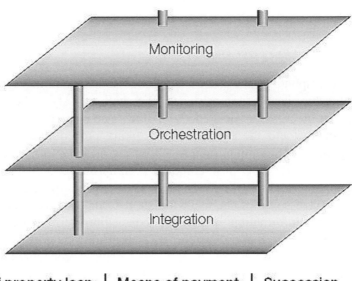

Staff property loan | Means of payment | Succession

Figure 7.12. *The three Allegro program platforms*

This architecture is not unique. We've seen it on other occasions, in other activity sectors and each time it has led to very large scale projects.

As far as Allegro is concerned we are talking about several thousand man days: an application that will be very difficult to supply in one day for a long time! The design led to the development of platforms that aimed at making it faster to implement future banking procedures.

Each level was constructed in two parts: a platform for sharing functionalities, then a specific project to transfer the banking procedure to this platform, the aim being to optimize the design from the technology, method and organization points of view to reduce as far as possible the porting time for all new procedures.

At the real-time monitoring layer, it is anticipated that the implementation of a new procedure will only take a few days from a technical point of view, by placing values in parameter setting tables: reusing a platform and generic balanced scorecards, limiting the quantity of code to be produced, and using a dedicated parameter setting console for all procedures.

In projects of this kind, the difficulty is the time it takes to construct a reusable and above all complete platform. Once the investment has been made in the solution, companies are very anxious to obtain results very quickly. Even if, in theory, they want to have a platform that will give them value-added services, particularly as far as faster development cycles are concerned, in practice they often reduce the scope of this platform to the absolute minimum in order to show results quickly. From then on, the train has gone and it will become more and more difficult to reattach the carriages.

7.4.3. *Real-time control*

As explained in the outline, monitoring the activity in real-time is one of the main components of the Allegro program. The aim is to provide back-office managers with the resources to reorganize their work depending on the events that occur in the course of a day.

Two main monitoring systems are available:

– monitoring current cases; and

– monitoring human activities.

On the other hand, managers need to be warned about operational malfunctions, and the monitoring system gives them different alarm levels: cases which are not processed within the normal timescales; work not allocated to an agent, or which has to be dealt with before the end of the day, etc.

Allegro gives managers the means to control the operational side of their work in real-time.

In terms of a technological solution, the program architecture has been completely entrusted to TIBCO, a pure-player vendor of transverse solutions and real-time integration software. As the developer of an event bus, which was installed into a large number of trading rooms around the world in the 1980s (and therefore with a large presence in the banking sector), TIBCO has been developing its full NISS range since the turn of the century.

Its latest offering, Business Events, is a CEP solution: it makes up the core of the Allegro real-time control platform.

On Allegro, the three platforms are completely separate and furthermore each one represents entirely separate projects. But for all that, the three levels must communicate with each other and exchange information. Luckily, TIBCO provides gateways between the different components of its offer.

Thus, the receipt of control events from the orchestration platform is native, via the iAP utility, which communicates with the message bus. This bus populates business events with information in order to:

– re-evaluate the activity control indicators in real-time;

– update the detailed data that makes up these indicators;

– detect when warning thresholds have been passed and warn the user that a corrective measure is necessary.

Control services are made available to users in the form of services, enabling them to be reused at different points of the program.

For example, some activity monitoring components will also be used in the orchestration consoles. The use of these services and therefore Web services once more encourages the reuse of balanced scorecards.

From the architecture point of view, it was necessary for this service display to connect business events with business works, the TIBCO solution that manages inter-application communication. In short, control services are supported by information retrieval services since the balanced scorecards are displayed on the Internet browser of a thin client.

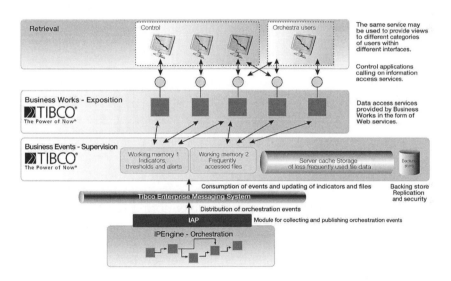

Figure 7.13. *The control construction site architecture*

7.4.4. *Complete control coverage*

In addition to real-time monitoring, Allegro contains two other dedicated monitoring levels: a retrospective analytical control system and a procedure performance control system. As the real-time dimension fades with the incorporation of more and more indicators, the solutions used are different from those used in real-time control.

For all that, the data sources are common and involve sharing the collection components between orchestration and monitoring.

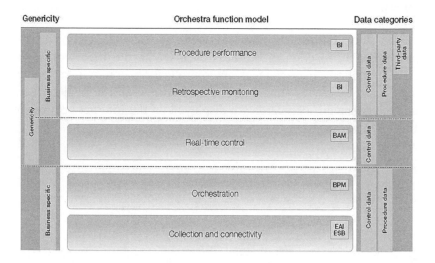

Figure 7.14. *The three levels of Allegro control*

Real-time monitoring only consumes data from the orchestration platform. On the other hand, the other monitoring levels will need to collect information from third-party applications to make up their indicators. For this reason, the genericity sought and obtained at real-time level is difficult to maintain on the other levels.

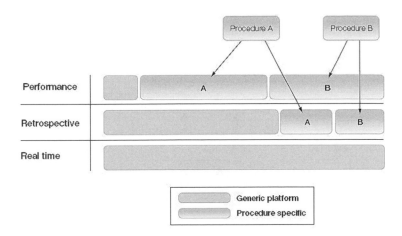

Figure 7.15. *The genericity of monitoring levels*

Real-time monitoring not only picks up generic information but also generic restored information, whatever the business procedure involved. Monitoring is completely independent of the procedures. These procedures become the main means of filtering information, depending on whether you want to have information for the entire activity or just for one procedure.

As soon as you get into the world of postponed time and analytical reporting, not only the indicators but also the restored information change from one procedure to another. The genericity part reduces, mechanically increasing the time taken to port new procedures. However, the impact on the technological platform and on the methods is reduced and it is at these points that it is necessary to factorize and find the project accelerators. This means, specifically, that with an NISS project, the design of the planned platform and the use of flexible methods will facilitate the transfer of skills, either for effectively managing the increase in capacity phases, or for replacing teams as time goes by.

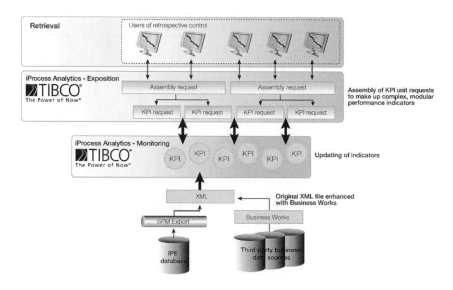

Figure 7.16. *Aggregated KPIs monitoring architecture*

7.4.5. *Conclusion*

Major NISS projects require several distinct, separate levels to co-exist. These levels must be able to fit together perfectly to provide a global, consistent platform. You will thus see that the use of Web services is not as widespread as in the previous case, although this is explained by the choice of the one supplier for the whole platform.

This case highlights the importance of dedicated NISS control, and the resources needed to set it up. The more solutions tend towards real-time, the more the monitoring systems must be inspired by the opportunities and threats inherent in this trend. Detecting a situation as quickly as possible is often the best way of limiting the damage that this could cause. This point will be developed in detail in Chapter 9.

Chapter 8

The Impact of NISS on Software Implementation

Steven Prentice, Vice-President and chief of research at Gartner, the American analysis and consultancy firm, likes to say that, as far as IT is concerned and, more generally, any scientific discipline, "That which seems most unlikely in the end has every chance of happening". A few years ago would we have thought it possible to store all the information handled by a human being on a card as big as a pin head? Or watch videos on our phone? Or leave our car to park itself without our help? Probably not. We would have been rather skeptical and the only place we could have entertained dreams of an improbable future would have been in the comfort of futuristic science-fiction novels.

A great fan of literature and a tireless opponent of scepticism, Steven believes less in the point-blank "it can't be done" statements that the most experienced consultants steadily bombard us with, than in the books of one Philip K. Dick. Thus, when Steven picks up the writings of the Master, he notes that this science-fiction novelist had clearly seen how our environment would develop 40 years into the future. The talking device as in Ubik? We already have that. Cells in the human body that warn when we are ill? That is just starting but we will get there sooner or later. Biometric marketing as depicted in *Minority Report*? It's coming on in leaps and bounds.

Thus, at the conclusion of the 2006 Gartner Symposium, when Steven announced that in 2012 the development of an application would take one day, just one single day, we felt somewhat lost. Should we believe him, or reimmerse ourselves in literature? What on earth did he mean by that? We returned feverishly to our Unilog offices, repeating these promises at every opportunity as if they were our own... only to face a unanimous reaction: "It can't be done...". And without the firm conviction of someone like Steven to give us strength, we looked like lovable idealists, very naïve and slightly simple-minded, blushing a little shamefully, convinced that the desire to believe had prevailed over reason.

And yet... monitoring the development of our market we had to admit that there was a distinct trend towards reducing implementation costs. This may make you smile and here is a small example to convince you of it.

In 2004 we sent one of our customers a business proposal to create a data exchange platform (an EAI). Based on previous experience of projects built on a solution for which we had a great deal of previous experience, our figures proved to be out of all proportion to the customer's budget. However, the customer gave us a second chance to redeem ourselves. They asked us to reassess our costings based on their own exchange technology, which was supplied by another developer. We drafted the specifications and two of the customer's specialist solution designers came to implement and test two perimeter flows. They actually spent less time on this than we had envisaged in our first estimate. By reevaluting all of our proposals on this new base, we arrived at costs of about 40% of the initial estimate, costs that we honoured to the letter (or to the figure, in this case) until the very end of the project.

With the latest, more specialized, innovative technologies, implementation and maintenance of the solution were considerably reduced. And, with the advent of new information system solutions, with service-oriented architectures, with agent or aspect-based development, event managers, the general implementation of rule engines and methodologies devoted to the reuse and integration of components, what could finally prove that in the future it would not take just one day to produce the work expected?

Thus it is important to construct new business solutions on a platform that is ready to meet permanent adaptation requirements. NISS will take part in this great convergence movement. Even if Steven announces fantastic results for 2012, which we probably won't get to see until 2020 or even 2050, we will forgive him; and go back to reading Philip K. Dick, because it can be done.

8.1. The process standard

Processes exist in all businesses but they are not necessarily visible. Business process formalization work is a starting point for mutual understanding of the activity by all the players, a linch pin on which the two communities agree. As a linch pin of the relationship between the business unit and IT, the graphic representation of business processes is also an innovation engine for the two communities. As we have already had the opportunity to write:

– innovation is constant work that also consists of modifying procedures or expertise on an almost daily basis;

– the business process is a working tool suitable for testing innovations. "If a process is transparent, effective and flexible, it is likely to be seen as innovative, both by internal staff and customers."[1]

---

1. Janelle Hill, *Business Process Improvement: From Process Understanding to Business Innovation*, Gartner, May 2007.

Business transactions must be more reactive to customer and market requirements. Flexibility is one of the major objectives of a process-orientated procedure – flexibility in the relationship between business unit and IT, and flexibility also in the ability to make existing assets evolve more quickly in the business sense.

For this reason, it must be possible to adapt processes and not present them as the finished article. Far from being a rehash of business process reengineering techniques, a dominant paradigm of the 1990s which ultimately garnered few significant results, business process management strategies promise to model a progressive world and not to model a fixed world perfectly.

In this context, modeling only makes sense as a starting point and not a destination. The process becomes paste to be modeled, clay to be shaped, always more accurately, always more effectively, following the multiple iterations that make up continuous change and constant progress.

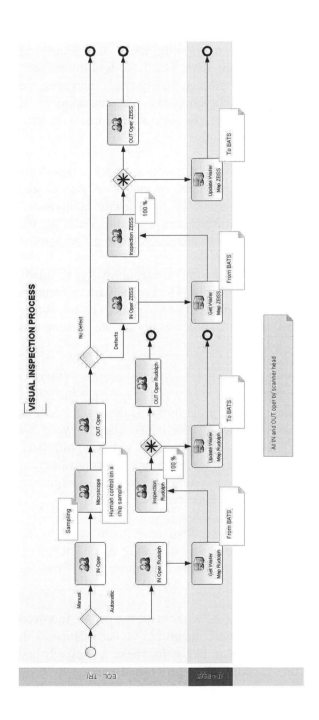

Figure 8.1. *Business process management in the semi-conductor sector*

The BPM process is a way of finding ideas and promoting innovation. If you go forward in the dark, you have less information and there are only a few ways to optimize your path. If, however, the company acquires increased visibility resources, it can improve its activity by acting at the process level, the level where processes join, over the whole value chain, transversally.

As processes are service consumers, it becomes easier to detect the points where expertise needs to be updated or improved. As services are consumers of master data, the whole NISS chain is involved. However, as data and services must ensure a certain stability, the process's responsibility is to involve all the progress identified points.

In this way and even if adjustments must normally be made between the business model and its IT counterpart, execution modeling is moved closer. Execution and control principles are similar to the points already dealt with in Chapter 7, during the presentation of the Allegro case.

Changes in the perception of model-driven architectures (MDAs) bear witness to this. Initially seen as a way to limit the production of code and therefore as a new way of programming, these architectures became, in principle, a way of looking for consistency between the model and execution on the ground, therefore, to put this point back into the context of our discussion, as a means of controling, of governing the transverse information system and, ideally, of exporting the corresponding model to its application context.

The adoption of such a process requires time, particularly in the initial stages of the procedure, since this operating mode inevitably must be accompanied by change… perhaps even more for IT than for the business unit.

Such a model cannot be established without all the people involved having an increased desire to work together, in accordance with innovative methods which are also likely to shake up established habits and responsibilities. Collaborative processes must be built up between the different groups, underlining the importance of the organizational work involved in the transverse information system.

New skills and methods must be developed on both sides of the barrier: if necessary, between so many others, a real-time monitoring culture on the business unit side (a topic dealt with in Chapter 9), and the ability to assemble composite applications on the IT side. To arrive at this stage, various barriers must be overcome for the acceptance of a marked or even generalized process orientation and the organization must gain the required maturity.

8.2. Towards assembly and beyond

Even if this is in no way their only dimension, SOAs explicitly involve software architecture and represent a different way of constructing applications, based on several major principles. One of the main principles is assembling. Assembling encompasses the whole NISS design. It alone justifies the existence of repositories devoted to the control of SOAs. The other principles are not unimportant for all that. Each of them helps to reduce implementation costs and helps to provide a faster delivery cycle for business applications.

8.2.1. *Principles and definition*

8.2.1.1. Principle number 1: assembling, a national sport

Once the services are created, developing a new solution is an activity that definitely changes its nature. Rather than designing applications as a set of functionalities, they will henceforth be designed as a set of services destined to fit together one inside the other, one with the other, to be assembled.

To illustrate this point, we shall start with an example found during the revision of an e-commerce application at a specialist mail order company. The functions offered to users of the Web channel are traditional for this type of operation: browsing the catalog, comparison engine, basket, news bulletin, online ordering, last products viewed, search engine, paper catalog ordering, etc.

In a traditional application development logic, these functionalities are not necessarily planned correctly. In fact, over time, the weight of the specific development on the software package platform initially chosen made everything inflexible and created points of complexity that increase the time required for new implementations.

Figure 8.2. *Interlinked functionalities making progress more difficult*

As the world of the Internet and e-commerce has experienced several changes since the end of the 1990s (are we not talking about Web 2.0?), the integration of new functions requires increasingly greater efforts and in the end threatens the stability of the whole platform. There are a large number of these new functions, as Figure 8.2 shows: integration of communities, real-time order monitoring, dynamic syndication of partner catalogs, online quotations, etc.

In order to integrate these new functionalities more rapidly, without threatening the stability of the platform, and to roll them out without side effects in the 26 countries where the group has a presence, designing applications following the principles of SOA was studied. This consists of planning and implementing the applications as you would assemble the pieces of a jigsaw puzzle, each piece being a business service and all the services not making an application but a function module with a clearly defined perimeter which is stable over time.

The assembly principle includes several front-office and back-office aspects to create applications:

– by assembling front-office services (access to messaging system, document search, business application interface), thus creating a new user work station; and

– by assembling business services (to construct transversal processes).

Figure 8.3. *Assembling composite applications: an iterative process*

The two processes are not at all orthogonal and readily complement each other to create business applications. In passing, this proves the scale of service-oriented architectures. It is wider than the initial range of inter-application integration.

Designing a new application becomes an assembly activity, hence the frequently used term "composite applications". The Allegro case, presented in Chapter 7, bears witness to this dual operating mode based on assembling.

From a process point of view, the idea is to rely as far as possible on already available services, to study the best way of assembling them, to identify which functional perimeters offered must be customized and which are to be implemented specifically to meet a need.

Once the functional perimeter has been defined, the divisions (and the decoupling) between the functions and services are identified in order to find the stable state based on the corresponding data model.

8.2.1.2. *Principle numbers 2 and 3: reuse and sharing*

Reuse is a principle that has existed for several years in our industry. It has, in particular, accompanied the development of object technologies, where service architectures are tributary and legatary. Reuse is a self formulated objective to significantly reduce the time taken to implement software, whilst maintaining the consistency of the whole. Reuse is an integral if not active principle within SOAs. It is not only implemented generally at the technical level (from where the object has found it very difficult to drag itself out), but also at the functional level. By using already existing services for new requirements, you maintain the functional consistency of the information system.

Sharing is simultaneously a construction principle for service architectures and an objective to be achieved. Where reuse must be seen in its functional dimension, sharing is more like a technological subject. A service is intended to be used by several consumers. Its purpose is to be shared. One part of the SOA return on investment is the hope that the largest number of business logic components can be shared.

In terms of maintenance, the benefit is obvious. A modification to the service will be promptly passed on to all consumers. This is particularly true of access services to master data. In terms of use, this raises a number of questions. Since the service interface is governed by the contract concept, how do you develop a service without increasing the number of versions each time a new requirement or a new consumer appears? There are different ways of achieving this, as there are different ways of creating a progressive relationship: the Brainsonic case, presented later in this chapter, will prove this.

The principles of sharing and reusing services are central to the SOA discussion. Can they necessarily be applied so easily? Some experts doubt it. As long as data is not properly organized, will it really be possible to achieve functional consistency and make services closest to the data redundant? It is likely that each information system will introduce constraints from its history and therefore it will be necessary to put up with it, even if it were at the cost of compromise, which you can well do without and which will change the "purity" of the model.

8.2.1.3. *Principle number 4: integration*

This dimension has already been mentioned more than once in the previous chapters. The previous principles do not only apply to new services. They also apply to existing services, already used or which can be used, by existing applications, and which any technology that connects to these services can benefit from. We know that Web services provide a standardized access level but we also know that they have not been implemented widely and that it remains vital to know how to manage the heterogenity: a role that data exchange platforms will still keep for quite some time – which is a euphemism.

8.2.1.4. *Impact on the implementation of applications*

The implementation of these principles goes alongside major revisions of the application implementation model. In Chapter 4 we learnt that from the dependencies experienced by the project manager until the developer divided up activities, SOA was not always a positive experience for the players. Applying the four principles shifts the responsibility for the construction even higher up the process, gravitating strongly around the information system planner or another enterprise architect. Guarantor of the consistency of the information system, reuse manager, guardian of assembling capacities, this is a lot of responsibility for a single role and yet this role must be taken up and not just in a consultative capacity. Important decisions must be made in terms of organization. But is it worth it? Of course, and all the company's management talent will manifest itself in the fact that each will help and contribute to the continuous drawing up of this model over time.

8.2.2. *Rolling out an international service architecture*

The distribution of functions as services is perfectly represented in the international roll out of the application platforms and new functionalities, where the logic of the puzzle mentioned above is broken down.

Above all it is a question of explaining the collaborative process which will lead to the construction of new functionalities. As we recommended in Chapter 4, organizing a working party which combines central posts and local correspondents results in the expression of a global need, from which you can define the service contract or at least:

– the specification of practical assembly details centered on the service interface; and

– the data used, whether it is master data or not, associated with the core model of the application or located in third-party applications.

From this, two models prevail:

– the functionality is implemented centrally and distributed to the local units as shown in Figure 8.4; and

– only the specifications are sent to the local units, which are then responsible for implementation.

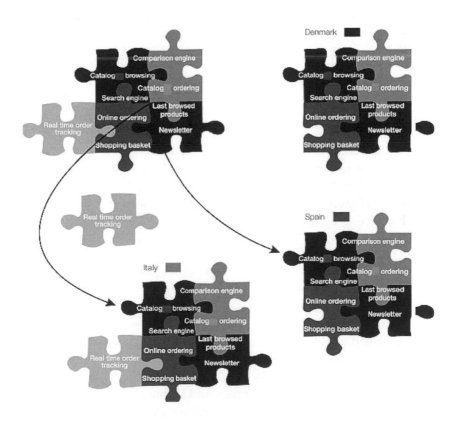

Figure 8.4. *Rolling out services internationally*

The two models can co-exist perfectly well. The central IT department implements a service and distributes it. This service may be customized in individual cases in the countries where it is rolled out, each country remaining free to roll out the functionality concerned or not depending on its own model. Any functionality can be enabled and disabled.

In both cases, there are as many independent platforms as countries involved. Each service implementation can be performed independently of each other. Each country thus has a free hand to modify one or more services in its functional block, as long as they respect the interface which provides stability for the model.

8.2.3. *Software as a service*

8.2.3.1. *The principles*

The software as a service model (SaaS) is a way of providing software to companies that is very similar to, what has thus far been called, the ASP (application service provider) model or even the on-demand model. According to this model, business applications are not supplied to companies in the form of project or perpetual licenses and operated within their premises, but managed externally by the software developer.

Starting with SAP, several major software developers have announced the provision of SaaS platforms for their medium-sized clients. Oracle will not be outdone and neither will IBM or Microsoft. Renamed S+S (software and service) by Microsoft, the model offers, amongst other things, to externally manage Microsoft clients exchange messaging systems. This represents another way of outsourcing the non-core business IT components and letting the IT department concentrate on the company's business.

A Gartner study published in 2007 showed that managing customer relations is a function for which the SaaS model is very well suited, thanks to players such as salesforce.com or Siebel on-Demand. The attraction for traveling sales forces is obvious, given that it enables staff to access the software using a simple Internet connection wherever they are.

SaaS is different from ASP in that it aims to provide users not with applications but with services and processes, with or without a graphic interface, ready to be assembled to bring value to companies.

In order to use SaaS software, companies use a pay-as-you-go system (invoiced on the amount used) or a "pay-as-you-grow" system (invoiced depending on the volume of information handled or the number of users). Salesforce.com thus invoices its customers based on the number of customers stored in its CRM database. This invoicing model based on the amount of resources consumed is interesting from the point of view of valuing information assets and particularly in a data valuation strategy, one of the targets of master data management (see Chapter 3).

Compared with the acquisition of a licence, analysts think that the SaaS model is less expensive than a traditional license for the first three years of operating the same version of the software. Beyond that, the acquisition of an on-site license is more attractive. The advantage of SaaS is to enable all users to benefit from upgraded versions of the software provided at much faster cycles, depending on user requirements and the acquisition of a new function. It is no longer necessary to wait for months or even years to have new functionalities. The length of the innovation cycle is considerably reduced. Finally, the question of investment in infrastructure or in skills no longer applies. The partner deals with all this.

8.2.3.2. *Brainsonic*

SOAs provide design methods that make it easier to apply SaaS principles. The following example is one of the most convincing illustrations.

Brainsonic is a company that specializes in the production and broadcasting of rich media content on the Internet via Web TV. Videocasts, audiocasts, conferences or live concerts. For the past five years the company has experienced accelerating growth, thanks to its ability to combine software industry concepts and undeniable expertise when it comes to the requirements and specific features of Internet video. The filming of 300 Microsoft TechDays conferences? That was Brainsonic. The live broadcast of Etienne Daho on the EMI web site? Brainsonic again. The "Pro" package of TV channels launched by Free, the French Internet service provider? Brainsonic once more.

In its asset portfolio, Brainsonic has developed a generic Web TV platform, first of all used for its own needs, as a showcase for its expertise: TV4IT[2] (pronounced "TV for IT") offers subjects associated with current new technologies.

Via this platform, Brainsonic provides its customers with their own communication tool on the Web: Adobe with AdobeWebTV, SSII Valtech with ValtechTV have this media, as do players moving outside the IT sphere, such as YooCuisine, a TV channel dedicated to the culinary arts, Vertbaudet or PrimeGolf, a channel that brings together Belgian golf clubs. For its part, Logica Management Consulting was responsible for putting online the first Web TV consultancy in France, Your Potential TV, on 13 November 2007.[3]

---

2. http://www.tv4it.net.

3. http://www.yourpotential.tv.

Figure 8.5. *TV4IT: Brainsonic's Web TV showcase*

8.2.3.3. *A shared service base*

Even if Brainsonic rolled out internal Web TVs to some of its clients, the principle of its Internet televisions is based on the SaaS model. Each Web TV uses a service platform that is common to other existing televisions: a list of available content, a search engine, tag clouds, newsletters, etc. Essentially it is a catalog that everybody can customize as they wish. For example, Your Potential TV does not use the tag cloud service but could easily enable this functionality on request.

Figure 8.6. *Your Potential TV, more than similarities: the same service platform*

The founding principles of the model are as follows:

– services are shared and any upgrade benefits all Brainsonic customers, while Brainsonic maintains the service;

– a multi-client logic or the same engine runs for all the beneficiaries of the model;

– services are configured and display context elements, including security; and

– the service layer is regularly updated for all clients.

Each front-office (each television) consumes part of the existing services and shapes the information according to the presentation logic appropriate for each channel. Brainsonic applies the founding principles of service-oriented applications to the letter. The addition of a new channel (Silverlight, podcast flows, etc.) has very little impact: "The increasing power of rich interfaces encourages awareness of the importance of service-oriented architectures", said Jean-Louis Bénard, CEO of the young company, during our interview in 2008.

8.2.3.4. *Managing updates*

How is the company able to manage demands for updates and modifications to existing services without threatening the flexibility of its platform? How does it manage the increase in versions of existing services over time? The answer is simple: by avoiding them as far as possible...

If you modify existing service interfaces, the impact is significant. For this reason, the interfaces have been designed in an extremely generic way. The typing level of some parameters has been reduced to gain flexibility. Passing on XML messages is prioritized by applying the hierarchical, fragmentary structure of the metalanguage.

Where an increase in the number of solutions remains the only solution, extremely rigorous versioning and configuration monitoring is required. As always, compromises must be found in individual cases to balance performance and maintainability. The parameters for a large number of components are stored in configuration files so that they can be modified on the fly without affecting services. This point is paramount in a platform standardization logic. Tools for setting parameters for these configuration files have been created. The advantage of this is a very high level of sharing.

In order to take account of highly specialized requests for updates, which would only involve one television out of all the others, Brainsonic has implemented a framework which is not part of the generic service model. The use of this workshop ensures that compromises that are too great which would affect the platform and threaten the integrity of the architecture are avoided. The points of complexity are thus shifted towards this framework which centralizes any non-generic update requests. However, its existence ensures an exit door to prevent hyper-structuring by the services, which would be more like a constraint than progress. In this way, the model remains controllable and its update rules are clearly defined, without increasing pressure on its flexibility.

8.2.3.5. *Managing the data model*

The data model is very structured, and is the most important component in a generic platform. There it balances the metamodel and the impact on performance.

As with services, a customized model is created at the same time as the generic model. A parallel model is administered for all the customized fields. When it becomes necessary to modify the existing tables, an initial impact level is determined at the level of stored procedures. Sometimes the impact is reflected at the service level. The existence of common tests enables problems to be filtered.

It is very rare that new data and new services cause major modifications to be made to the existing platform. However, creating a new service, even a simple one, requires time because a top-quality design is required which takes into consideration the various integration scenarios. The objective is traditional in an NISS context: grasping the unknown, planning for the unforeseen. What are the consumers of services and what could they be in the future?

8.2.3.6. *The method used*

The company is a consumer of flexible methods and iterative development: the construction method for Internet televisions combines XP (eXtreme Programming) and Scrum. The iterations are very short, a few man days, with milestones that are very close together. The common tests are run automatically, with tools that offer a very standardized approach to the whole project cycle. It is up and running very quickly.

The point of short iterations is the option to reprogram all, or part, of the project in the event of new, high-priority requirements. This ability ensures that it stays abreast of customers' issues. For Brainsonic, Jean-Louis Bénard states that "SOAs make using flexible methods easier. The iterative aspect reduces risk taking. This is the key point. The main objective is alignment: priority to the business unit." The service platform is constructed on Microsoft service architecture and on the .NET framework. According to Jean-Louis Bénard: ".NET makes it easier to implement these types of architecture."

8.2.3.7. *Conclusion*

Since it was brought into service in 2004, the platform has supported several dozen televisions and is still ready to cater for others. It is giving no sign of loss of impetus and the updates are always accepted calmly, a sign that the complexity inherent in the model has been mastered. Updates are made to it respecting the constructed model and new functionalities are assembled on the existing platform to expand it in new directions. The Web TV model in SaaS accompanies the clearing that Brainsonic carries out within this market segment, where innovation is a daily occurrence.

8.2.4. *Redefining an R&D model: who has the power?*

Given that it is supposed to represent all or part of a business model, a service architecture must be suitable for the context of the company concerned. Once it has been written, the strategic dimension of this architecture and its stable appearance are clearly revealed and it strikes us that only these issues are likely to encourage the construction of such a procedure.

For their part, the major software developers are trying to set out the functions of their solutions in the form of services. In this way, they offer their client companies service models which are custom-made for the application context of their software. Even if some services can probably be used and reused, because they are generic (placing orders, availability of an article in stock, consulting customer data, etc.; and dozens, even hundreds of others of this type), nothing can guarantee that the granularity of these services will be suitable for the company, that the service model outlined is complete. There too, the role of the service integration bus, with its ability to enable the co-existence of the most heterogenous packages, proves to be vital.

Who has the responsibility for defining the business model for entire business sectors? The developers? The service companies? The companies themselves? The answer is far from simple.

Software developers have always, or almost always, been responsible for companies IT research and development. Irrespective of whether they are criticized by their customers for their ability to impose certain innovations, the fact remains that this outsourcing model is viable and profitable for all concerned, as long as the technology is stable (in the short term) and supported (in the medium term). In addition, as developers have tried to promote models that are not solely based on technology, but which have a degree of verticality, they have sometimes been welcomed with open arms by their clients. But isn't this just a sales argument that companies ignore once the contract is signed?

In their eagerness to obtain a high level of added value, companies have, to a large extent, encouraged developers to advance in this direction, even if it means losing autonomy and abandoning the ability to innovate, both from the business and from the IT point of view. How do you ensure alignment if the business model is provided by an external company, especially when that company is the developer of the software? Are we to conclude from this that the field of possibilities opened up by SOAs is already doomed? And if we look into it more closely, is it reasonable to claim that we are seeking out more flexibility when we remain dependent on services provided by others?

But let us not succumb to despair. This analysis asks more questions than it provides answers for, which is not unusual. We are only at the start of these initiatives. Companies are still far from having made a massive migration towards this model, all the more so since the developers themselves are still announcing certain delays in delivering the complete model.

You can imagine that some companies will continue to rely on an externally provided model if it suits them. You can also imagine that other companies will try to customize this model if it proves to be strategic and they have the organizational abilities to be responsible for it, and to develop it. These companies will take charge of this R&D business model which is largely the domain of the business architect, a profile whose role will be introduced in Chapter 10. For technical R&D, software developers will keep the role that they have always held until now. Each company will decide how much importance it wants to attach to the SOA.

In fact, the SOA is not necessarily a strategic subject, except in the case of companies that want to see it as an opportunity for growth. For the others, it is "only" a dominant architecture paradigm which has to be developed at the instigation of the developers and with which they will comply when they are ready – with more or less preparation, which is another subject.

8.3. Model-driven architecture and docking

As we already mentioned at the beginning of this chapter, model-driven architectures (MDAs) have seen their role and their scope change since their birth in 2003 in a document published by the Object Management Group and co-signed by a large number of players in the IT industry.

The initial intention was geared towards new methods of programming, intended to restrict the production of code and to create a physical application model from models that could be called business or logical models, even if this was not the actual terminology used (the document instead used the term "platform-independent model").

Since this founding act, little has been said of MDA in truly significant terms. However, in 2006 IBM delivered its Websphere Process Server suite, the first large-scale initiative that tried applying the virtuous loop, shown in Figure 8.7, in a global and comprehensive way.

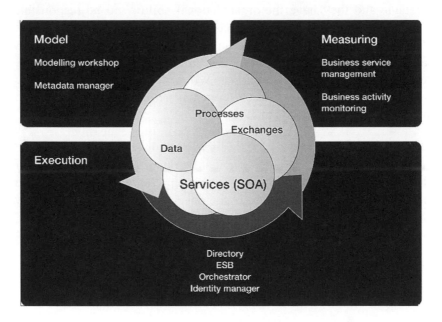

Figure 8.7. *The virtuous loop*

The idea is to optimize relationships between the model, the execution of this model and measuring the performance of this execution. In this way, you can identify the points of contention and the performance bearings both from the business unit and IT points of view.

Armed with this knowledge, it became easier to decide how to develop the model: by acting on the process, on the services, on the data or, at the same time, on all the assets. In practice, you rarely see the last stage of the loop. The transition from measuring to (re)modeling is far from effective.

Big Blue is probably the first developer to have developed this approach on a large scale, in a complete suite, from modeling to monitoring. For this reason, it appears that this suite is still reserved for major projects and that companies still prefer to concentrate on the execution engine, which can be used independently of the other modules. Would the MDA approach be reserved for very large projects?

Initially, no. The desire to align the execution on the model directly is found in other, smaller scale solutions. This is the case with Oslo Suite, produced by the French developer Oslo Software, where there is very little coding.

From representations of the real world constructed in this workshop and from a set of rules specifying the objectives to be achieved, Oslo Suite has created and exported a set of agents, object-orientated objectives, exchanging amongst themselves to reorganize their activity automatically depending on the behavior of their neighbors (for more information on this subject, see Chapter 4).

Examples are seen in the dynamic allocation of resources for processes that are too complex to be modeled and which are mainly used to specify objectives.

The important thing is to keep the three levels separate. Each level must be able to be used independently of its neighbors. The modeling workshop should ideally serve as a repository. Standards exist, based on the XML metalanguage, to transmit the model's information assets to execution: XML diagrams for data, WSDL (web services description language) for Web services, BPEL (Business Process Execution Language) or xPDL (process definition language) for business processes. This gateway between modeling and execution should work in a bi-directional way, so that the modifications seen in the field can easily be integrated into the model. This involves an ability to "version" the models and to devote oneself to specialized impact analyses.

In this context, rather than model-driven architecture we talk about the docking between the model and the execution. This docking concept is an integral part of our discussion about new information system solutions. Effective control of information assets requires the ability to map the use of these assets at any time.

As long as the tools for providing real, constant visibility are still lacking, we can only hope that developers like IDS Scheer or Mega will show shortly that they are able to support the growth of the transverse information system, both for the good of IT departments and for company performance.

8.4. A "sourcing" process to be defined

While reading through the contents of this chapter, you will have noticed that the question of sourcing occurs frequently. Our past observations have thrown up some exceptions. Recently, an industrial company wanted to launch a business process management procedure by entrusting its implementation to an offshore platform.

After some months, it noticed that not outsourcing this strategic platform would have been much more sensible. However, the SaaS model encourages outsourcing. How do you find your way through this field of possibilities?

eSCM (enabled sourcing capability model) is a repository that gives companies the means to define their sourcing strategy. It is comprised of 95 practical components, like the sourcing strategy (what should be outsourced and/or dealt with internally?) or value management (how can the value of the sourcing service provision be maximized?) that companies may adopt selectively or more globally to achieve the certification levels. You first of all try to diagnose the practical components, then prioritize them: the major benefit of the model is its iterative aspect. Companies thus construct their own customized route and, most importantly, try to create a dynamic and then perpetuate it.

In all cases, the NISS response must be dealt with by keeping in mind a desire to be geared towards rapid delivery cycles. These will provide the flexibility necessary to turn away from the constraints of the technical question and keep in mind the importance of the business unit, the search for innovation and the control of the constructed system.

Chapter 9

From Implementation to Measurement

Could you imagine driving a car without its instrument panel? Probably not, and you can easily imagine the risks you would run. Suppose the oil ran out. You would only know when the engine seized up. You would then waste valuable time finding out why you had broken down and you would realize that it would be very expensive to repair, whereas if you had found out in good time this would certainly have avoided a breakdown. In the same way, not all work on information assets can be restricted to ad hoc modeling, a meticulous design and effective implementation of execution platforms. This fine package would still be incomplete and potentially ineffective, if not dangerous, without the option to measure that it is working properly.

This chapter sets out specific solutions for controlling new information system solutions: they are the business activity monitoring and SOA management solutions. Not only do these solutions ensure that the complexity involved with rolling out NISS is controlled but, in addition, they make a real contribution to performance by guiding it towards operational excellence.

9.1. Towards operational excellence

9.1.1. *Issues and objectives of operational excellence*

Operational excellence is a subject that could take up a number of volumes. You will have already realized that it does not make up the subject matter of this one. However, a considerable part of operational excellence now depends on the performance of the NISS.

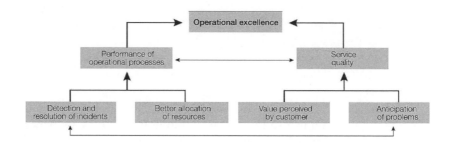

Figure 9.1. *The objectives to be achieved*

Operational excellence is broken down into two groups of objectives, which themselves are sub-divided into two subgroups of objectives:

– *The performance of operational processes*: this is arrived at firstly by reducing the time devoted to the detection and resolution of operational errors and incidents and secondly by better allocation of resources during activity peaks.

– *Service quality*: this is measured not only quantitatively but also qualitatively on the basis of the customer's perceived value. It is maintained and improved by putting in place systems that are likely to anticipate problems.

Process performance is geared more towards managing internal processes and organization. Service quality is a matter of communication and is more outward looking, towards the customer.

The two points are of equal importance, as the following anecdote shows. The marketing director of Orange UK explained to us that in the UK, the companies Syst and Test Mobile (the names are made up) shared the same network infrastructure. Syst's customers were convinced that the bad quality of Syst's network infrastructure was the reason for the problems they encountered when using the network, whereas Test Mobile's customers were particularly satisfied with the network. Performance indicators provided by Test Mobile backed this up. Proof of performance does not make a system work better but it at least ensures that customers do not focus on factors that are sometimes just an impression. In any case, the evaluation of these indicators shows a measuring process that can be carried out directly at ground level.

Since business units are IT's main customers, this logic also applies internally within the company. Controling process performance is another way of improving the relationship between the business unit and IT and honoring the commitments made. Figure 9.2 shows one of the answers given by the IT department panel consulted for the 01 DSI study. The question was: "From your point of view, what are the best ways to improve the relationship between the business unit and IT?" As seen in Figure 9.2, priority is given to reporting.

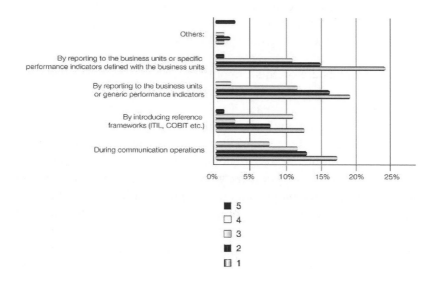

Figure 9.2. *Improving the relationship between the business unit and IT*

Contrary to received ideas, introducing a set of performance indicators is better than introducing or organizing specific communication operations. After all, reporting is also a means of communication and communicating on the organization's performance. It is seen as a reliable tool that can re-transcribe all the investments provided specifically and not superficially.

You will note that IT departments attach more importance to specific indicators than to generic indicators. The example of the Allegro program, shown in Chapter 7, gives us some additional pointers on this subject. For Allegro, real-time control was aimed at all business units, based on generic indicators. Analytical reporting itself was subsequently customized for each of the business procedures monitored. Considering the scale of Allegro, we do not have examples to deduce that this assertion is generic. It will be interesting to keep this division in mind when analyzing future implementations.

9.1.2. *Operational excellence and its IT variations*

Rolling out architectures based on new information system solutions has many advantages. One of the most obvious is the speeding up of the information processing cycle, so that it more closely matches the rhythm imposed by the business unit. This acceleration, however, creates new points of complexity. You must be able to master and control this information whose movements are increasing. Dealing with the NISS question solely in terms of its implementation and execution is not enough. You have to be able to concentrate on monitoring this execution, knowing about and anticipating the circulation of information internally and beyond.

From the point of view of solutions, several monitoring and control levels are connected in order to supply real-time monitoring of the activity at transverse information system level, for each of the information assets. Depending on whether it is aimed at data, services or processes, there are different categories of solution on the market:

– Data quality management: this subject, which must lead to a real rise in data value, was dealt with in Chapter 3.

– SOA management: this subject, which monitors the performance of a service architecture in real-time and compliance with SLAs, was described in Chapter 4.

– Business activity monitoring (BAM): this subject is dealt with in detail in this chapter. BAM is geared particularly to business users. It may or may not be connected with monitoring business processes.

These control levels are supplemented with monitoring processes more geared towards IT and used for several years by operating departments for the monitoring of applications and infrastructures.

These two levels are covered by more conventional types of solutions which are, in any case, normally already present in most companies at operation department level. Players in this market include BMC, Computer Associates, IBM and HP. Their aim is to get back-up to the high levels of the model shown in Figure 9.3. Currently their solutions are evolving to include particularly service and process monitoring components but, having a very marked IT background, they do not yet offer the full range of functions provided by the pure players in each of the segments.

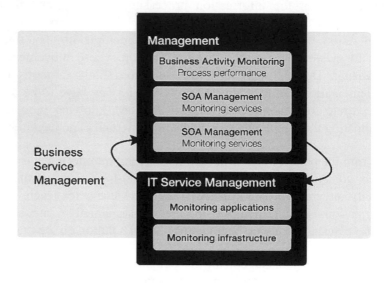

Figure 9.3. *Links between control levels*

In any event, measuring the performance of the information system on a global scale is a vast project that is still quite unusual. From the business unit point of view, there is little justification to launch such projects and this justification is vital to obtain budgets. In a more fragmented way this justification exists, as shown in the examples in the next part. We are now going to witness the construction of modular control platforms which will, at best, combine two of the three levels mentioned.

If you reposition the different control levels on an architecture diagram you will see the complementarities that Figure 9.4 demonstrates.

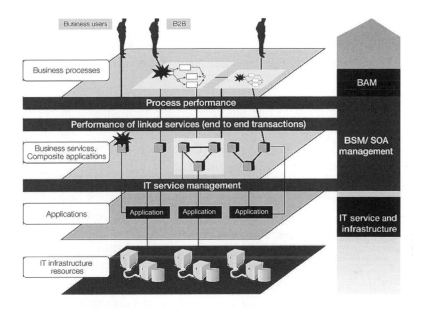

Figure 9.4. *Links between control levels in an NISS architecture*

The new monitoring solutions are aimed at information system components and have nothing to do with the technical part, which infrastructure monitoring solutions can already manage. The application concept definitely swings in the direction of the IT system.

9.2. Business activity monitoring

BAM is an approach that consists of setting up real-time monitoring of processes and company operations. This approach aims to set up key performance indicator balanced scorecards for monitoring that are essentially geared to business users.

We prefer the term approach to solution because, just like all technologies, using a BAM solution without appropriate organization and methods would not provide a great amount of added value. In addition, we are dealing with a transverse information system here, the purpose of which is to expand over time, corresponding to the capacities of these solutions. To consider implementing BAM for a single requirement is not sensible. New projects are bound to follow over time.

BAM alerts users in real-time of trends and malfunctions for better decision-making, by analyzing and comparing indicator values. In some cases you can even draw on past experience to detect problems in advance. We call this predictive analysis.

This approach is based on value-added software, a market where the main players are TIBCO, Systar, WebMethods, IBM/Cognos/Celequest, Progress/Apama, or even Oracle. The real-time dimension is the main added value of these solutions.

Where previously in the IT field you could only find control tools retrospectively, BAM solutions have provided a dimension that cannot be separated from the operating mode of new information system solutions.

9.2.1. *The place of BAM in the IT landscape*

As a technology dedicated to real-time activity monitoring, BAM is clearly linked to the theatre of operations. Such measuring technologies exist in other industries, on production lines, for example. With the advent of NISS in management information systems, it became necessary to provide monitoring resources suitable for on-the-fly concepts and real-time information.

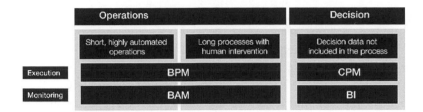

Figure 9.5. *The place of BAM in the IT landscape*

These solutions are not in any way in competition with business intelligence or corporate performance management solutions, the weapons of administrative and finance directors. You normally find BAM solutions in business process monitoring. These may be long-term solutions and include human interaction (see the example in Chapter 7) or they may be short and highly automated. They are not used to execute processes, a role that business process management solutions are already performing with aplomb.

In this sense, BAM solutions have found their own place in the landscape and occupy a field that has been hitherto unoccupied. It isn't every day that you discover virgin territory in the IT industry. This territory remained because the real-time dimension was less significant before the transverse information system asserted itself. This is no longer the case now; in fact, giving up occupying this terrain leads to exposing yourself to serious inconveniences such as those that we shall set out later in this chapter.

Ideally here we are trying to free ourselves from IT considerations. BAM is geared primarily to end users. It is ideal for monitoring the operational performance of business processes and, primarily, transversal processes. If orders are stuck in the pipeline because of marginal problems, users must be alerted, at least at the end of the day.

9.2.2. *Monitoring means of payment*

There are critical, extremely real-time processes in each retail bank – processes for managing means of payment. Every day, information on credit transfers and debits for companies and individuals arrives at banks. As far as their customers are concerned, banks are committed to publishing this reprocessed information before a certain time, the cut-off time. At the cut-off time, the information is sent to the inter-bank clearing center (in France, this is the CRI or SIT for domestic transactions or the SWIFT network for international transactions).

Between the time the information arrives in the bank's information system and the time it leaves, the transaction passes through a number of applications that each performs a significant activity in the life cycle of this transaction. In practice, this entails exchanges between the applications, interspersed by the production of files when they leave the application, transporting them and then integrating them into the final application. All these exchanges must be done at a certain rhythm, so that the information is processed within the correct timescale.

Under the pressure of this deadline, you expect to find control systems suitable for the intraday (the process executed in a single day) nature of the activity. But this is not always the case. A major foreign bank was recently unwittingly forced to break its service commitment for a volume of transactions exceeding a billion euros. The amount of penalties incurred was in proportion to the amount held up. A derisory 1% penalty would already represent a phenomenal sum and the actual percentage was a great deal more.

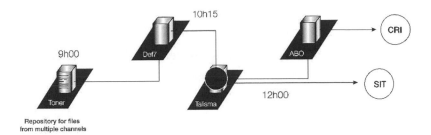

Figure 9.6. *A process with a number of milestones*

Aware of this assessment, the banks are now turning towards solutions that can help them to monitor this type of process in real-time. A BAM solution is a good way to achieve this, owing to the transparency it gives to the conducting of transactions, and its ability to alert people immediately of any incidents encountered. Figure 9.6 illustrates an incident that occurred during the day. The information should have been sent out at 12.00 and this was not the case. The alert that resulted from it was linked to the detection of a non-event and this is also one of the characteristics of BAM.

It is vital to be able to detect incidents the very moment they happen. To go back to a well-known metaphor, if you drive a car and the warning LED does not come on as soon as you have no oil left, the absence of information risks putting you in a much more serious situation than simply having to top up the oil. This is the BAM principle. The earlier you are warned about problems, the less impact they will have, and if you can detect the warnings even before a problem has occurred, then you can only be more efficient.

The case set out above is one of the cases most frequently encountered when implementing BAM solutions.

9.2.3. *The functional model*

The BAM functional model is created on three distinct levels, collection, analysis and reporting. Each of these levels combines specific functionality modules as shown in Figure 9.7.

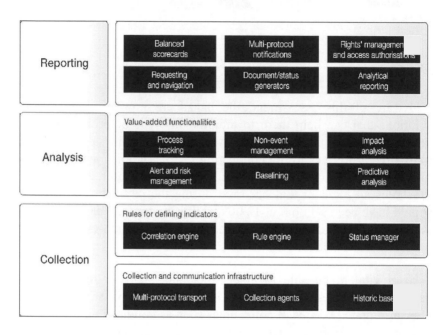

Figure 9.7. *The three functional levels of BAM*

9.2.3.1. *Collection*

We store two distinct sets in collection:

– on one side, the actual collection and communication infrastructure;

– and on the other, the rules for defining indicators.

As such, collection, is organized around three functionality sets (see Table 9.1).

Multi-protocol transport	Ability to transport data and events over multiple protocols, synchronous as well as asynchronous.
Collection agents	Connectors, probes and agents for capturing data and events within and outside of applications.
History base	Ability to set up an analytical reporting base at the same time as real-time monitoring.

Table 9.1. *Collection and communication infrastructure*

The rules for defining indicators merge three distinct groups dedicated to organization (see Table 9.2).

Correlation engine	Ability to link the events captured to each other on the ground to determine whether they involve the same process instance or business object.
Rule engine	Ability to trigger actions (calculation, comparison, filtering) for an event depending on its type, where it came from, its status, etc.
Status manager	Ability to manage the map of possible statuses an object may have and analyze the validity or the consequences of changing the status.

Table 9.2. *Rules of defining indicators*

The heart of this organization is undoubtedly the correlation engine. The two other groups do not feature in all the products. On the other hand, it is impossible to find a BAM solution without a correlation engine. It would not have any other way of linking the information together and giving meaning to the data captured in the operations field.

9.2.3.2. *Added-value functionalities*

This set describes the real services offered by a solution as part of the real-time control of the activity. It involves going beyond measurement and helping the user in his recording of the activity and in his decision-making. It is the completeness of the solutions that normally determines the use of a developer's solution to meet the control requirements expressed, and differentiates the solutions from each other (see Table 9.3).

Process tracking	Monitoring the execution of a process, instance by instance.
Non-event management	Ability to generate alerts resulting from a non-event within a fixed time or on a fixed date.
Impact analysis	Correlation of business unit → ← IT malfunctions. Ability to identify the effects of an IT malfunction on a business process.
Alert and risk management	Generation of a warning to inform the process owner of a malfunction, with the associated corrective measure. Workflow functionalities associated with dealing with the warning, escalation measures.
Baselining	Integrating variations of activity into passing thresholds. Ability to take into account the seasonal nature of an activity to adjust threshold levels dynamically depending on an historic, already created base.
Predictive analysis	Retrospective identification of the probability of encountering an error within a set time from the determinist diagrams.

Table 9.3. *Value-added functionalities*

One of the most typical functionalities is undoubtedly the baselining functionality, which is used to note deviations from the standard course of a process, while taking into consideration the seasonal nature of the activity.

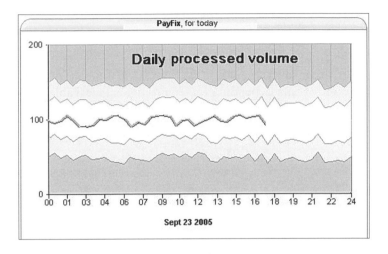

Figure 9.8. *Baselining*

This screen is taken from the Business Bridge application, which is published by French vendor Systar. In it you can see the adjustment of the alarm and alert thresholds depending on the time of day. This baselining function highlights the fine line between real-time control and analytical reporting. To create a seasonally-related history, indicator values must be kept for a longer or shorter period. From this you can compare momentary indicators and indicators that reflect structural trends.

For this reason the Allegro project, described in Chapter 7, comprised different control levels with indicators created and aggregated differently depending on these levels, their temporality and the hierarchical level it was aimed at. For this reason the control levels were separated and the solutions were different depending on whether it was real-time control or deferred control.

For its part, predictive analysis has been based up till now on statistical functionalities that analyze and detect, for example, standard deviations and can warn the users concerned of such deviations. Truly predictive functionalities, which enable real anticipation, are mainly still under development in the key market products.

9.2.3.3. *Presentation*

Reporting covers the means available to users for monitoring and controling their activity, with different degrees of autonomy in handling control data depending on requirements (see Table 9.4).

Balanced scorecards	Standard BAM tool reporting method: in the form of balanced scorecards in fat or thin clients. The functionalities of these balanced scorecards vary greatly from one product to another.
Multi-protocol notifications	Ability to route alerts to the process owner in different formats and protocols: email, SMS, pager etc.
Rights and access authorisation management	Ability to connect to a company directory (normally LDAP) to manage the user list, their privileges and to customise the balanced scorecards depending on the user's role in the process.
Requesting and navigation	- Devices for interrogating the events database or data database to access full or filtered information. - Browsing through data, from the most aggregated information to a single unit of data (drill down/ drill up). - Transversal navigation between analysis axes (drill across) Ability to handle data and provide the user with autonomy of analysis.
Document/statement generator	Creating and issuing paper or Web statements for printing.

Table 9.4. *Presentation*

9.2.4. *Other applications*

BAM is dedicated to monitoring processes in real-time. These processes are executed between applications. Each single application normally provides its own monitoring facilities (or at least we must hope so.) The most frequently monitored processes are normally those associated with financial flows and service quality:

– Monitoring orders: some B2B (professional clients) distribution companies have built their success on the quality of their delivery service. They can deliver the goods with a very quick turnaround if orders are placed before a certain time. To be more proactive with these processes, they want to be alerted to malfunctions in their major clients order processes in real-time. These malfunctions can, for example, be spotted by the fact that an order quantity falls below a normally noted average, resulting in a deviation from this average. Users are then warned and can contact their client to check the situation or take immediate corrective measures. In this way the distribution company exceeds its prerogatives and provides a type of monitoring for its clients.

– Provisioning: transversal provisioning processes distribute information between several data sources. You can find them in telecommunication operators information systems, when it involves activating authorizations for the different options to which a subscriber is subscribed. You can also find them in human resources when it also involves triggering all the authorization sets in the systems involved (training, meals, pay, badges, etc.).

– Supply chain management: logistical real-time monitoring is an activity that has become tricky because of the number of applications or even partners involved in the process. The same is true for real-time monitoring of orders and deliveries, the main type of application encountered, with the introduction of more and more information systems.

– Factoring: invoicing processes are the subject of a large number of cases we have been involved with: allowing a holding to monitor the payments of its different branches, or to monitor the invoice generation process from telephone call statements in the telecommunications sector, as shown in Figure 9.9. In both cases, these chains are vital since they directly affect the returns and cash flow of these companies. Monitoring them permanently, chasing up and alerting at the right time may mean that considerable amounts of money are saved.

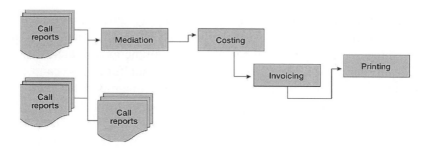

Figure 9.9. *Invoicing chain*

The use of BAM applies to cases that are sometimes obvious or improbable, depending on your point of view. We have thus positioned these technologies at the heart of an architecture for counting the number of visitors to the staff canteens of a major French bank. The number of people passing through the different physical points of the restaurant are captured on the ground, at the entrance, going through the cash desk, the dining room, etc. The number of places still available in the room, when it fills up and when people leave, the average waiting time before they get to the room – these are as many indicators as are supplied by the event collection for diners going through the sensor points.

What is the point of this measuring and who does it apply to? With the construction of a new building and two new restaurants, this bank has five restaurants physically distributed in several locations. At lunch time, staff members want to know in which restaurant they will be able to find a place most easily and in which the waiting time will be shortest. This will avoid the risk of making a wasted journey to a full restaurant. This information is shown on the company's Intranet or on screens in the corridors, in the lift lobby, in the lifts, etc.

The architecture created is based on a BAM engine combined with a complex events manager, a solution category described in Chapter 7.

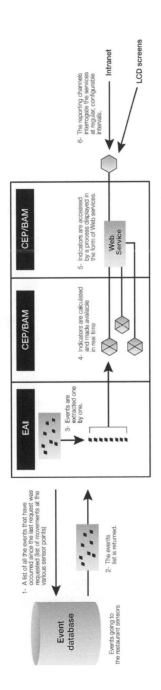

Figure 9.10. *Footfall counting architecture*

On the left is the counting events database. Whenever a person passes a sensor point, this movement is stored. Since the sensor solutions cannot manage the event aspect and produce information as they go along, it is the monitoring solution via its EAI integration layer that collects the events at regular intervals, which shows the complementarity between the exchange and integration manager and the real-time monitoring solution. Managing events using a dedicated set of rules ensures that the indicators are updated.

These events are offered to the different display channels in the form of services: the company's Intranet on the one hand and the set of LCD screens on the other. The service aspect shares the production of results.

There too, the information is not driven towards its destination but requested at regular intervals, which corresponds to the frequency required to refresh the information. In *L'EAI au service de l'entreprise évolutive*, we have already shown how much real-time/on-the-fly management could require arbitration in order to keep pace with the speed of the business unit.

The restaurant case illustrates it perfectly. There is no need to refresh the information constantly. It is more important to know at what times the restaurant tends to fill up and its remaining capacity, two simple indicators that enable the staff to make their decision as to their choice of restaurant.

9.2.5. *BAM and exchange bases*

Normally, a BAM tool can work on the collection and sensor agents that belong to it. In fact, it is possible to use a business monitoring solution without involving any other NISS in the construction. For this reason the pure market players, such as Systar, offer a connection architecture that enables them to interrogate the data sources they have available.

In this way, they mimic the connection and collection devices that already exist in the exchange and integration platforms. You may therefore wonder about the point of "connecting" a BAM solution to an exchange platform in order to share the whole collection, transport and transformation level.

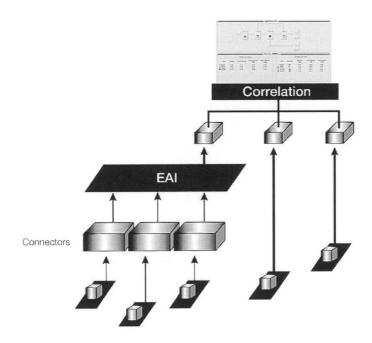

Figure 9.11. *BAM and the exchange manager*

As for the other NISS, the use of a dedicated exchange manager provides added value and an undeniable architectural consistency. It is pointless repeating a connection to the same information sources from different managers several times.

You might as well benefit from the existing data flows and capture the information that they are transporting, thereby leaving each application system to manage what it manages best: flows for the exchange manager, balanced scorecards for the BAM solution.

Information that is not yet available, if any, will be the subject of new flows. It will then be time to determine whether they can pass through the integration platform or if they must be processed autonomously. Ideally, it is preferable for all the flows to use the exchange manager, although there too compromises may occur depending on the situations. This explains why the main integration market players also position themselves on the market with BAM solutions, simultaneously dedicated to real-time monitoring separated from the rest of their offer.

When setting up real-time business monitoring, you will note that complex event processing applications are used at the same time as integration solutions are implemented. This is particularly the case with the TIBCO or WebMethods developers range.

9.2.6. *In full development*

Real-time monitoring is gradually winning its spurs. Although it has been restricted to the banking market for a long time, it is gradually freeing itself from this and is starting to aim at all activity sectors.

At the end of 2008, it remains a niche market but is starting to assert itself, and people are becoming less and less skeptical than they were when it first started ("real-time BI", "no application outside the bank", "a way of making the user resolve IT problems", etc.).

The concept was developed at the end of the 1990s based on the products of two software developers. The first developer, Vitria, was a major company application integration player at the beginning of the 2000s but subsequently lost its grip over the market. The second, Systar, specialized in this area and was one of the leaders, perhaps *the* leader, being the only player in the market to make BAM its means of survival and therefore its priority.

They have both contributed to making the real-time monitoring of business activity more popular, dragging in their wake all the big names in the market, and with some of the smaller players.

Since then, other developers have appeared and taken up an interesting position, with excellent products that are likely to change the existing balance of power. TIBCO, Progress Software, WebMethods, Oracle and Axway are the main ones.

The rollout of NISS, which makes the use of real-time widespread or, should we say, makes it easier for IT to adapt to the pace of the business unit, increases the need for real-time measuring systems that can react, alert and, if need be, anticipate. Consequently it would appear that the future is bright for the BAM market.

9.3. SOA management

Monitoring business processes is aimed directly at users who are responsible for finding out how to resolve problems when they occur, and to determine whether the resolution methods must be requested from the business unit or IT. This monitoring may be accompanied by the rollout of additional measuring systems. As regards the rollout of SOAs, monitoring the performance of the rolled out services is vital.

We have seen that one of the main application contexts leading to the construction of SOAs is the collection and distribution of information in the multi-channel mode.

In most cases, this results in the information system being opened up to partners. This opening up must be controlled. It is not only that customers will be confronted with operational difficulties when they use a sales channel, all the more so if it is partners who are involved. It is important for your partners to be up to the job and that they can prove a minimum, constant level in the quality of service supplied.

But there again, this service quality must be measured. Without this, some problems may not be noticed. And when they are revealed, you will not actually have the means to measure the extent of the damage. In the same way, partners have the right to demand a service of constant, measured quality from the intermediary company.

These complex architectures create criticality points. If a service is not available or responds wrongly, all the company's business and that of its partners may find that they are penalized by this.

Drawing up service contracts between the players creates a way to prove performance and to determine the respective penalties incurred by a player who does not comply with them. As in the BAM case, any problem must be detected as quickly as possible so that it can be controlled as soon as possible.

Figure 9.12 shows the control of a service model. We have used the Actional Solution produced by Progress Software, which is described by Forrester Research as the market leader. In this example, a deterioration in the service response time has been noted. The assembly logic creates chains to link services. It isn't necessarily the service that has been called up directly that poses the problem, rather one of those that it calls up in turn. In this way the SOA management solution creates a list of dependences between the services and shows them to the supervisor. To find out the origin of the problem, the supervisor navigates graphically between the services and locates the service(s) where the response times have actually dropped. As is the case for BAM, real-time alerting is one of the functions offered by these solutions, according to this logic which consists of identifying problems as quickly as possible. From all these measurements taken on the ground, summary scorecards can be created which illustrate once more how close real-time monitoring and retrospective reporting are.

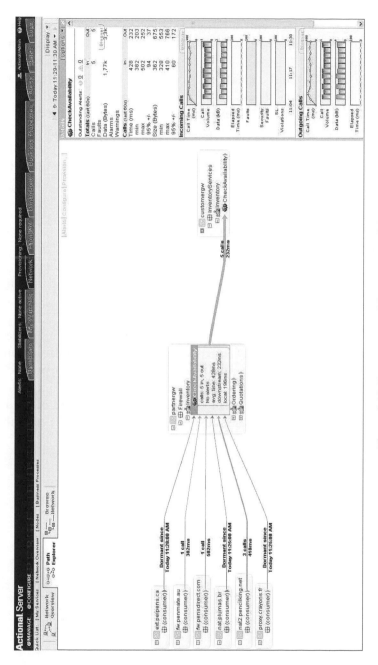

Figure 9.12. *Investigation of the service model*

The SOA management solution thus supplies its performance analysis of the architecture, with its filters and its analysis lines, and determines the SLA values to facilitate arbitration and decisions between a company and its partners, or between an IT department and its business customers. These solutions enable a service model to be evaluated to determine, for example, how to invoice the use of resources depending on their actual consumption by such-and-such a partner or by a particular business department, which is useful for internal sourcing and for operating a solution in software as a service mode.

9.4. The loop is completed

Even if they are not always widespread, the means to measure the performance of the new information system solutions do exist. They provide a permanent link between the solution itself, from a technological point of view, and the information assets that it handles. They thus encourage exchanges between staff in the business unit and the IT teams. You can determine the origin of an incident precisely and find out whether the cause is to be attributed to the business unit or the IT department. You can also determine the effects of an IT problem on all the business processes and services. This is how the monitoring systems bring these two groups together.

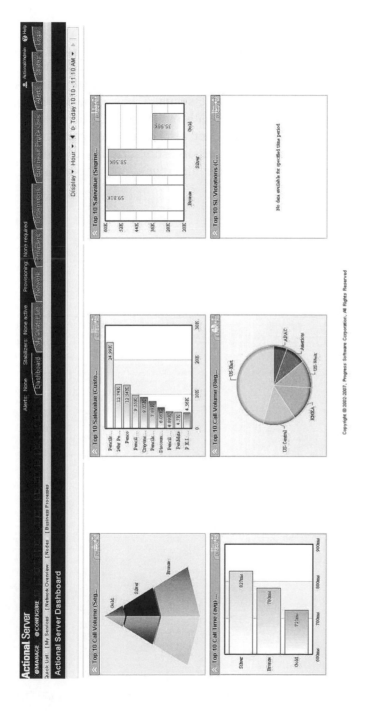

Figure 9.13. *Balanced scorecards*

But let us not dream, since there is still a great deal to do to bring these two groups together. Even so, in the context of aligning the information system to the business unit requirements, a significant step has just been taken. For this reason, BAM and SOA management solutions are quite simply becoming essential. They close the loop described in Chapter 8, which starts with modeling and continues to measuring performance. While it is not yet possible to monitor the whole process in a fluid loop, there are solutions for controling information assets over their whole life cycle, in a continuous improvement process.

Chapter 10

Contribution and Impact of NISS
on Organization

In Chapters 3 to 7 we described all the information assets and the solutions for managing them. We also outlined the issues and questions associated with each of them. In Chapters 8 and 9 we mentioned the question of methods applied to manage them, from creating the applications to measuring performance. In this chapter we shall deal with question of transforming the organization using the technology and the methods with a view to achieving efficiency.

Rolling out new information system solutions gives a company the opportunity to try new technological, method and organizational systems. Some software developers willingly confide in their customers that the success of a project does not depend on the technology but more on the quality of the integrator, on his ability to provide a method and enhance the range of the product in a consistent and future-proof fashion. The success of the transverse information system includes adoption of these new systems by the company.

There is no point in having flexible technologies if they are not used properly or if they are used with rigid organizations which cannot adapt to the specific features of the technologies. Given that the technology must be able to blend in with an organization, the organization must always take a step towards the technology for the graft to take. The smaller this step is, the more organic the method.

10.1. From the business unit to IT: a new fluency

The point of NISS is to increase the flexibility and the alignment capacity of the information system. And yet, however well designed they are, it is hard to imagine these solutions applying the good governance rules by themselves. We all know that technology does not work on its own and that without proper organization, using it may turn out to be counter-productive. The question must therefore be asked: what sort of organization is to be recommended? How can the potential of NISS be exploited to its best advantage? Are there specific roles and responsibilities?

Unlike technologies, methods and processes, organization is a subject that is considerably less malleable. Even when the decisions to be made seem obvious, they may take a long time to become a reality: the difficulty of finding the ideal profile for a new post, imbalance of current operations, tactful distribution of responsibilities: there is no lack of excuses to postpone making a choice with a preference for doing nothing rather than causing an upset.

As far as NISS and the transverse information system are concerned, and this is a subject that sometimes lies fallow, some decisions must be applied immediately and others can be embarked upon gradually, over time. Some rely on existing systems and others may have a massive effect on the normal operation of an IT department – that is, if there actually is one. The information systems director is principally responsible for finding the right fuel. The director has to take into consideration the objectives and the strengths available to put decisions together in a consistent order and enable the development of the initial vision.

For all these reasons of alignment, flexibility and business–IT correlation, implementing NISS requires increased collaboration between the functional departments and this support function provided by the information systems department.

10.1.1. *A tighter link*

When organizing a project traditionally, the cycle going from the expression of the requirement by the business units until the solution is implemented, sometimes lacks co-ordination and communication. Project ownership and studies associated with managing the project all collaborate to create the solution. The organization is set up for the project under consideration and is then maintained for as long as the solution is maintained, over a potentially extended period. The number of intermediaries does not make it easy to apply the new requirements quickly.

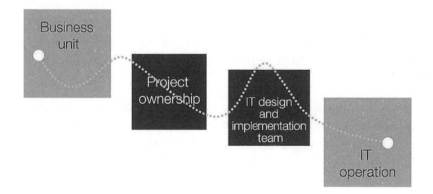

Figure 10.1. *IT organization in project mode*

More and more frequently we companies are undertaking to implement the organization in a three-layer system, a configuration that is particularly suitable for the new information system solutions. This organization stipulates that the project owner, IT design and implementation teams and a production representative all collaborate to draw up the solutions, so as to make up a single team, a single intermediary between the business units and the operation.

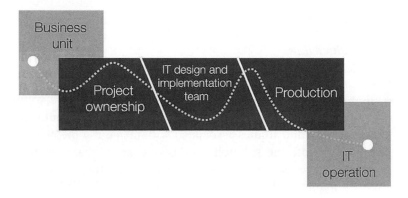

Figure 10.2. *Organization in phase with the business unit*

The idea is not only to establish such a connection during the projects but to maintain it over time. This presupposes that the teams specialize in the technologies in question. Thus constant organization is provided around this technology. This means that the choices are structuring and that the right choice is vital.

If you want the investment to be safe, new investments must not be associated with a single project but with a set of projects. On the one hand, the investment may thus be considered as an asset and recorded as CAPEX (capital expenditure). On the other hand, investment in teams, in organization and in methods will eventually yield a profit in the long run, as the number of projects increases. It is also this increase in numbers that enables you to start with a small platform and to expand this platform over time as the standardization requirements grow.

10.1.2. *Organization in project mode*

All these profiles provide responsibility for managing information assets, a recurrent responsibility since consistency in the long term must be assured. In project mode and particularly in the design phase, the following connections could be observed.

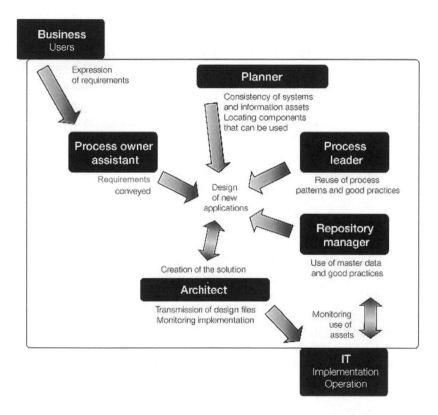

Figure 10.3. *Connection of roles in the project design phase*

This model breaks down the model described in Figure 10.2, an outline that we shall continue to scrutinize in the following pages. This model highlights the new role of the information system planners, at the heart of projects.

In 2004 we had looked into making the post of information system planner more important. We found that their planning work was little used, badly used and even, unfortunately, not always useful. More seriously, they were described as sometimes expensive and having no effect on results. This is what the man in the IT street thought at the time.

The planner's task in some cases did not seem to have anything to do with the preoccupations of the people who would operate the system. It had no weight and was defined by rules enacted like decrees, rules which were unreal because they were never introduced at the right time and did not actually help. This resulted in a kind of covert cold war, a break in communication between the ivory tower and the battlefield. However, in 2004, with the acceptance of transverse information system components, it suddenly appeared that the situation could be reversed and the atmosphere could lighten up a little. The planner once more became the privileged witness of the information system.

In fact, the planner occupies a choice, unique place at the intersection between the business unit and the technology: being practically the only one with a dual (business unit and IT) panoramic view (over the whole information system). The planner is the governance component that maintains the consistency of the information system. In this way we have created an anchorage point for planning, which is intended to ensure that the planner's decisions are closer to the ground. This anchorage point has never really seen the light of day. In fact, we only anticipated it without knowing what service-oriented architectures and later NISS would confirm.

In an NISS context, a transversal vision is vital to supply the expected reuse and sharing processes, to define the granularity of services which leads to a stable state, to define the responsibilities for master data, services, exchanges and transversal processes. In an NISS context, a multitude of micro-projects that are interdependent on each other are assembled, leading more to the idea of a program than the idea of a project.

The planner is now directly involved within the program and is empowered. This contribution can be directly seen. It is specific, applied to the context and vital, since it is made at the initial stages of a large number of decisions. Furthermore, the planner remains in the best position to act as coordinator with the "central" planners and at the same time to work at maintaining consistency.

The center benefits directly from the contributions from the ground to remodel and adjust its design, where previous governance models were rather unidirectional and "meteoric" (only coming from a sky that was then falling on your head).

Contrary to the claims of those who protest when the SOA is taken back by consultancy companies which are hungry for a lack of transparency and profit, NISS are not the backdrop for a military coup by planners. They are the backdrop for their return to grace.

10.1.3. *Business architect and enterprise architect*

Another job that is gradually emerging is the business architect, whose role is to be one of the business innovation drivers, transversally, for the whole company. The business architect reports directly to the operations manager (chief operating officer or COO) working transversally with the local business architects and business analysts.

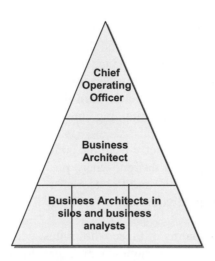

Figure 10.4. *The Business Architect's position*

This transversality is also manifested later. For example, in the pharmaceutical sector, the measurement of return on investment of new products is complicated because, after the R&D phase, it is broken down into the distribution of expenses and profits between the functions. The role of the Business Architect is to make this type of measurement possible.

It is interesting to note that the transversality of IT resources is reflected in the transversality of interrogations associated with the business unit. This balance is the most reliable guarantee of the permanence of the model that we are describing.

It is no longer surprising to note that organization centered on a business architect is echoed in the organization of the IT department and in the appearance of the information asset exploitation model.

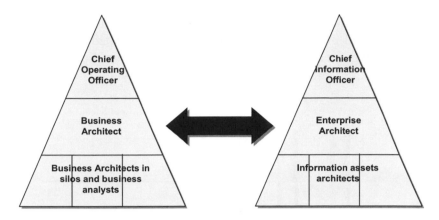

Figure 10.5. *Connection between the Business Architect/Enterprise Architect*

The relationship between the Business Architect and the Enterprise Architect is key to the success of the creation. As they are both guardians of transversality, it is vital that the collaborative processes between these two roles run smoothly and effectively and that the two players enjoy working together for the benefit of the whole company.

There will be no efficient transversal information system in the long term without efficient, smooth organization between these two vital players.

10.2. Governance of information assets

10.2.1. *The new roles*

The gradual rollout of good governance practices has enabled each person's roles and responsibilities to be formalized more clearly by the creation of new posts. The subject of transversality is not new but it has not been dealt with sufficiently until now or, at least, has not been dealt with taking into account the new requirements mentioned in this book.

Generally, 62% of decision-makers questioned in the 01 DSI study are convinced of the necessity for new jobs dedicated to this area. Figure 10.6 gives a more accurate idea of the jobs identified.

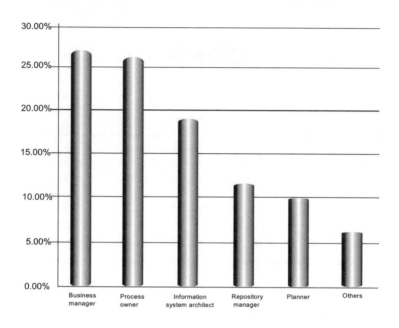

Figure 10.6. *Management of transversality and new posts*

Some of these posts are already found in an IT department. Others are considerably less traditional: you may be surprised to find process owners and master data managers in this figure. Let us examine them.

10.2.1.1. *First place: business manager*

The business manager, also known as the "IS Coordinator", is a generic name for all personnel who provide either support to project owners or a link with the business units. A business manager is ranked in first place among the responses submitted, a position which testifies to the importance of this link as regards the issues raised in these pages. This role is not only to collate information, but also to disseminate it, in order to alert contacts to the opportunities and benefits to be derived from the use of technologies which may or may not already exist within the company.

A business manager is not only the business unit's intermediary in its relationship with IT, but also the innovation intermediary with respect to the business units and is tasked with breaking down certain mental barriers, certain unwitting acts of self-censorship. In terms of the relationship with the business units, data, services and processes become the cornerstones on which the relationship is built: an asset platform, a common relationship base. They enable relationships to be forged based on a cohesive company legacy, to amass a useful body of information and to guarantee a certain cohesion, which nevertheless allows for both adaptation and progression.

10.2.1.2. *Second place: process manager*

The second place ranking of a process manager underlines the importance of business processes in transversal asset management. *It is essential to appoint transversal asset managers, who are half-way between the business unit and IT.* Transversal processes bring together the company's functional silos. Responsibility for their performance can only be situated transversally to these silos. However, business organization is not yet attuned to these possibilities. On the business unit side, there is no transversal processes manager; the same is true on the project management side. For now, and until such time as the visibility of the transversal information system is increased, we will continue to see responsibility for these processes entrusted to IT.[1] Is this situation likely to persist long-term? Probably not. It is directly dependent on the enterprise's acquired perception as to the importance of transversality and issues related thereto. For the time being, it is still a marginal and tactical situation. In the future, it must be established as a growth lever. If it turns out that distinct business unit

---

1. In Chapter 4 we presented a textbook example of this situation.

responsibilities are dedicated to the management of these processes, then the shift will occur by itself. In that event, all that will remain on the project management side will be an operations manager tasked with developing the process and monitoring it, both in real-time and retrospectively.

10.2.1.3. *Third place: information systems architect*

The information systems (IS) architect is the final member of our winning trio. Do we still need to know exactly what is meant by the term "architect"? Is this an enterprise architect? In which case strong links would be maintained with the business unit, and this would considerably affecting our trio of roles and responsibilities. Or is this a technical architect, responsible for implementing the decisions of the first two roles out in the field?

Our opinion is that an IS architect manages to consolidate both of these aspects. We could even use the name "New IS Solutions Architect", such is our conviction that the transition between business unit and IT must be guaranteed at this level. This is particularly clear for SOAs: did we not mention that service was a component which inherently contains the business dimension and the technological dimension? The architect must integrate these two dimensions into construction work and into model evolution.

NISS require significant integration with existing systems, which in itself justifies this source of transversal expertise whose task is to strengthen the agility of the information system. Moreover, NISS are innovative and complex and generally involve state-of-the-art new technologies. It is important that IS architects work closely with experts in these technologies, unless they already have a thorough understanding of all of the implied technologies (which is rarely the case).

10.2.1.4. *Fourth place: the database manager*

The role of database manager does not seem to be clear. This position bears witness to the fact that it is probably "easier" to start a procedure which is focussed on processes rather than data. Thinking about data is often the opportunity for a large-scale project at information system level and existing application level. It is actually the opportunity to review the foundations and, in this capacity, it may have more of an impact than a process approach which plonks itself down like a hat on existing components.

The two approaches are complementary but you can better understand in this context all the interest that companies have for managing data and, paradoxically, all the resources they can provide to launch such projects. In addition, if no master data project has yet been launched, the database manager only deals with the semantic level, an activity for which planners are normally responsible.

Finally, data governance considerations are still, normally, less widespread than those dealing with service governance, for example. The need is probably not felt so keenly. That is why the database manager occupies this fourth place.

10.2.1.5. *Fifth place: the planner*

Of all the individuals in our classification, does the planner wear the dunce's cap? Why isn't this position further up? The role and responsibilities should give an extra importance, this is a vital role as soon as the transversality of resources is mentioned. Although planners have been promoted to deal with these questions, until now their role has often been both functional and technical, consultative and instructional, without there being a real balance between all these dimensions.

There is probably a governance problem surrounding the role of planners. In a project the planner is often someone who you will try to convince, to whom you must prove your credentials, a control and validation body, a Cerberus guarding the gate, from which we would be very happy to obtain the key. While acting as guardian of the temple (one of the sought-after dimensions), the planner does not necessarily help with the development and evolution of the information system faced with project requirements. Planners constrain rather than judge, over time becoming reluctant to change, creating a dichotomy between project requirements and the subject for which they are responsible. Can permanent change management be part of these responsibilities? The results of the study seem to prove that this is not the case.

To improve the operation of the information system, as a result of constantly helping with projects, the planner will, over time, have a role that is halfway between the business unit and IT, that of guardian of information assets. This implies that the planner is also in a position to make recommendations on the architecture. As transversal systems are taking on an increasingly important role, it is logical that transversal functions will grow with them.

10.2.1.6. *And the service manager?*

In the transversality governance model that seems to be forming, it seems odd that one profile does not appear – the service manager. In reality, this choice is positioned 8th in our rankings. We think that companies are generally close to committing themselves to opting for SOAs.

As a result of this, the center of gravity of considerations is being moved towards technological matters and away from organizational matters, a frequently observed phenomenon. When the decision is in the distant future, you take a step back to think about organization but you very often remain at the thinking stage. When the decision is getting nearer, organization often takes a back seat without clear-cut decisions having been made. It is a paradox but that is what happens.

Companies are more worried about succeeding with their initial implementations than managing a service platform over time. You can see at the technological decision level that the service repository that is to organize the architecture and be the service manager's tool is not often regarded as one of the short-term requirements. This requirement will grow as the number of services increases. This does not make the requirement for a service manager disappear, but delays his appointment, which may turn out to be detrimental. It is generally up to us to emphasize this requirement and to ensure that this role is not forgotten. Thus, initially, we recommend that a member of the planning team is reserved for this role. He will then be free to specialize in this activity and to entrust it to someone else later, when it will be organized as a result of the initial projects getting under way.

10.2.1.7. *Conclusion*

The IT department is often the driving force for creating new posts. In fact, these new posts are incorporated into the IT organization while a good number of them ought to be the responsibility of the business units. However, the feature of all the posts under review is to be mixed:

– The business unit coordinator is an innovation intermediary and must be able to promote innovation to the business units.

– The IS architect must control the functional dimensions associated with information assets.

Finally, each of these roles, each of these responsibilities is a trustee, at its own level, of a part of the consistency of the information system and its transverse dimension.

These roles also co-exist in project mode processes. Figure 10.7 shows the association between the different roles involved and outlines a collaboration framework in the design phase.

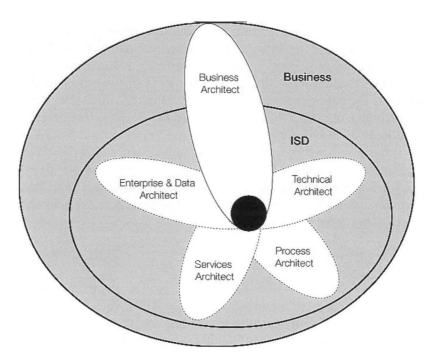

Figure 10.7. *The different facets of enterprise architecture*

Loosening the relationship between the business unit and IT, making the operational alignment of the information system easier, requires all the collaborative models which manage information assets; continuous integration of innovation and the acceleration of projects to be identified in the company's particular context. It is not certain that all the IT process repositories emphasize the specific features of transversality. In the following pages we shall see that the effects on IT governance involve revising existing models.

10.2.2. *Specific roles for master data management*

In Chapter 3, which was devoted to managing master data, we mentioned the creation of a type of academy, responsible for drafting a dictionary of company data in order to establish the semantics and their meaning. We also mentioned initiatives essentially driven by IT and the lack of support encountered on the part of the management who are difficult to convince of the importance of the project. But once support is obtained, who should make up this academy? Who are its members, the members of the French Academy (Académie Française)?

10.2.2.1. *The data owner*

The data owner is a member of a business unit who combines the roles of:

– metadata owner;

– quality manager, but restricted to defining the level of quality required for the business unit's performance.

The data owner is responsible for defining the business unit objects and, in particular, the semantics of the attributes. This responsibility also extends to defining the quality criteria and the security level required for the business unit's performance.

10.2.2.2. *The data architect*

The data architect works in the information systems department. In English-language literature he also goes under the name of data steward. As far as information is concerned, the data architect is its legal trustee and the representative of the information system security manager for security matters.

The data architect is a role in the IS chain with the following tasks:

– capitalizing the data models (including their semantics) and ensuring they are consistent;

– describing and capitalizing the data flows and the transformations from a source format to a target format;

– ensuring that the data is relevant, correctly used, efficiently shared and of the required quality level;

– helping the business unit to understand data management and associated technologies;

– resolving and anticipating conflicts with data and detecting opportunities for improvement (for example: making the data consistent, changes in repositories, improvements in quality); and

– ensuring compliance with the business unit and IS standards, with regulatory constraints on data and security rules.

As far as the job profile is concerned, the data architect understands business processes that handle data, is familiar with the corresponding applications, and has mastered modeling tools, data management and data quality technologies.

10.2.3. *Roles specifically for managing services*

Service governance is a fashionable concept at the moment and one that is difficult to escape. It describes all the roles that go to make up SOAs.

Whatever it is, there are certain to be impacts on methods. Specifications dedicated to service architectures are necessary. A service-based application is not designed in the same way as a traditional application.

10.2.3.1. *The service manager*

The service manager is the person you turn to for a new service or to modify existing services. They are a service model trustees who know how to construct a service: working closely with the architects who create service models for new projects, in order to establish the impact on existing services in the event that certain of these services are shared, reused or phased out.

The service manager's working tool is the service repository from which models are constructed, metadata is allocated, impact analyses are performed and the need to shift away from existing services is identified. The service repository must be the weapon for reusing services.

10.2.3.2. *The domain manager*

The domain manager is the controler of a functional set of services, and is responsible for carrying out studies on them: possibly deciding to modify a service model if this refines the search for the stable state.

If the service model is restricted (as is the case if it is being implemented for the first time or the company is of moderate size), a service model manager would be appointed rather than domain managers, since the size of the architecture does not lend itself to specialization.

The domain manager also has a part to play in measuring service quality and monitoring the service level agreement; regularly providing proof of the performance of the architecture to business unit colleagues based on product reporting. The SOA management tools provide a warning in the event of an alert.

10.2.3.3. *The SOA manager*

The SOA manager works in the operations department, controling the execution and operation of the service model, knowing the solutions on which this service model is based (orchestrator, SOA manager, etc.), or relying on internal or external skills if necessary. The SOA manager is informed when an alarm is raised, either by being in the front line when it comes to resolving the problem or by being ultimately responsible for resolving an incident detected by other managers. This role works together with the operating engineers for other platforms.

10.2.4. *Roles specifically for managing business processes*

Just as for data and processes, business process management involves focussing on specific posts:

– a process owner and process leaders;

– process function experts, e.g. business analysts and business architects;

– technical process function experts, e.g. process analysts;

– technical process experts, e.g. architects, integrators, operators.

10.2.4.1. *The process owner and process leaders*

These roles are used to establish the authority required for managing processes. Normally, critical processes are likely to have a specific owner. We came up against this case with the process of responding to an invitation to tender in a major industrial group. The process owner has a duty to be independent of the functional areas that the process goes through, unless the process in question only belongs to one area. Consequently, with a transversal process, the process owner should ideally report directly to the Board. It is also highly recommended that the Board should be involved with the quality procedure process.

Process leaders are local managers responsible for the business process. In operational terms they report to the process owner but may belong to a different hierarchy. They may be functional or technical managers (IT). The former are responsible for executing and controling the part of the process that goes through their territory, the latter for the IT infrastructure involved with the process.

Normally, the process owner belongs to a business unit. This is also the case for functional managers. On the other hand, technical managers are logically attached to the IT department.

10.2.4.2. *Business analysts and business architects*

Business analysts have detailed knowledge of the functions of all or part of their process. They have mastered in particular:

– all the possible scenarios depending on the process execution conditions;

– the functional exceptions;

– the organization of the people involved;

– the infrastructure used by the process; and

– the information consumed and produced by the process.

Business analysts are therefore functional referral agents and normally occupy project owner posts for BPM projects.

Business architects have a broader view of the company's business. They are not solely process-orientated. However, they play the essential globalization role in the BPM process in order to guarantee a homogenous approach throughout all the business processes. Business architects are normally attached to planning departments.

10.2.4.3. *Technical experts*

Technical experts have a detailed knowledge of the technical infrastructure used by business processes. By restricting our study to the IT infrastructure, we see these post holders have mastered in particular:

– the business applications that the processes go through;

– data and document bases;

– the inter-application flows involved in processes; and

– technical exceptions.

Technical experts normally occupy project management posts in BPM projects.

10.2.4.4. *Process analysts*

As you know, business units and IT experts do not always speak the same language. Business and IT problems are not the same and it isn't unusual for the differences in preoccupations and constraints between the two worlds to lead to poor communication between the functional departments and the IT departments.

The way a member of a functional department depicts a process will always be different from the way a member of the IT staff will do it. The member of the functional department will aim to model the tasks carried out by human players and will highlight the business rules that structure the process. The IT expert will be more concerned with the data structure and flows that result from the functional model. To be executable, the process model requires levels of detail, formality and rigour that are quite useless for the member of the function department who is more into a documentation logic. While the IT expert is involved with programming, the member of the functional department is into description. These two activities therefore require very different skills and serve as completely different objectives.

The role of the process analyst is to act as a mediator between the business unit and IT, between business analysts and IT staff. In this capacity there is a duty to master functional problems as well as technical problems. The main task is to translate functional models into formal models that can be used by technical experts. As this post requires a high degree of formality and method, it isn't unusual for it to be occupied by an IT expert with good business awareness. These qualifications are still unusual in businesses, which often call upon consultancies to provide this key post for the whole BPM process.

10.2.5. *Shared responsibilities*

After such a description of all these roles, some of which are not specifically for managing assets, it is not easy to determine what profiles are to be created immediately and which could be left until later in the adventure. In other words, how is the organization going to progress based on the solutions?

An initial response consists of considering the approach initiated by the company. Is it to create a data repository? To roll out a business process manager? To organize a service-based architecture? The impact will not be the same. Business process management does not necessarily involve having a full time data. If the NISS are complementary, they can also exist autonomously. The organization will reflect the choices made.

However, some projects may involve working with three types of assets. The link between services and master data may be quite strong, for example in the creation of a virtual repository such as described in Chapter 3. Similarly, business processes are consumers of services. Thus, an SOA project may cater for all dimensions. Such a project forced the bank, described in Chapter 4, to appoint process owners.

10.3. Organization methods

Are IT department organizations the most efficient at catering for NISS rollouts? How can organization come before technology, when it remains a component that is much trickier to develop than technology?

10.3.1. *From the matrix model to the transversal model*

The emergence of the matrix model is already the culmination of ideas on sharing and transversality. It bypasses the restrictions inherited from the hierarchical model, which was formerly predominant but presented a major disadvantage in terms of the construction of silos.

The matrix model provides a unique point of entry for each project. Each project manager provides transversality of directed resources by providing an interface to the different contact people on the operations, architecture, planning and security sides, etc.

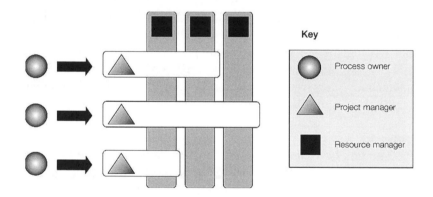

Figure 10.8. *The matrix model*

The matrix model ensures that the best use is made of resources but reduces the number of people involved in process ownership between:

– projects on the one hand; and

– units responsible for the IT expertise on the other hand.

The project manager's responsibility is to ensure efficient coordination of the experts in order to supply an integrated solution. However, one silo remains: the project. There is no mechanism able to share resources between projects.

10.3.2. *A transversal model: competence centers*

With the advent of ERPs, companies were able to organize themselves into competence centers. Sometimes, they were only a self-conscious way of avoiding using the term "service center": the competence center was, above all, a workshop dedicated to implementing new applications and maintaining existing applications. The attraction of the model lay in specializing in a technology which may have seemed contrived but wasn't. By using this model, significantly improved links were noted between the business unit and IT. These are the main benefits from this model. Thus, as part of the 01 DSI study we asked for a description of competence centers. The answer says it all.

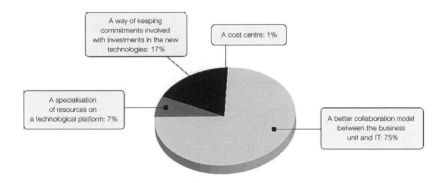

Figure 10.9. *Definition of the competence center*

It is interesting to note the low number of those surveyed who opted for cost center as their main reply. This leads us to believe that appropriate organization may enable competence centers to prove their efficiency and their contribution to performance, a benefit obtained jointly by:

– faster alignment to the business unit, by a better relationship between the different people involved and explicit collaborative processes;

– an ability to provide upgrades and new projects more quickly, thanks to increased specialization in the technology and better management of information assets, from modeling to monitoring; and

– performance measuring made possible with suitable indicators in real-time and retrospectively.

In fact, the model as a competence center (or semi-matrix model) provides:

– stable points of contact for project management, and maintained consistency, which the matrix model did not allow;

– mobilization of all the expertise required for the project; and

– the sharing of requirements between project owners, and the sharing of resources to meet these requirements, both from the human point of view and that of the information capital handled.

In this context, the competence center is not restricted to a service center in the strictest sense.

Implementation may be entrusted to business project management teams, a service company specializing in the technologies involved or an internal or external service center. Most importantly of all, it is necessary to have:

– a high-quality design, respecting the existing one;

– firm control, with no concession to the use that is made of the assets and the planners by verifying that the assets have been used properly; and

– experts controlling the implementation machinery to ensure that the points of complexity are properly located where they are meant to be.

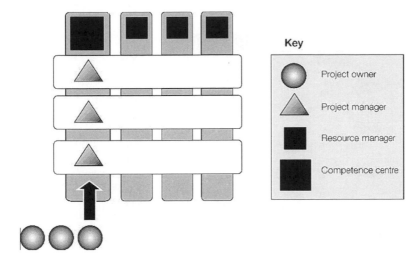

Figure 10.10. *A transversal model of competence centers*

Competence center

The competence center provides a one-stop shop for project owners to express what they want. It is responsible for measuring its performance.

For NISS devoted to transversal information assets, our study showed that IT departments considered organization into competence centers to be more efficient than organization in matrix project mode.

This point is important because the definition of competence centers is itself open to varying interpretations depending on who is talking about them. Real centers of expertise for some, they become development workshops, even application maintenance workshops for others. In all cases, they form the organization's specialization points in meeting transverse requirements.

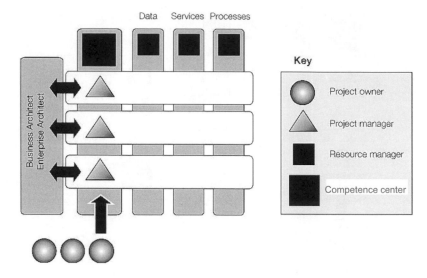

Figure 10.11. *The competence center model translated into the transverse information system*

The business architect and the enterprise architect play a part in design and analysis. The aim is to benefit from increased added value, to seize opportunities, to create future-proof solutions respecting existing assets and to ensure consistency of the whole when these assets are forced to change.

This begs the question of invoicing resources. Setting up a model based on ABC (activity based costing) methods was successfully tested with some of our clients.

The point is gradually to achieve a model for increasing the value of assets which takes account of the quality of the model created.

10.3.3. *An example of an EAI competence center*

In order to go into competence centers in more detail, on the next page we have provided an example of such an organization designed and rolled out as part of installing an EAI exchange platform.

The competence center is organized according to the four major role sets:

– project mode, organizing the creation of new flows;

– pre-production and production, rolling out, approving and using flows and managing incidents; and

– recurrent activities, a set of added value activities which will give the precise appearance of the competence center and its purpose. You will find there, for example, functional architecture activities (mapping, impact analysis, etc.).

Some of the transverse activities can be dealt with in more detail:

– A generic capitalization model: for each new requirement issued by the project owners, an analysis of the existing requirements must be made in order to identify whether existing interfaces or objects can cover all or part of the new requirement. If this is not the case, it will be a question of defining and capitalizing new components (if they can be applied generally to more than one interface). A dictionary of canonicals listing all the objects and their generic function must be installed in order to speed up this study.

– Service contract: the commitments made between the exchange platform and its application partners must be summarized in a document distributed to everyone. This is used to clarify the expectations and constraints of each party.

– Object life cycle: this is to define the logical link of interfaces to the same business object in order to identify whether specific rules must be implemented (application or flow level) to guarantee the consistency of the flow links.

– Business processes and rules: these are used to validate with the application responsible for managing business processes that the events sent to the exchange infrastructure is correctly organized.

The point of this presentation is to show how thinking about exchange platforms may hold the answers to the whole current debate on the transverse information system.

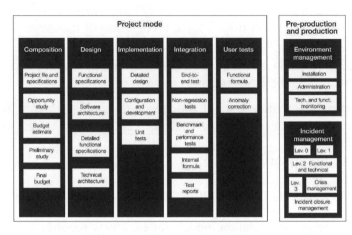

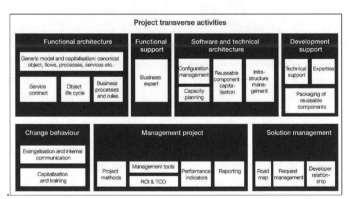

Figure 10.12. *An example of an EAI competency center*

10.4. Managing change and maturity stages

The company is probably going to want to avoid a change that is too major or fast and will develop in stages to adopt this policy gradually. As part of a modest operation, the company will try to refine its practices and to integrate them into its processes and its structure. The roles and systems described in this chapter, their job descriptions, the collaborative processes: all these factors will be fleshed out as the NISS practice, the recognition of transversality, the means to prove the performance obtained, become established.

It is a question of time but also of organization. It is up to the company to identify the maturity stages to be cleared, to manage consequential change and to bring the NISS practice to a higher stage of maturity and standardization. This work is just as much in-depth as it is recurrent. Sustainable development is a concept that empowers those who practice it. You do not embark on an NISS investment with the idea that, finally, at the end of the springboard, events will follow on positively by themselves. It is up to the organization to retain the structuring dimension in the NISS without this turning into a restrictive dimension. Only a proactive approach will guarantee permanent control of the points of complexity and their evolution.

Chapter 11

How to Get the Best Out of NISS

This chapter, which we could have called "Before starting with NISS", consolidates all the factors that must precede the effective implementation of the solutions described in this book. As for any structuring investment, the value creation lines and benefits must have been identified both for the company and for the information system. This work is done during the preliminary stages.

11.1. The initial phases

Any emerging technology, any architectural paradigm, any innovative solution is the subject of a great deal of discussion covering the whole range of possibilities, from unconditional, naive enthusiasm to sheer reluctance. The reality is always somewhere in the middle. It is well known that initially enthusiasts will break down all barriers. It is also well known that later, others will have to put up with a few teething troubles and will let everybody know about it. They cast doubt on what the consultants have said for fear that they have confused consulting and raw experimentation, client and guinea pig. Finally, they will go along with increasing standardization to integrate a technology that has eventually passed the tests and demonstrated all conceivable fields of use.

Whenever a company decides to embark on a technological adventure, the initial stages are vital. They are vital to understand its benefits and impacts right from the start. They are vital to foster awareness on a wide scale, to adapt to the concepts and prepare the future creation with a fair idea of the services that the said technology will be able to offer. It is also vital for the company to make an early decision or for the technology to be rolled out on a large scale already. The aim is still to decide on what value to produce for the business unit and how to generate it.

11.1.1. *Creating the vision*

The example of Sokourov proved that successful innovation is often the work of a person or a team which can keep the target in the line of sight even if the path is being built step-by-step, as progress is made. The fruit of a founding vision that drives the entire project and gives it permanent life, successful innovation is also reliant on the resources which enable it to be developed without disappearing like a mirage.

As we have seen, these resources largely go beyond the framework of the technology. We have more than once maintained in these pages that structuring technological choices involves a dedicated organization. These choices must be made with full knowledge of the facts, including assumed ones. Consequently, creating the vision consists not only of demonstrating the value created but also of measuring all the effects – financial, organizational, methodological and, finally, and perhaps only finally, technological.

Businesses want to understand what these technologies represent for their business, for their practices, their teams, their information system. They want to look at it from every aspect before plunging in.

They want to be educated. This is the moment when they are going to be confronted with the reality of these technologies:

– first of all, the reality of the innovation, with the compiling of business cases suitable for using the technology in the context of the company;

– next, the reality on the ground, with feedback on previous experiences which sometimes have as much evidential value as counter-examples;

– also the reality of integrating this technology into their context with impact analyses and change plans; and

– finally the reality of the initial investment with an appropriate budgetary framework.

When these four dimensions have been dealt with in all their aspects, the company will have created its very own vision for using NISS in its context. Knowing how to perpetuate this vision will be the major issue to be dealt with in the medium term.

11.1.2. *Identifying business cases*

The first question to be asked is: what contribution is the solution going to make to the business? What value will it create or contribute to creating? It is vital to create the first business cases and to evaluate their impact on the company's value chain.

Figure 11.1. *Identifying business cases*

Several levers can be identified, for example, system information levers or method levers. They remain confined within the IT department. Only business levers provide a basis for communication between the business unit and IT. The internal relationship with the business architect must help to draw up these business cases and have them validated by the business units.

11.1.3. *Calculating proof indicators*

In the short term the key is to be convincing. Estimating proof indicators helps in this process.

Within the NISS framework, creating the vision is also a question of evaluating the metrics intended to prove the solution's contribution. This contribution is just as valid for the business unit's performance as for the information system's performance. This performance is measured with indicators that are suitable for each of the domains.

11.1.3.1. *Value added to the business unit*

The value added to the business unit is an indicator that shows what the benefits or the savings may be from installing an NISS. It proves the direct contribution of the NISS to the company and information system's performance. For example, if a new exchange platform allows a business process to be executed in two hours rather than in two days, then we would consider that this indicator has an added value of 24 (48 hours/2 hours).

This indicator is always linked with a given business context in a given technological context. It is not financial, even if it may be calculated financially to estimate the profit or savings made, before ending up in an ROI evaluation. The values of the different gains may be added up to define an overall value, even if this comes down to adding cabbages and carrots. It would be better to divide the results into types of performance gains on the one hand and on the other hand by separating pure gains from potential savings or penalties avoided.

This indicator is used to justify business priorities when choosing pilots or projects based on an NISS platform. It can be used as an indicator on the flow chart of a competence center manager.

11.1.3.2. *The integration coefficient: case by case*

The integration coefficient shows the ability of the applications involved in a business process or in an exchange to integrate easily into an exchange platform while respecting the state of the art of the process: transmitting on-the-fly, managing different protocols and time of exchanges, the ability to manage the exchange from a semantic point of view and without the clumsy configuration of the exchange manager... The more difficult the application complexity is to manage, the poorer the integration coefficient is.

For example, with a product data synchronization flow, the target application is expected to integrate the updated data incrementally (only for modified products) and on-the-fly. If the application is only capable of integrating a whole file, without distinguishing between modified and unmodified items and in batch mode, then we would say that its integration coefficient is, in this case, very low.

We have thus graded the integration coefficients between 0 and 1.

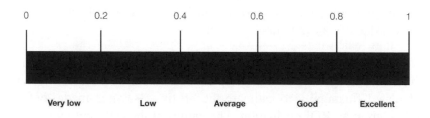

Figure 11.2. *Integration coefficient values*

The integration coefficient always relates to a fixed context. For some business cases it may be good and in others much weaker. It must therefore be evaluated case by case. In addition, you must consider the role played by the exchange manager who increases automatically in some cases, by his own abilities, the integration coefficient of some applications. Finally, as an indicator of proof, the integration coefficient must be linked to the intrusion rate to give its real importance.

11.1.3.3. *The intrusion rate: an impact analysis*

The intrusion rate shows the effects of implementing NISS on surrounding applications, whether they are involved in a business process or in synchronizing reference data. The intrusion rate measures the complexity of opening an application and the work load that it needs to connect it if necessary to the rate imposed by the exchange rhythms. All these factors make up parameters for measuring this rate.

The intrusion rate is characterized by the impact analysis:

– light when it is a question of connecting directly to a database table (on the other hand, the application integration coefficient will be low);

– moderate when it is a question of displaying the procedures stored in the form of Web services; and

– high when it is a question of developing specific modules on a mainframe to generate data files, or creating a service layer in an existing application.

The intrusion rate is in addition to the integration coefficient to describe an integration solution. For example, accessing database tables is often possible and the corresponding intrusion rate is low. However, the integration coefficient is also low because the exchange platform does not manage a semantic model at the level of the application that it integrates.

Combined with the integration coefficient, the intrusion rate assumes a certain importance. This indicator will judge between business requirements and the reality of existing applications. If these applications cannot be integrated easily, it may be necessary to review the scope of a pilot project or revise the path to be followed (see section 11.3).

11.1.3.4. *Total cost of ownership*

The total cost of ownership (TCO) gives an indication of the investment budget and the recurrent budget necessary to implement and administer NISS over a longer or shorter period. Factors involved in TCO include:

– software licenses including maintenance;

– hardware platform based on the target technical architecture;

– installation and configuration of the solution on the server and client platform (e.g. for development);

– modification of existing applications to improve the integration coefficient or reduce the intrusion rate;

– training of implementation and operations teams, project managers, help with change and transfer of skills;

– controlling and implementing identified pilot projects;

– migration from the existing platform to the new platform;

– putting in place the means to measure performance;

– recurrent technical and functional operating costs; and

– costs of creating and operating the competence center.

Evaluating the TCO is also a means of negotiating with the teams from partner companies.

11.1.3.5. *Return on investment: difficult to assess?*

Cases where evaluating the return on investment (ROI) is desirable but turns out to be complicated are not rare. The concept of ROI is interesting in that it is either relatively simple to evaluate and may be calculated without any possible dispute, or extremely complex and subject to a number of assumptions or interpretations.

Let us take the example of the means of payment described in Chapter 9. It is easy to know the amount of penalties incurred periodically by this bank and the reasons that led to these penalties. These are obviously dealt with by the rolled out solution. You can reasonably assume that the said solution would prevent 80%, 50% or 30% of these penalties over the period, depending on whether you are an optimist or a pessimist. Compare this value with the total cost of ownership of the solution over the same period and check that the solutions provides a quantitative value as a result of the savings it makes.

However, the qualitative part proves difficult to put a value on. How do you measure the improvement in value perceived by the customer in financial terms? How do you define the contribution of this improvement to the ability to gain new customers in the invitation to tender phase? A drop in the customer attrition rate (fewer customers leave, more customers taken on) is qualitative data that may be valued if necessary. The marginal cost of a customer can be calculated. However, it remains an aggregate, a composite indicator that will remain a subjective component.

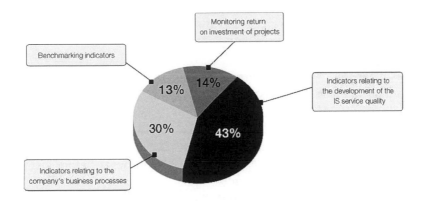

Figure 11.3. *Preferential indicators*

43 + 30 = 73%, i.e. ¾ of people questioned were concerned about efficient, improved reporting for business units. While it is logical when proving the effectiveness of the governance to align the IT indicators with a business unit reading, the 30% allocated just to business processes is always surprising. The profiles of process leaders, the second transversal job highlighted to improve the governance exercise, must be compared. The importance of the business process turns out to be greater than we thought.

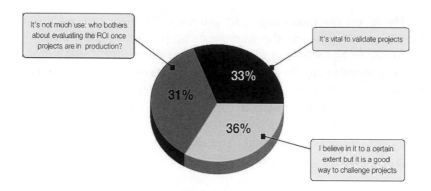

Figure 11.4. *ROI trends*

It is clear that ROI is a concept which is used more in the initial stages than later on and thus remains above all useful for qualifying the investment. However, there remains palpable skepticism as regards its validity. At working party meetings, we have noted that ROI was first of all investigated by IT (how, thanks to innovations, I can reduce the operating costs of my IT department) before being eventually understood by the business unit.

However, this indicator is above all relevant for the business unit. In fact, taking into account the points raised in this part, implementing new solutions must at best generate an IT ROI of nothing. The increase of dedicated teams offsets economies of scale, including the reduction in development cycles.

For the business unit, value creation must be tangible, even if it may be difficult to evaluate. What are the benefits of integrating a new product partner quickly? What savings are obtained by increasing performance and service quality for a critical business process?

ROI is a concept that cannot be ignored. Thus, it remains essential for proving the relevance of an investment.

11.1.4. *Evaluating solutions*

In the NISS context, a number of solutions and products may still be described as emerging:

– in France at least, the projects for which they have been rolled out are far from exhaustive;

– skills are still difficult to find, even in French development companies which market the solutions;

– methods are still sometimes in the stabilization phase and not enough feedback can be found to build an exhaustive vision.

In addition, some developers still find it difficult to transfer their sales cycles to the reality of such solutions. Having been used to selling volume technological solutions or software packages, their sales forces must now understand the consultation dimension and the sales cycles for this software. The iterative approaches implemented for these investments are explained by these numerous uncertainties. We have been used to running these selection processes for ten years. Each process is an opportunity to scan questionnaires containing hundreds of criteria, but with the reduction in the number of players and solutions on the market, the processes are becoming more and more direct. The technologies are closer and closer and the much talked-about questionnaires are becoming more and more difficult to differentiate.

Companies want to see the solutions before choosing, so that they can form an opinion from the graphical, ergonomic and then functional point of view. You no longer count the number of selection studies that include the creation of a prototype in one day. It is no longer a question of rewarding the best prototype. It is first and foremost a question of determining the solution which most closely matches the requirements and culture of the company.

11.1.5. *The importance of the initial phases*

Far from being a luxury, the initial phase is a breathing space that precedes the great race. Breathing space, because the company is giving itself precious time to prepare itself before launching operations, and because it will be a question of not running out of steam once the operations have been launched. In itself, this phase does not represent an enormous investment, if you take account of the fact that the investments that will depend on it will be significantly greater and will commit the company permanently. The initial phase also represents the means to convince everybody of the validity of the approach, to find sponsors and to integrate them at company or group level.

11.2. The foundations: creating platforms

Once the vision has become reality, the number of players involved with the technology increases significantly. They rarely know the whole background of the situation. If they do have all this information they do not necessarily share it. In turning into reality, the vision is diluted.

In a way, once the platform has been created, this gives form to and perpetuates the vision. For this reason, it is not only restricted to the technological aspects of the NISS response. For a large number of reasons, the creation of a platform is a vital concept for this type of architecture:

– the platform is an engineering concept intended to standardize the expertise acquired and to capitalize on the prior implementation of the solution for other projects;

– the platform sets the factorizing points. You will know precisely what to reuse, how and under what conditions;

– the platform shows the expected points of complexity and gives all the keys to prevent the solution losing flexibility over time.

Figure 11.5 shows the example of the Allegro program which comprises three distinct platforms for each part of the program.

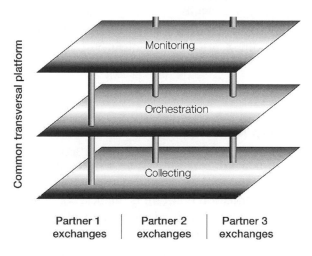

Figure 11.5. *The platform: a stable construction*

Once the platform has been set up, the aim is to significantly reduce the porting and rollout time of each of the bank business unit procedures. You sort of "plug" the procedures into the rolled-out platform.

The points of complexity are mastered and are an integral part of the platform. Porting a new process is a monitored, standardized procedure reduced to the minimum (a little parameter setting and configuration according to a rigorously described procedure).

The platform is just as vital for doing things quickly as for doing things well, which means respecting the consistency of the practices and technologies implemented, and respecting the information assets. It is not restricted to the technological dimension but also covers the organizational, methodological and business aspects of the platform.

11.2.1. *Organizational platform*

The organizational platform implements the recommendations issued in the initial stages. These recommendations may cover all or parts of the points dealt with in Chapter 10 – creating new roles, allocating responsibilities, creating a dedicated competence center or not, etc.

11.2.2. *Information platform*

Implementing a new information system solution indicates that the company wants to control its information assets better. The construction of an information platform is the best way to have a bank of reliable assets which are standardized and suitable for use in the projects with which they are involved. This platform is normally constructed by modeling the assets and allocating metadata to describe and facilitate how to manage them. It normally includes a tool in a modeling product and suitable mapping.

In a way, the information platform is the control tower for rolling out NISS. The users who are in the best position to orchestrate it are the business architects and the enterprise architects, whose complementarity is ideally expressed in this platform.

11.2.3. *Technological platform*

The technological platform comprises several aspects:

– it provides all the shared services provided by the selected solution, which are then customized and used by all the context elements to be executed on the platform: the alert manager for a BAM platform, the transcoding manager for an exchange platform, etc.;

– it incorporates the framework set up to extend the native capacities of the selected solutions,[1] a framework which itself provides shared services for the whole platform;

– it allows for docking between information asset management tools and execution platforms,[2] to transfer the model's context elements to the implementation repository; and

– if need be, you may integrate hardware and infrastructure elements into the platform, particularly in a framework where the architecture is based on grid computing (which turns out to be completely suitable for constructing SOAs), or create a complete monitoring system from the business unit to IT.

11.2.4. *Methodology platform*

The methodology platform is made up of documents to accompany the project mode. Although it varies in size depending on the size of the platforms and the projects, we can mention the following documents that are encountered regularly when constructing what we would normally call the foundations of the model:

– The process guide: outlines the activities, inputs, deliverables, documents and software components produced at each stage from the initial phases up to operation including the project. It is accompanied by document models that describe the project mode (for example, general and detailed, functional and technical design documents), and specifies when and how to use each of the documents listed below.

– Impact and reuse analysis guide: identifies processes that lead to maximum reuse and sharing.

– Architecture document: describes the functional, application and technical architecture of the NISS implemented.

---

1. As described in Chapter 6.
2. As described in Chapter 8.

– Organization and collaborative processes: provide a list of roles and responsibilities in the projects and in everyday life, and mark the collaborative processes involving the people concerned.

– Platform installation guide: specifies the installation procedures and parameters for the different environments in which the platform is executed.

– Implementation guide: provides the norms, standards and good practices for creating components in project mode. This maintains a certain consistency between the work of the different producers which will make the maintenance phases easier.

– Standards and naming conventions: these provide the means of giving names to components handled during the design and production phase, as well as to make handovers within the team and the reading of application components easier.

– Delivery guide: explains how to package and deliver technological platform applications.

– Operating guide: is aimed at operating managers and may be accompanied by script models.

– Monitoring guide: is aimed at monitoring managers and shows how to interpret any errors encountered and how to remedy them.

– Guide for using and configuring the framework: covers all the components that are not provided within the selected solution.

You can easily understand that the methodology platform is highly upgradeable and that it will become hardened with each new project implemented. This platform generally shows the maturity level reached by a given company when using NISS.

11.3. From the process angle

An NISS project is a potentially complex project that includes some risks to bear in mind:

– sufficient mastery of the technology, both by the company and its partners;

– scope initially too wide, leading to the scope being reviewed during the project, with the pressure and disappointment that involves and the negative effect that it will not fail to produce on the teams involved and on the technology itself. Solutions, methods and organization are all sensitive, complex subjects to be run in parallel. Too big a picture leads to maximizing risks on all sides. If you want to remain on the tightrope permanently at all costs, you normally end up paying for it.

– lack of understanding of the challenges and impact of the technology by the people working in the company. We remember the rollout of an SOA where our contacts would regularly tell us that this type of design would not change the way things had always been done in IT. Very well. A great deal of effort leading to an anticlimax.

No project is successful initially and this applies to NISS just as much as to all the others. Mastering this type of engineering requires a certain expertise.

It is difficult for us to take all the techniques and practices that enable a project of this type to be secure and squeeze them into a book like this. Instead we shall make do with giving some important facts.

11.3.1. *An iterative framework*

It is important to note that iterations can only occur in the design phase and that the implementation stage must not be the place for new iterations. Some players in the market favor this type of approach and justify it by maintaining that is an indispensable condition for authorizing flexibility and speed of development. While this operating mode may seem attractive at first, in reality it is a backward step that may lead to the project having to be (re-)designed. The design burden then becomes greater than it should have been. Why authorize a practice that goes against those established in the majority of IT projects for an

NISS project? The favorable signal is the one where the initial design phase is more important than for a traditional IT project, given that its effect will be an automatic contraction of the production phase. The approach that we propose is an approach built on successive, repeated meetings with the business unit users and the IT users. The role of a consultant is to act as a prism to judge between business unit requirements and IT constraints, in order to reach the most balanced judgement and a satisfactory initial scope for all parties. This is done by adopting a gradual approach based on interviews and workshops where the two departments are first of all separated before getting together for a final round to correlate the workshops.

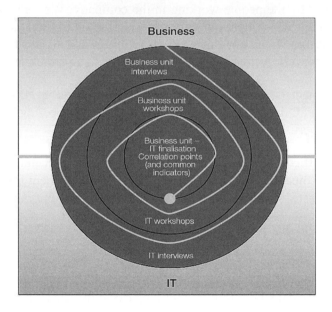

Figure 11.6. *The iterative approach*

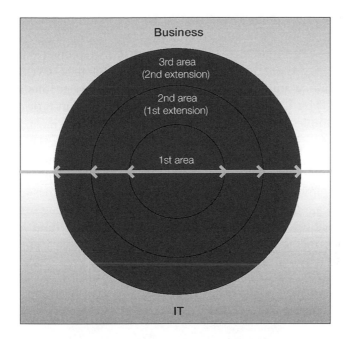

Figure 11.7. *Definitions of the project scope*

This approach enables you to define the most satisfactory area and to anticipate from the start of the process, the type and scope of the extensions to come. You then have a progressive expression of requirements that provides a framework for the successive areas to be covered.

Each project is seen as a nucleus around which the different extensions will expand the initial scope. Reasoning based on information assets allows for the possibility of this iterative operation, based on assembly.

11.3.2. *The methodology package*

There is no single way of making an NISS project successful. Unilog Management has created a complete method based on the Praxeme public initiative, although there are other methods on the market (SOMA UOS, etc.) and, without a lot of effort, you can find further examples by consulting market players.

These methods have a common specific feature, in that they focus top-down and require a complete analysis of the company's business to break it down into its IT aspects. You therefore use these methods for large-scale projects (projects involving the overhauling of a part of the information system, for example). At the same time there are approaches that will provide results more quickly based on iterative techniques drawn from flexible methods.

11.3.2.1. *Praxeme and RUP*

Praxeme is based on a top-down approach which starts with the company's business and breaks down into different models and layers to supply a complete analysis. In order to cover the complete project cycle, we have been forced to combine the Praxeme models with rational unified process disciplines.

As well as its model-driven architecture-based approach,[3] Praxeme provides something invaluable, in that the organization and the company business unit must be clearly separated in the model. Combining one with the other ultimately reduces flexibility. One of the main features of using this method lies in the option to separate them, in order to free a detached business semantic model from any organizational consideration. From this model, Praxeme breaks down its model into all its information system components. Praxeme considers several levels of representation that are broken down and supplemented with each different contribution: the topology of the company's system. The semantic model is the closest level to the

---

3. See Chapter 8.

business unit. From this, Praxeme generates a pragmatic model that introduces the action, the players and the organization.

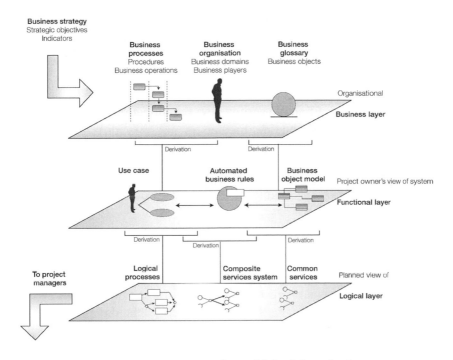

Figure 11.8. *Praxeme: the model divided into levels*

Thus, Praxeme provides a global method that is aimed at the whole transverse information system. It is clearly up to the modeler, when modeling, to follow the rules that apply to the fringe of the NISS for which he is starting to create platforms. If the first stone is to construct a data repository, you will only follow the part that describes the definition of the company's data model. If the first stone relates to services, other principles will be followed, etc.

11.3.2.2. Flexible methods

As described in Chapter 8, the Brainsonic example shows us that applying flexible methods to the SOA context has yielded pleasing results. The company favors iterative approaches, particularly because they enable a road map to be revised easily in order to stick closely to the new business priorities. The iterations are very short, a few man days, with milestones that are very close together.

The aim is to continue to supply new functionalities efficiently and quickly. This implementation method is not very different from a business concept carefully carried out in the initial stages of the project with the use of different repositories to help control the impact of new implementations. In other words, the two approaches can be completely mixed:

– a very high level approach, which controls the assets; and

– a very pragmatic approach providing fast delivery cycles, aimed at business priorities respecting existing assets.

11.4. Here and now

There would be no books on the transverse information system and on the new information system solutions if they did not lead to modifications or even major breakthroughs in a generally familiar landscape. You can see that method and organizational components already exist to provide the efficient promotion and orchestration of these solutions. What has changed is the position of the cursor: certain roles, certain responsibilities and certain methods have been completely re-evaluated with regard to the customary perception of their contribution. In a way, it's normal. IT organizations have been in existence for long enough to have already done or tried everything, with more or less success.

This book has tried to show the means, the action levers and the ideas that will allow a business to adjust the respective weighting of the different components to give its project the required timbre. Do not forget that this transformation will not be instantaneous and that, whatever happens, the process is iterative. Do not also forget that the transverse information system is a wasteland for a good number of companies, and that it is not too late to act. In fact, it is far from being too late. It is here and now that the major operations are being launched.

11.5. Bibliography

ABOU HARB G., RIVARD F., *L'EAI au service de l'entreprise évolutive*, éditions Maxima, 2003.

ALBERGANTI M., "Transformée en ordinateur, la cellule analysera sa propre santé", *Le Monde*, 9-10 September 2007.

BONNET P., DETAVERNIER J.-M., VAUQUIER D., *The Sustainable IT Architecture*, ISTE, 2009.

CASEAU Y., *Urbanisation et BPM*, Dunod, Paris, 2008.

REGNIER F., GABASSI M., FINET J., *Master Data Management*, Dunod, Paris, 2008.

RIVARD F., PLANTAIN T., *L'EAI par la pratique*, Eyrolles, Paris, 2002.

Index

R

reporting, 62, 66, 74, 78, 182, 217, 249, 250, 258, 259, 261, 262, 270, 293, 315

reuse, 22, 25, 35, 39, 103, 104, 107, 108, 178, 180, 214, 215, 221, 228, 230, 240, 280, 293, 318, 321

S

SAP, 72, 73, 77, 84, 89, 115, 232

scorecard, 182, 209, 213, 215, 253, 267, 270, 273

Scrum, 238

semantic, 56, 57, 58, 61, 62, 83, 84, 91, 105, 174, 175, 193, 287, 291, 311, 313, 326

service level agreements (SLA), 113, 251, 272

service-oriented enterprise (SOE), 193

sharing, 8, 20, 34, 36, 38, 54, 97, 99, 104, 200, 213, 216, 228, 229, 237, 280, 298, 300, 321

Siebel, 72, 186, 233

Software AG, 115, 151, 165

software as a service (SaaS), 232, 233, 234, 235, 239, 244

standardization, 37, 38, 57, 62, 68, 89, 111, 133, 134, 153, 154, 156, 160, 237, 278, 305, 307

Sun SeeBeyond, 182

supply chain management, 263

sustainable, 6, 23, 24, 25, 26, 27, 35, 44, 82, 170, 184, 210, 305

SWIFT, 16, 256

syndication, 226

Systar, 254, 261, 266, 268

T

thresholds, 214, 261

TIBCO, 73, 115, 120, 151, 156, 162, 196, 214, 215, 254, 268, 269

training, 101, 123, 167, 184, 263, 314

transactions, 1, 5, 103, 115, 126, 133, 136, 143, 176, 194, 222, 256, 257

transformation, 27, 67, 78, 92, 93, 110, 116, 120, 146, 156, 163, 171, 174, 175, 176, 180, 181, 267, 292, 329

tunnel effect, 103, 187

TV4IT, 234, 235

V, W

Veolia Environment, 182, 187

Vitria, 162, 182, 268

Web services description language (WSDL), 244

Web, 28, 75, 76, 79, 83, 85, 89, 90, 92, 93 95, 99, 102, 106, 107, 109, 110, 111, 146, 148, 160164, 174, 180, 198, 207, 208, 209, 215, 218, 226, 229, 234, 235, 239, 244, 313

WebSphere, 63, 67, 72, 242

WebMethods, 156, 165, 182, 254, 268, 269

WebServices, 28, 76, 79, 85, 89, 90, 92, 95, 99, 102, 106, 107, 109, 110, 160, 174, 207, 208, 209, 215, 218, 229, 244, 313

work station, 111, 207, 208, 227

X, Y

XML, 110, 237, 244

Your Potential TV, 234, 235, 236